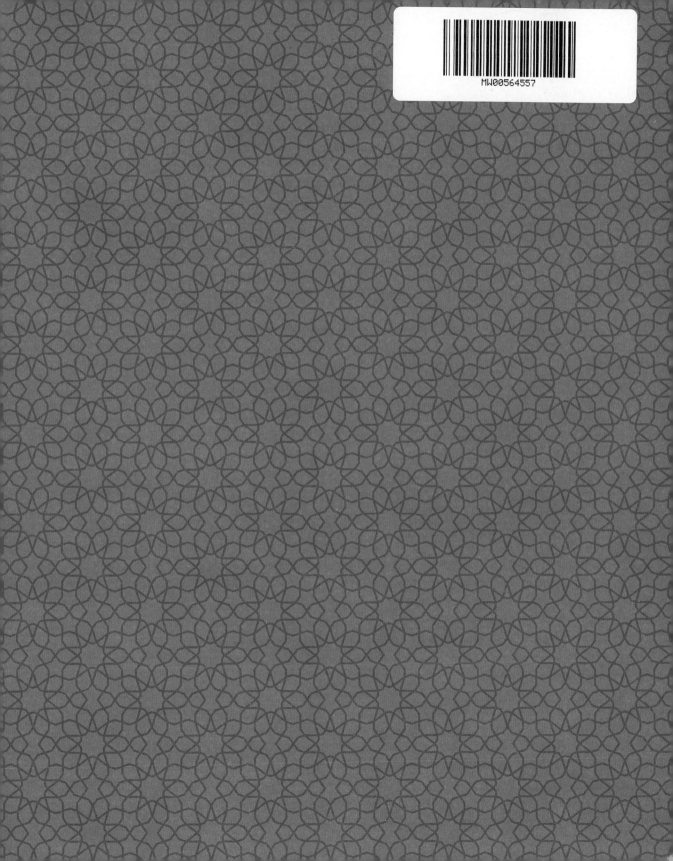

GATHER & GRAZE

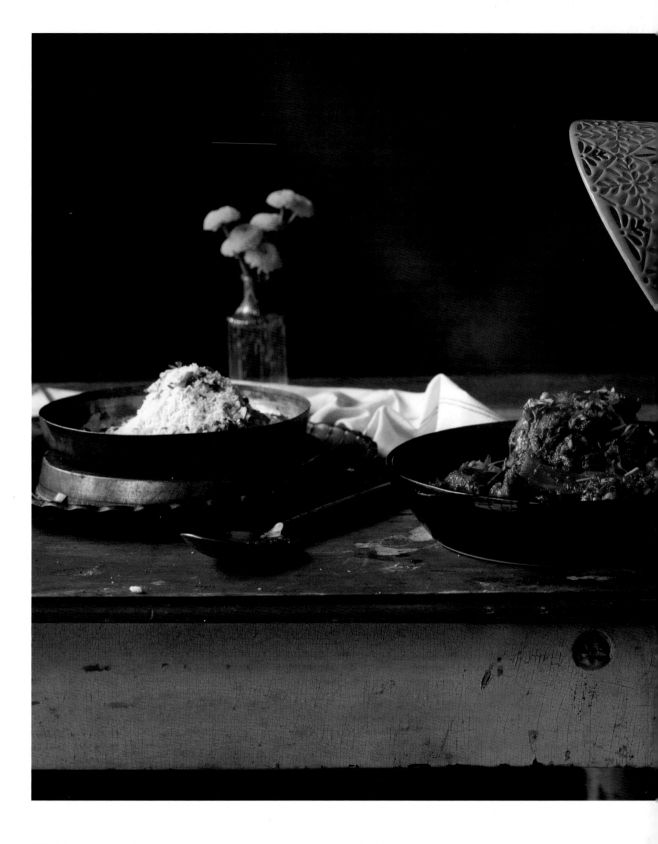

GATHER
&
GRAZE

Globally Inspired
Small Bites *and*
Gorgeous Table Scapes
for **Every Occasion**

MUMTAZ MUSTAFA & LAURA KLYNSTRA
FOREWORD BY SHARMEEN OBAID-CHINOY

SKYHORSE PUBLISHING

Skyhorse Publishing books may be purchased in bulk at special discounts for sales promotion, corporate gifts, fund-raising, or educational purposes. Special editions can also be created to specifications. For details, contact the Special Sales Department, Skyhorse Publishing, 307 West 36th Street, 11th Floor, New York, NY 10018 or info@skyhorsepublishing.com.

Skyhorse® and Skyhorse Publishing® are registered trademarks of Skyhorse Publishing, Inc.®, a Delaware corporation.

Visit our website at www.skyhorsepublishing.com.

10 9 8 7 6 5 4 3 2 1

Library of Congress Cataloging-in-Publication Data is available on file.

Cover & interior design: Spice & Sugar
Food photography: Laura Klynstra
Food styling: Mumtaz Mustafa and Laura Klynstra
Travel photography: Mumtaz Mustafa and Laura Klynstra, Pakistan photographs on pages 1, 36, 39 by Syed Muhammad Abid Rizvi. Turkey photographs on pages 72, 75 by Renee Brunsting, Netherlands photographs on page 132 by Wilma Freeley
Author photograph: Mehreen Jabbar
Editor: Nicole Frail

Print ISBN: 978-1-5107-7701-9
Ebook ISBN: 978-1-5107-7702-6

Printed in China

Celebrating the fierce women of my world,
both by heritage and heart: your enduring strength,
boundless dreams, and nurturing camaraderie
fill me with immense pride as I share my table with you.
—M.M.

For every person brave enough to cross borders—
you have made my world richer,
my horizons wider, and
my table more abundant.
—L.K.

CONTENTS

FOREWORD

My most vivid early memory of Mumtaz dates back to the late 1980s, gathered around my grandmother Azra Syed's dining table, a place of culinary magic and warmth. Azra, a pioneering female chef in Pakistan, would hold summer cooking and baking classes in her home, where Mumtaz, with a big wooden spoon in hand, deftly mixed batter with the expertise of someone beyond her years.

Those classes were a bustling hive of activity. We, the young apprentices, were entrusted with preparing ingredients, buttering pans, and the most delightful task of all—taste-testing our creations in the afternoon. Our culinary adventures didn't just end there; each home we visited, belonging to friends or family, was a new world of flavors. These tables, laden with dishes steeped in family history, were more than just places to eat. They were spaces where stories unfolded, where we, as children, were captivated by the rich tapestries of tales that accompanied each meal. This was more than food; it was a celebration of culture, history, and the joy of shared experiences, a cherished part of our childhood that continues to inspire and nourish us.

When Mumtaz shared this book with me, I was instantly transported back to my childhood. She and her collaborator, Laura, are both artists, and they take on food with the same keenness of the eye as they take on their art. This book is an extraordinary culinary journey and a collaboration between two remarkable women who have ventured beyond the traditional bounds of recipe creation.

It is a vibrant testament to the power of cross-cultural friendships in deepening our understanding of the world. As their diverse backgrounds meld in the kitchen, each recipe becomes a dialogue, a celebration of their unique cultural heritages, and a bridge between seemingly disparate worlds.

From the alchemy of recipe development to the eloquence of writing, from the artistry of food styling to the precision of photography, and finally, the aesthetic finesse of design, this cookbook is a deliberate and thoughtful process, echoing the fusion of their distinctive perspectives. Each page is not just a recipe; it is a narrative of friendship, a blend of traditions, and a celebration of culinary exploration.

It is a chronicle of passion, creativity, and the unyielding spirit of collaboration. As you turn the pages, you are not merely learning to cook; you are being invited into a vibrant dialogue with flavors, textures, and colors, orchestrated by two women who have poured their hearts and souls into every detail. Welcome to a culinary adventure that transcends the boundaries of the kitchen, where every recipe is a story, and every photograph a captured moment.

—SHARMEEN OBAID-CHINOY

INTRODUCTION

———◆———

"If you really want to make a friend, go to someone's house and eat with him. The people who give you their food give you their heart." —CESAR CHAVEZ

We met in the HarperCollins art department in New York City, and have been connected through book design over our twenty-year friendship. Although design is our primary occupation, food was our real passion and our true connection. Coming from totally different worlds, we enjoyed swapping stories and cooking together. We planned parties and served up delicious food for friends. Brainstorming menus and working through our collective culinary histories kept us talking and connecting with each other and with others. We quickly discovered that food was our primary love language—nothing made us happier than knowing people loved what we prepared.

MUMTAZ

My love for sharing delicious food is deeply rooted in my life growing up in Karachi. The hospitality of the Pakistani people is an element as essential to the experience as the food itself. The warmth I felt each time I was welcomed into a home, the way no one would let you leave without partaking in a hearty meal, is a hallmark of the deeply ingrained tradition of togetherness. Food is a binder, a catalyst for community, exemplified brilliantly by our cuisine. For me, these aren't merely memories, they're chapters in a book of resilience, love, and identity, sealed with the spices and aromas of Pakistani food. Whether it was a humble cup of tea at Bohri Bazar or a grand Friday breakfast, each experience was a stepping stone in understanding the duality of my existence—anchored both in tradition and the sprawling complexity of modern Pakistani life. On weekends we would pile into the family car for faloodas. Being the youngest, I was always wedged in the middle. Those car rides culminated in moments of pure, unadulterated joy as we all—parents included—let our guards down, relishing the ice cream, rose syrup, and vermicelli noodles. It was like every spoonful dissolved a layer of everyday worries. Fridays were my dad's day to bring home a breakfast that felt like a feast. Halwa puri and channa graced our dining table, rendering the day ahead not just manageable but eagerly anticipated.

When I moved to Rhode Island and later New York, I took my love of food and the traditions of hospitality with me. Meeting people from all over the world and getting to experience many places abroad, I came to love gathering around tables with myriad cuisines and flavors. After I met Laura, we began to cook together. We talked about our grandmothers and how food brought everyone together. We hosted internationally themed potlucks and laughed till we cried. I got to meet her family and cook with them. Those moments reminded me so much of home, where everyone cooked and ate together.

When Laura left New York, we lamented the end of our small cookouts, and all the gatherings with conversation and time to slow down and savor great fellowship. We started our Instagram, Sugar and Spice, as a way to stay connected through our favorite creative outlet—food. We also set a goal to make something positive to counteract the divisive moment we found ourselves in. At a time when welcoming the stranger was replaced by talk of walls to keep people apart, we wanted to focus on all the things that bring us together. There is nothing so uniting as a table set for family and friends, no place we connect better than gathered around a delicious spread of home-cooked dishes.

LAURA

My family was never big on spices or even fresh herbs. I grew up in a community of Dutch descendants in Michigan. We were quite happy with simple flavors and we built our diets on local produce and comfort food. When there was an illness or a death, our community shared love in a casserole dish or a pie plate. Potlucks were the favorite way to gather and my mom's dishes were always among the favorites shared at parties. It was a time that packaged foods were well established and, like many Americans, we usually had a bag of sliced squishy bread in our house. I made my first trip out of the country at eighteen and discovered the bread of Europe and fell in love. Early every morning, my friend's Oma would go to the bakery to buy fresh Brötchen and everyone would share in the crusty rolls with butter and cheese—a breakfast my ancestors must have eaten daily, but somehow Americans had replaced with boxed cereals. As I traveled more and lived in urban areas, I discovered much about food and its personal history. Memories of family meals and recipes passed through generations are ingrained in our sense of self and culture. Mumtaz shared much of her world with me through her stories of food. How unlikely could our food friendship be—her from a land of spice and me from the comparatively bland Midwest? What we realized is that how people connect is the same whether over a potluck casserole or a warm plate of dal. Comfort comes in many forms. Perhaps our histories became our methods for making food. Mine went back to the perfect Brötchen in Germany and a love of baking. Mumtaz's fondness of spice has made savory cooking her passion. As we wrote this book, we didn't divide the recipes by origin, but mostly by whether they were made in an oven or cooked on the stove.

Researching this book made me believe that food is often like people—traditions mix across the globe. Historically, as people traveled and emigrated, they took their heritage and their recipes with them. I grew up believing that I was all Dutch, but in fact my ancestry also includes British, Scandanavian, and German. My son has that and Mayan, with a sprinkle of Spanish and Italian. The origin of food is likewise complex and varying. Churros originated in Spain but have become so intricately woven into Mexican cuisine, they seem to belong to both countries. The United Kingdom claims Chicken Tikka Masala as its national dish—a meal they brought over after colonizing India. Developed by an Italian while living in France, is frangipane Italian or French? Bitterballen are a quintessential bar snack in the Netherlands but are clearly influenced by Spanish croquettes. Sometimes we had to debate which section a food belonged in or who owned a specific recipe. In the end the answer is like us; we may hail from a specific place but our diaspora places us and our traditions all over the world. We can take pride in our origins and our foods while also knowing that many heritages came together to build our cuisines—just as my son's heritage stretches from the new world to the old, the ancient pyramid-builders of Mesoamerica to the builders or windmills and canals in Amsterdam.

We hope you will use this book to build a variety of beautiful table spreads and boards from a large party to a small intimate gathering. The dishes and flavors will inspire conversation, treat people to new experiences, and elicit nostalgia. We have done our best to be true to the flavors of each region we included while working to make recipes accessible to all. We do not intend this to be a comprehensive sampling of world cuisine, but rather a love letter to all the tables around the world where we have gathered and the many people from all over the globe who have broken bread with us. It is a celebration of the multitude of spices, sweets, and flavors we have tried, the complexity of stories and culture, the joy of coming together around abundant platters and dishes, and most of all the universality of this one simple act—sharing food as a form of love.

MUMTAZ'S PANTRY

GHEE

Clarified butter essential in Indian cuisine, ghee provides a rich, nutty flavor ideal for cooking.

TOASTED SESAME OIL

This oil, made from pressing toasted sesame seeds, brings depth and a subtle nuttiness to East Asian dishes.

EXTRA VIRGIN OLIVE OIL

The defining oil of the Mediterranean, fruity extra virgin olive oil shines in Italian, Spanish, and Greek cuisine.

SOY SAUCE

This fermented sauce with wheat and soybeans delivers savory umami and saltiness to various Asian cuisines.

TAHINI PASTE

Ground sesame seeds create this tangy, creamy condiment central to Middle Eastern foods like hummus.

GINGER PASTE

Fresh ginger gets pulverized into this spicy, citrusy paste that punches up curries, stir fries, and teas.

GARLIC PASTE

Minced raw garlic blended into a sharp paste contributes flavor and aroma across global cuisines.

DATES

Sweet, sticky dates are used in Middle Eastern desserts and entrees, also lending natural sugar to smoothies.

POMEGRANATE MOLASSES

Sour pomegranate juice reduced into a syrup adds sweet-tart depth to Middle Eastern dishes like muhammara.

CHILI CRISP

Fried chilies and aromatics in oil lend this condiment crunchy heat and umami flavor to Asian cooking.

GOCHUJANG PASTE

The fermented Korean chili paste brings sweet yet spicy umami and a touch of vinegar to various dishes.

SESAME SEEDS

Nutty, oil-rich sesame seeds get sprinkled on breads and in Asian dishes for texture and subtle flavor.

Saffron (Kesar)
The "golden" and costly spice, hand-harvested saffron lends its vivid color and unmistakable flavor to Indo-Pakistani delicacies.

Spices have long played a pivotal role in global trade and culinary traditions. Portugal's conquest of the spice trade beginning in the 1500s brought once-obscure flavors from Asia and Africa to Europe, irrevocably shaping the country's cuisine. Intrepid voyages in search of pepper, cinnamon, nutmeg, and more influenced trademark Portuguese dishes like piri piri chicken and pickled fish. Meanwhile, spices arriving in the UK from colonial Indo-Pakistan—most notably curry powder—left an enduring mark on British food culture. Today, tikka masala and coriander are quintessential ingredients. But nowhere is the impact of spice more evident than in Indo-Pakistani cooking. Over centuries, spices like turmeric, cardamom, and saffron have become essential across regions—woven into curry blends, infused in rice dishes, dusted onto meats. Whether providing heat, aroma, medicine, or preservative powers, spices' role in transporting people across distance and time is unmatched. Ultimately, the demand to cultivate, sell, buy, and savor these flavors of faraway lands connected civilizations in trade and forever transformed foodways.

Red Chili Powder (Lal Mirch)

This quintessential spice traces its origins to the Americas but became indispensable across the regional cuisines of Indo-Pakistan for its intense red hue and fiery bite.

Paprika Powder

Once a pillar of Silk Road Spice Trade, sweet Hungarian paprika brings a burst of red and a touch of smoke to European and Indo-Pakistani dishes alike.

Black Peppercorn (Kaali Mirch)

The "King of Spices" journeys from India's Malabar Coast to ancient Rome and beyond, imparting its distinctive heat and aroma.

Carom Seeds (Ajwain)

Tiny, flavor-packed carom seeds infuse Indo-Pakistani curries and breads with thyme-like notes, also aiding digestion.

Cumin Seeds (Jeera)

This smoky, earthy spice essential from Mexico to the Middle East provides warmth and depth to Indo-Pakistani cuisines.

Coriander seeds (Dhaniya Seeds)

Fresh, grassy coriander seeds flavor curries, spice blends, and breads from Indo-Pakistan to the Mediterranean.

Cardamom (Elachi)

Regarded as "Queen of Spices," floral cardamom from India and Guatemala stars in Indo-Pakistani sweets and curries.

Bay Leaf (Tej Patta)

Playing both aroma and medicine, the ancient bay laurel leaf flavors pilafs and sauces of Indo-Pakistan and the Mediterranean.

Curry Leaves (Kadhi Patta)

Fresh curry leaves offer citrus and herbaceous notes that define southern Indo-Pakistani dishes.

Fenugreek Seeds (Methi Seeds)

Bittersweet, earthy fenugreek seeds blend into Indo-Pakistani curries, breads and teas to aid digestion.

Nigella Seed (Kalonji)

Ancient nigella seeds bring oniony notes, popping texture, and black sesame beauty when sprinkled on Indo-Pakistani breads.

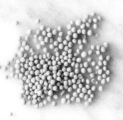

Mustard Seeds (Rai)

Pungent, nutty mustard seeds temper Indo-Pakistani curries, pickles, and oils through their crackling-hot finish.

Nutmeg (Jaipal)

This once-prized protected spice provides warmth and balance from Indonesian eggnog to European baked goods.

Sumac Spice

Tangy, burgundy sumac encapsulates Middle Eastern fare with its citrusy zing and pretty purple hue.

Turmeric Powder

Earthy, vibrant turmeric colors and flavors rice, curries, and teas from India to the Middle East; also touted for health benefits.

LAURA'S PANTRY

MEASURING FLOUR

To measure flour it is best practice to first stir or sift the flour to fluff it up. Add flour to measuring cup by scooping it with a spoon until measuring cup is over-full. Use a flat knife to level off the flour, scraping extra flour back into the flour container. Avoid using the measuring cup to scoop the flour as that compacts the flour, resulting in more than the recipe calls for.

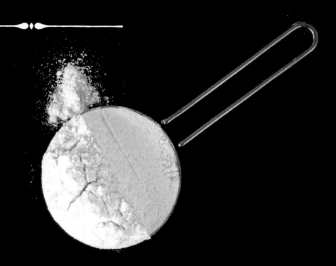

FLOURS

Since this book covers many regions, it also contains a variety of flours. Western baking typically uses wheat flours. Along with wheat flours the recipes in this book contain many other flours to add new flavors and for those who prefer gluten-free options.

All-Purpose Flour

As the name implies, this flour will work for most savory and sweet baking. All-purpose flour is made from a mix of hard and soft wheat and has a medium level of protein / gluten.

Bread Flour vs. Cake Flour

Bread flour, made from hard wheat, is on the high end of the gluten spectrum, making it perfect for chewy bagels and crusty breads. The low gluten level in cake flour produces a fine, light crumb.

Whole Wheat Flour

Whole wheat flour is milled from whole unprocessed wheat kernels, leaving in the germ and bran. This makes whole wheat flour higher in fiber, nutrients, and flavors. It has a high protein content and creates a denser end result.

Semolina

Made from hard durum wheat, Semolina is a high-gluten flour with a coarse texture, commonly used in pasta and couscous. Semolina is often used in Europe and the Middle East.

Rice Flour

Rice flour originated in Asia and is a gluten-free flour used in dumplings, baked goods, and as a thickener. We use it in our beer batters and in Tijgerbol (page 131). It is high in protein and dietary fiber.

Teff Flour

High in fiber and protein, teff flour is more nutritious than wheat flour and is also naturally gluten free. Teff is a grass that grows in the Horn of Africa and is an essential ancient grain in Ethiopian cooking. It comes in a variety of colors including brown and ivory.

Almond Flour

Almond flour, made entirely from blanched almonds, is a gluten-free flour commonly used in baked goods such as macarons, amaretti, and frangipane.

Masa Harina

Masa Harina means "dough flour" in Spanish and was first developed in Mesoamerica hundreds of years ago. It is still a staple in Mexico and Central America. This gluten-free flour is commonly used in corn tortillas and tamales and comes in a variety of colors depending on the corn it was made from.

Chickpea Flour

Chickpea flour is made from ground garbanzo beans and is frequently used in Middle Eastern, Pakistani, and Indian cooking. It is also known as besan or gram flour.

YEAST

I always use active dry yeast in my recipes. If you swap it out for instant dry, you can subtract some time from the rise. Rise times will always vary based on your room temperature. If your house is on the cold side, place your dough in the oven with the oven light on. Store opened yeast packages in the refrigerator.

BUTTER

It's always best practice to use unsalted butter in baking recipes. One can never tell how much salt is in the salted variety, so the only way to control salt content is to use unsalted butter. I prefer American butter (from grass-fed cows when I can afford it) when baking and European butter for pretty much everything else.

EGGS

Look for pasture-raised versus free-range or cage-free eggs. Avoid eggs that say vegetarian-fed, as the only way to make natural omnivores into vegetarians is to deny the hens access to the outdoors. You know you have a good egg when the yolk is much closer to orange than yellow.

Most baking recipes in this book call for room-temperature eggs. This is to keep the butter in your recipe from hardening which will destroy the light and fluffy butter-sugar combination and will reduce the rise and crumb in your final baked good.

CHOCOLATE & COCOA POWDER

Chocolate and cocoa are ingredients that vary greatly in quality. You really do get what you pay for when it comes to chocolate. Inferior, cheap ingredients will make your final baked goods taste mediocre. Valrhona makes excellent chocolate and cocoa. Guittard is also a favorite —with excellent flavor and fair-trade production, it is a great staple to keep in your pantry. When melting chocolate, it is best to melt from a coarsely chopped chocolate bar or real chocolate melting wafers. Chocolate chips are designed to hold their form so they are not the best for melting.

VANILLA

Vanilla is the heart of flavor in baking—the most essential extract to keep in your pantry. Pure vanilla extract is made from dried vanilla beans soaked in alcohol for months—not to be confused with imitation vanilla, which is chemically synthesized vanilla flavor—only one of vanilla's three hundred flavors. Real vanilla is complex and is the second most expensive spice (after saffron) in the world. In this book, we use three forms of vanilla: extract, bean paste, and beans. Vanilla bean paste and beans have stronger flavor and will also add dark, tiny flecks to your baked good. I make my own vanilla extract with vodka and vanilla beans. Since I cut my beans open before making my extract, I get vanilla bean seeds in all my sweet baking.

OTHER EXTRACTS & FLAVORS

We use almond extract, peppermint extract, rose water, and orange blossom water in this book. The main thing to look for when shopping for extracts is *pure* on the label. Try to avoid artificial flavors.

HONEY

Honey is a key ingredient in Mediterranean and Middle Eastern cuisines. It's good to have on hand to add to boards and as an ingredient. Store honey outside of the refrigerator in an airtight container for up to one year.

PUFF PASTRY

We use so much puff pastry in the recipes in this book that it seemed important to also include a recipe on how to make it yourself. Don't worry if you don't have the time or inclination to make your own. It is easy to find in the store and your recipes will still turn out great if you would rather buy puff pastry than make it. When purchasing puff pastry, check the ingredients on the back of the package. Be wary of pastry that doesn't have butter as the first ingredient. Be more wary of packaged puff pastry that has no butter at all. Packaged puff pastry with real butter does cost more, but it also tastes better and isn't filled with hydrogenated oils and chemicals.

ROUGH PUFF PASTRY

Rough puff pastry is the easier version of the more intense, real-deal, butter-block, lamination method of making puff pastry. With some care, you can make something just as buttery, flaky, and delicious. The process is similar to making pie crust—just with more steps to create layers. Be very careful to not overmix the dough. It is essential to have chunks of butter, which will steam when they hit the oven, creating the puff. It is also helpful to make in a cool kitchen, on a cold surface like a marble pastry board. Melting butter is the enemy of getting the dough to layer properly.

2⅔ cups all-purpose flour

⅔ cup bread flour

1 teaspoon salt

1 cup + 5 tablespoons unsalted butter, very cold

⅓ cup ice water + more if needed

1. In a medium bowl, mix the flours and salt. Slice the butter into 1-teaspoon pats and toss into the flour-salt mixture. Toss the butter with your hands to coat with flour. Flatten each piece of butter between your fingers, tossing flour to recoat the butter. You should still have large, flat pieces of butter.

2. Sprinkle the ice water over the crumb mixture. Toss to combine. Squeeze the crumbs together until a dough forms. If the dough doesn't come together, add more ice water 1 tablespoon at a time until you get the dough to form. Flatten dough into a 2-inch-thick rectangle and cover with plastic wrap. Refrigerate for 30 to 45 minutes. Don't refrigerate too long or the dough will get too firm and won't be pliable. If you do leave it in refrigerator for too long, take it out a let it set on counter for 10 minutes before rolling it out.

3. On a lightly floured surface, roll out dough into a rectangle, ½ inch thick. Use a bench scraper to neaten the edges to make them as straight as you can. They don't have to be perfect. Fold the dough as you would a letter. With the short side closest to you, fold the top third down and the bottom third up. (see photos on the next page). Rotate 90 degrees and roll it out to a ½-inch-thick rectangle again. Repeat the letter fold. Wrap dough in plastic wrap and refrigerate 30 minutes.

4. Remove dough from refrigerator and repeat step 3, rolling and folding the dough two more times. Divide in half and wrap each portion tightly in plastic wrap and refrigerate for 1 to 2 hours. The dough is now ready to use.

CONTINUED

5. To store dough for a later use, roll out each dough half to about ¼-inch thickness, cover with a sheet of parchment, roll or fold dough. Place in a resealable plastic bag and freeze for up to 2 months. Thaw frozen puff pastry dough in refrigerator for 4 hours before you need to use it.

NOTES: If at any time you notice that the butter is starting to melt, place your dough back in the refrigerator to firm up. If your kitchen is too warm, you may only be able to do one fold between each refrigeration.

The type of butter you use matters. American butter has a lower fat content and is harder than most European butters. That makes the American butter easier to work with—it doesn't melt as fast. However, the extra fat in the European butter adds better flavor and more puff to your pastry. You can use whichever you prefer. Just be ready to add more refrigeration to your process if using European butter.

This recipe calls for a mix of bread flour and all-purpose flour. The added gluten in the bread flour gives the dough a little more strength to help hold layers together. You can switch to 3⅓ cups all-purpose flour and eliminate the bread flour. The taste will not be altered; you may just have slightly less puff.

Each portion of dough will weigh about 1 pound, which is close to the weight of one package of store-bought puff pastry.

MAKES ABOUT **2** POUNDS

BUILDING BOARDS & TABLE SCAPES

Whether hosting an intimate dinner or lively cocktail party, thoughtfully designed spaces encourage guests to gather, graze, and connect. Your table should complement, not overpower, the cultural nuances of the food. Research table customs to inform choices like utensils, dining formats, and menu progression.

STYLING IDEAS

Opt for natural materials like wood, marble, geode, slate—each adds unique texture. Rough-hewn woods provide organic beauty while polished marble lends elegance. Layer boards of varying sizes and materials for interest. Try incorporating unexpected platters like terracotta tiles or reclaimed metal for rustic charm. Cluster ceramic vases, mercury glass votives, and bud vases for ambiance.

Narrating a Culinary Tale: Immerse your guests in a gastronomic adventure by aligning the theme of your table scapes with the cuisine being served. This could be achieved through the choice of board, garnishes, or complementary table adornments.

Fresh Flowers: Intersperse fresh flowers or edible blooms amidst your culinary creations. Choose flowers whose colors harmonize with the food and tableware.

Layering: Elevate your display by using tiered serving platters or stacking some items on cake stands. This creates dimension and makes the table more engaging.

Textiles: Incorporate linens, napkins, or table runners to add layers and colors. Select colors that resonate with the theme of your gathering or the season.

Personal Touch: Infuse your personal touch by incorporating unique or quirky serving pieces that reflect your style. Showcase treasured linens, heirloom silver, handmade bowls with a story.

HELPFUL SERVEWARE

Wooden Boards: Ideal for a rustic or homely setup, and perfect for cheeses, charcuteries, and bread.

Marble Boards: Adds a touch of elegance, best for displaying fruits, desserts, or cold appetizers.

Slate Boards: Chic and modern, a slate board can be used for a variety of foods and is great for labeling cheeses or charcuterie items with chalk.

Pinch Bowls: Employ petite pinch bowls to hold dips, spreads, and pickled delights. These not only add color but also provide ease for guests to help themselves.

SERVING HACKS

Preparation: Pre-slice charcuteries, breads, and cheeses for effortless grazing. Check out the Make Ahead section for ideas to reduce work on the day of the gathering.

Labeling: Label food items for guests' convenience; this is especially beneficial for those with dietary restrictions. Add chalkboard signs or reclaimed wood plaques to write on.

Temperature Control: Ensure cold items remain cold and warm items stay warm by using chilled or heated serving ware accordingly.

Garnishing: A final flourish of fresh herbs, fruit slices, or a sprinkle of nuts can enhance the visual appeal and taste.

Scale: Use the chapters as a guide to build your menu, but scale it to what works for your group and your schedule. Many of these table scapes required both of our full attention to build. If there is only one of you preparing food, you might need to reduce the items on the menu. You can also mix and match to create an international table scape or board.

CHEESES

What could be more inviting than a platter laden with cheese options to welcome guests? If hosting a party showcasing a specific region, research the most popular cheeses from that region. Higher-end grocery stores have a wide selection of delicious imported cheeses. They will normally organize them by region. If you want to know more about a specific cheese, the employee in that section will often be able to answer your questions. Creating a cheese board is an exercise in personal expression. Use these guidelines as a base and then let your preferences and creativity guide you to your unique masterpiece.

* Aim to have a balanced mix of textures and flavors on your board. A soft cheese like Brie offers a creamy texture, while the firmness of Manchego brings a different tactile sensation. A blue cheese like Roquefort can introduce a strong flavor profile, contrasting nicely with milder varieties.

* To truly appreciate the intricate flavors, always serve cheese at room temperature. It's advisable to take it out of the refrigerator about an hour before your guests arrive.

* Fresh fruits such as grapes or apples add a touch of sweetness, while olives and pickled veggies introduce a tangy contrast. Make sure to include a selection of crackers or some fresh crusty bread. For those who enjoy meats, prosciutto or salami complements cheese wonderfully.

* A wooden board or a slate plate can be your canvas. Lay out the cheeses with some spacing, and if you're hosting a larger group, consider labeling them. This can be both decorative and informative.

* While wine is a classic partner for cheese, the specific type depends on your cheese selection. Reds, whites, and sparkling wines all have their pairings. For those preferring non-alcoholic beverages, a sparkling water with a hint of citrus is both refreshing and neutral.

* Ensure you have appropriate cheese knives for each type. Different cheeses demand different tools, from spreaders for soft cheeses to sturdier knives for the hard ones.

"It seems that the more places I see and experience, the bigger I realize the world to be. The more I become aware of, the more I realize how relatively little I know of it, how many places I have still to go, how much more there is to learn."

—ANTHONY BOURDAIN

PAN-ASIAN TABLE

"It's very simple; in every culture and language, food is love." —DAVID CHANG

Pan-Asian cuisine brings together a variety of culinary traditions from across the diverse regions of Asia. It began with simple exchanges of recipes among Asian communities, growing over time into a shared culinary identity. As travel and migration became easier after the 1950s, the appeal of Pan-Asian cuisine reached beyond Asia, allowing people worldwide to enjoy a blend of Asian flavors. Today, this cuisine continues to contribute to the global food culture, showcasing the rich history and traditions of Asia through every dish. The recipes we've chosen capture the essence of Pan-Asian cuisine, blending flavors from different parts of Asia. From the savory Sesame Shrimp Toast with a sweet chili dipping sauce from China, the spicy kick of Gochujang Dipping Sauce from Korea, to the bold spices in Thailand's Chicken Meatballs, each dish tells a part of the larger story of Asian culinary heritage. While each recipe has roots in its native land, together they provide a delightful journey through the flavorful world of Pan-Asian cuisine. The love for this food is evident in New York City, where many have embraced the unique flavors of this culinary style. The city's food scene has been spiced up with the introduction of Asian condiments like spicy chili crisp and gochujang dipping sauce, which have quickly become favorites among New Yorkers. These additions have not only become staple items in many kitchens but also added a dash of Asian flair to the multifaceted culinary landscape of New York, showcasing the broad appeal and delicious versatility of Pan-Asian cuisine. —M.M.

MAKE AHEAD

You can make the Bao Buns in advance. Allow them to cool and store them in an airtight container. Re-steam them to warm them up before serving.

You can wrap the Asian-Style Shrimp Wontons in advance and freeze. No need to thaw; you can fry them straight from the freezer.

Prepare the Bulgogi marinade, Sweet Chili Dipping Sauce, Asian Dipping Sauce, and Gochujang Dipping Sauce up to two days in advance. Store it in an airtight container in the refrigerator.

EXTRAS

Chili crisp

Fish sauce

Thai chili paste (like Nam Prik Pao)

Gochujang paste

Hoisin sauce

Mirin

TIME SAVERS

Bao buns, sweet chili dipping sauce, and Asian dipping sauce can be purchased instead of making.

Styling Ideas

Adorn your table with fresh fruits such as lychees, dragon fruit, and oranges to add vibrant color and texture.

Embellish with cherry blossom branches, orchids, or bamboo shoot. Arrange them in traditional vases or lay them directly on boards and platters.

RECIPES

Sesame Shrimp Toast with
Sweet Chili Dipping Sauce ✕ 7

Mini Scallion Pancakes ✕ 8

Asian-Style Shrimp Wontons ✕ 11

Korean-Inspired Beef Bulgogi Lettuce Wraps ✕ 12

Sticky Gochujang Shrimp Baos ✕ 15

Spicy Thai Chicken Meatballs
with Sesame Chili Dipping Sauce ✕ 18

SESAME SHRIMP TOAST WITH SWEET CHILI DIPPING SAUCE

Sesame Shrimp Toast is a beloved Chinese Cantonese-style appetizer that's found its way to hearts and menus globally. Its origins are deeply rooted in the Guangdong province, where the art of dim sum—small bite-sized portions of food—was refined. This dish is a delightful rendezvous of finely minced shrimp, seasoned and perched atop slices of crisp, golden brown bread, then generously sprinkled with sesame seeds.

SHRIMP TOAST
1 pound raw shrimp, shelled and deveined

1 tablespoon soy sauce

1 egg, lightly beaten

1 tablespoon chopped green onions

1 teaspoon grated fresh ginger

6 slices of bread

2 tablespoons sesame seeds

Frying-grade oil for frying

SWEET CHILI DIPPING SAUCE
½ cup sweet chili sauce

1 tablespoon rice vinegar

1 teaspoon soy sauce

1 teaspoon grated fresh ginger

1 tablespoon chopped green onions

1. **To prepare the shrimp mixture:** In a food processor, combine the shrimp, soy sauce, egg, green onions, and grated ginger. Process until a smooth paste forms.

2. **To prepare the bread:** Trim the crusts off the bread slices and cut each into 4 triangles. Spread a generous amount of the shrimp mixture onto one side of each triangle. Sprinkle sesame seeds over the shrimp mixture, pressing gently to adhere.

3. **To fry the shrimp toast:** Heat frying-grade oil in a large pot until it reaches the appropriate frying temperature. Use a thermometer to accurately monitor the temperature. The oil should be about 3 inches deep.

4. Carefully lower the bread triangles, shrimp side down, into the oil. Fry for about 1 to 2 minutes until the bottom is golden brown, then flip and fry for an additional minute or until the bread is golden and crispy. Work in batches to avoid overcrowding the pan. Transfer the finished toasts to a plate lined with paper towels to drain any excess oil.

5. **To prepare the dipping sauce:** In a small bowl, whisk together sweet chili sauce, rice vinegar, soy sauce, grated ginger, and chopped green onions.

6. **To serve:** Arrange the shrimp toasts on a platter and serve immediately with the sweet chili dipping sauce on the side.

MAKES **24**

MINI SCALLION PANCAKES

Mini Scallion Pancakes, or "cong you bing," are a cherished staple in Chinese cuisine, often reminisced as a warm morning delight or a companion to the evening tea. Originating from the bustling streets and age-old eateries of China, these savory pancakes have now found a cozy place in the global culinary scene.

SCALLION PANCAKES

2¼ cups all-purpose flour + extra for dusting

1 teaspoon sugar

¾ cup boiling water

⅓ cup cold water (adjust as required)

3 teaspoons toasted sesame oil

Kosher salt to taste

½ cup finely chopped scallions (ensure they are dry)

¾ cup vegetable oil for frying

¾ teaspoon red pepper flakes (optional)

ASIAN DIPPING SAUCE

2½ tablespoons soy sauce

1½ tablespoons rice vinegar

1 teaspoon sesame oil

1 tablespoon sugar

1 green onion, finely chopped

½ teaspoon red chili flakes

1. To make the scallion pancakes: In a bowl, combine flour and sugar. Gradually pour in boiling water, stirring consistently. Add the cold water bit by bit, mixing until a cohesive, non-sticky dough forms. Adjust with additional cold water as necessary.

2. On a floured surface, knead the dough for about 3 to 5 minutes until smooth. Cover with a damp cloth and allow it to rest for 1 hour.

3. Once rested, divide the dough into 20 equal-sized balls. Roll out each ball on a floured surface into a 3-inch circle.

4. Brush each mini circle lightly with sesame oil. Sprinkle a pinch of salt and a bit of the chopped scallions on each. Roll each circle into a tight cylinder, then coil each cylinder into a snail-like shape, tucking and pinching the end underneath. Let them rest under a cloth for another 20 minutes.

5. After resting, take each coiled dough and roll again into a 3-inch circle. They're now ready for frying.

6. Heat the vegetable oil in a frying pan over medium heat. Once hot, fry the mini pancakes until golden brown on both sides. This might take around 1 minute per side, but keep an eye on them to avoid overbrowning. Transfer to paper towels to drain excess oil.

7. To make the Asian dipping sauce: In a bowl, whisk together the soy sauce, rice vinegar, sesame oil, and sugar until sugar dissolves. Stir in the chopped green onion and red pepper flakes, if using. Serve with Mini Scallion Pancakes.

MAKES ABOUT 20

ASIAN-STYLE SHRIMP WONTONS

The humble wonton embodies culinary universality, transcending borders to find a place in many a culture's gastronomic narrative. As Shrimp Wontons grace our Pan-Asian Table, they echo a common language of food that speaks through delicate folds and savory fillings. From China's cherished tradition, the essence of wontons meandered across cultures, inspiring variations such as Italian ravioli and Eastern European pierogi. Each culture, while maintaining the essence, imparted its own flavors and techniques, turning a simple dumpling into a global culinary icon.

1 pound shrimp, peeled, deveined, and finely chopped

1 tablespoon sesame oil, divided

1 teaspoon chili crisp oil

½ lime, juiced

1 green onion, finely chopped (optional, for added flavor)

Kosher salt, to taste

Wonton wrappers

Frying-grade oil for frying

1. To make the shrimp filling: In a mixing bowl, combine the finely chopped shrimp, ½ tablespoon of sesame oil, chili crisp oil, lime juice, and green onions. Mix until well combined. Season with a pinch of salt if desired. Taste and adjust seasoning if needed.

2. To wrap the wontons: Lay out a wonton wrapper on a clean surface. Place about a teaspoon of the shrimp mixture in the center. Dip your finger in water and moisten the edges of the wrapper. Fold the wrapper in half to form a triangle, ensuring no air bubbles are trapped. Press the edges to seal. Pull the two opposite ends together and press them, forming a wonton shape. Repeat with the remaining wrappers and filling.

3. To fry the wontons: Heat frying-grade oil in a large pot until it reaches the appropriate frying temperature. Use a thermometer to accurately monitor the temperature. The oil should be about 3 inches deep. You can test the oil by dropping in a small piece of wonton wrapper; if it bubbles and rises to the surface quickly, it's ready.

4. Gently place a few wontons in the hot oil, careful not to overcrowd the pot. Fry the wontons until they are golden brown, which should take about 2 to 3 minutes. Remove the wontons with a slotted spoon and place them on a plate lined with paper towels to drain any excess oil.

MAKES **20-25**

KOREAN-INSPIRED BEEF BULGOGI LETTUCE WRAPS

The journey of Bulgogi is rooted deep within Korean history, tracing back to the Goguryeo era (37 BC–668 AD), evolving over centuries into the savory, sweet, and tender grilled dish we savor today. The very term "Bulgogi" translates to "fire meat," a tribute to the traditional cooking method over open flame. Our rendition pays homage to this age-old practice, preserving the iconic sweet and soy flavor profile, while introducing a contemporary spin with the lettuce wrap.

LETTUCE WRAPS

2 pounds flank steak

¼ cup soy sauce

2 tablespoons rice vinegar

3 tablespoons light brown sugar

4 tablespoons toasted sesame oil, divided

5 cloves garlic, minced

1 tablespoon fresh grated ginger

½ Asian pear, grated

⅛ teaspoon red pepper flakes

1 tablespoon gochujang paste

2 tablespoons sesame seeds

¼ cup finely sliced spring onion

Iceberg lettuce leaves, washed and drained and dried

1. To prepare the beef: Partially freeze the flank steak. This should take around 1 to 1½ hours. This will make it easier to cut. Using a sharp knife, slice the partially frozen flank steak against the grain into thin strips.

2. To prepare the bulgogi marinade: In a mixing bowl, combine the soy sauce, rice vinegar, light brown sugar, 2 tablespoons of the toasted sesame oil, garlic, ginger, Asian pear, pepper flakes, gochujang paste, and 2 tablespoons of sesame seeds. Whisk the ingredients until the sugar dissolves and the marinade is well combined.

3. Add the sliced beef to the bowl and ensure each strip is well-coated with the marinade. Cover the bowl and refrigerate for a minimum of 1 hour. For best results, marinate for at least 4 hours or overnight.

4. To cook the bulgogi: Heat the remaining 2 tablespoons of sesame oil in a large pan or skillet over medium-high heat. Add the marinated beef strips, ensuring not to overcrowd the pan. You might need to cook the beef in batches.

5. Cook each side for about 2 to 3 minutes or until they are nicely browned and cooked to your desired level. Once cooked, remove the beef strips from the pan and set them aside.

CONTINUED

GOCHUJANG DIPPING SAUCE

3 tablespoons gochujang paste

1 tablespoon soy sauce

1 tablespoon toasted sesame oil

1 tablespoon water

1 teaspoon light brown sugar

1 teaspoon sesame seeds (for garnish)

GARNISH

Fresh cilantro

1 carrot, cut into matchsticks

1 green onion, finely chopped

6. Alternately, you can grill the beef on a gas or charcoal grill. Ensure the grates are clean and lightly oil with vegetable oil to prevent the beef from sticking. Preheat it to a medium-high heat. Once the grill is heated, lay the marinated beef strips individually across the grates. Ensure you don't overcrowd them to get proper char and grill marks. Grill each side for about 2 to 3 minutes. Once they have a nice char on each side and are cooked to your preference, remove them from the grill and set aside.

7. To make the gochujang dipping sauce: In a small mixing bowl, combine the gochujang paste, soy sauce, and toasted sesame oil. Stir until the ingredients are well blended. Add water 1 teaspoon at a time until you achieve your desired consistency. Then stir in the light brown sugar until it's completely dissolved in the sauce.

8. To serve: Take a leaf of the iceberg lettuce, place a couple of beef bulgogi strips in the center. Top with some sliced spring onions, matchstick carrots, and a sprinkle of sesame seeds. Garnish with cilantro. Serve with Gochujang Dipping Sauce.

MAKES **12–14**

STICKY GOCHUJANG SHRIMP BAOS

Bao buns have roots in Chinese cuisine, but this recipe brings in a Korean twist. Encased in soft bao buns, the shrimp is glazed with a sweet and spicy gochujang sauce. The fusion of Korean gochujang's spicy kick with the gentle texture of Chinese bao buns creates a dish that showcases the beautiful culinary blend that arises when different Asian flavors meet.

EQUIPMENT
Bamboo steamer

KOREAN BAO BUNS
2¾ cups all-purpose flour + extra for dusting

1½ tablespoons skim-milk powder

1 teaspoon baking powder

1½ teaspoons instant dry yeast

2½ tablespoons white sugar

2½ tablespoons vegetable oil + extra for brushing

¾ cup warm water

14 squares of parchment paper (4×4 inches)

1. **To make the bao buns:** In a large mixing bowl, whisk together flour, milk powder, baking powder, yeast, and sugar. In a separate bowl, combine the vegetable oil and warm water. Create a well in the center of the dry mixture and pour in the liquid mix. Begin mixing with a spoon and gradually knead with your hands until a dough forms. If the dough feels sticky, sprinkle in additional flour, 1 tablespoon at a time. Once combined, move the dough to a floured surface and knead until smooth, about 5 minutes. Place the dough back into the bowl, cover, and allow it to rise in a warm area for about 90 minutes or until it doubles in size.

2. Once risen, transfer the dough to a floured surface. Knead for another 6 to 8 minutes, focusing on removing air bubbles. Roll out the dough to ³⁄₈-inch thickness. Lightly brush the surface with vegetable oil. Using a 3-inch diameter cookie cutter (or a similarly sized cup), cut out circles. Gather and reroll any excess dough. Fold the cut circles in half, gently press down to flatten slightly, and place each on a parchment paper square. Lay them in bamboo steamer. Cover the folded dough circles and let them rise again for 30 minutes.

3. Fill a wok or deep pan about one-third full with water and set it over high heat. Once boiling, place the bamboo steamer over the wok. If you don't have a bamboo steamer, you can use a metal steamer but make sure the buns don't touch the water. Steam the buns for 12 minutes. After this, turn off the heat but leave the steamer lid on, allowing the buns to sit over the hot water for an additional 5 minutes.

CONTINUED

CRISPY SHRIMP

1 lemon, juiced

2 teaspoons soy sauce

2 tablespoons mirin

¼ teaspoon ground white pepper

1 pound medium-sized shrimp, washed, peeled, and deveined

1 cup + 2 tablespoons cornstarch

Frying-grade oil for frying

STICKY GOCHUJANG SAUCE

¼ cup soy sauce

¼ cup light brown sugar

1½ tablespoons apple cider vinegar

3 tablespoons gochujang paste

2 tablespoons ketchup

1 tablespoon chili crisp

4 cloves garlic, minced

OPTIONAL TOPPINGS

Sriracha mayonnaise

Pickled Red Onions (page 290)

Green onions, chopped

Sesame seeds, toasted

4. **To prepare the shrimp:** In a mixing bowl, combine the lemon juice, soy sauce, mirin, and ground white pepper. Stir well to mix. Add the shrimp to the bowl and toss. Cover the bowl with plastic wrap or a lid. Refrigerate for at least 30 minutes.

5. **To prepare the sticky gochujang sauce:** In a saucepan over medium-high heat, combine soy sauce, light brown sugar, apple cider vinegar, gochujang, ketchup, chili crisp, and minced garlic. Bring the mixture to a simmer. Cook for roughly 5 minutes or until it slightly thickens. Once done, set aside to cool down.

6. **To fry the shrimp:** Place the cornstarch in a flat plate. Toss each shrimp in the cornstarch, ensuring they are well-coated. Shake off any excess cornstarch and set them aside.

7. Heat oil in a large pot until it reaches the appropriate frying temperature. Use a thermometer to accurately monitor the temperature. The oil should be about 3 inches deep.

8. Fry the shrimp in batches, ensuring not to overcrowd the pan. Fry each batch for about 5 minutes or until the shrimp turn golden brown and are fully cooked. Remove and drain the shrimp on a wire rack with paper towels below to catch any excess oil.

9. **To assemble the bao buns:** Gently open a bao bun. Spread a thin layer of sriracha mayonnaise on one side of the bun. Place 2 to 3 crispy shrimp in the center. Drizzle gochujang sauce. Add pickled onions and chopped green onions. Sprinkle with toasted sesame seeds.

NOTE: You can serve the shrimp on their own, generously brushed with the Sticky Gochujang Sauce.

MAKES **12–14**

SPICY THAI CHICKEN MEATBALLS WITH SESAME CHILI DIPPING SAUCE

Thai cuisine often marries the heat of fresh chilies with the umami depth of fish sauce and the aromatic notes of herbs like cilantro and basil. These meatballs are no exception, embodying the tradition of blending a variety of spices and herbs to achieve a complex, layered flavor profile.

MEATBALLS

1 pound ground chicken

1 teaspoon minced garlic

½ teaspoon grated fresh ginger

¼ cup roasted peanuts, finely chopped

2 tablespoons roasted sesame seeds, ground

¼ cup finely chopped spring onions

¼ cup chopped mint leaves

2 tablespoons fish sauce

1 teaspoon fresh lime juice

1 teaspoon brown sugar

1 red chili, finely chopped

1 teaspoon soy sauce

Oil for frying

DIPPING SAUCE

2 tablespoons soy sauce

1 tablespoon hoisin sauce

2 tablespoons fresh lime juice

1 clove garlic, minced

1 tablespoon minced fresh ginger

1 tablespoon honey or brown sugar

2 tablespoons sesame oil

1 teaspoon Thai chili paste

1. **To prepare the meatballs:** In a large bowl, combine all the meatball ingredients except the olive oil. Mix until well combined.

2. Shape the mixture into small balls, roughly the size of a golf ball.

3. In a skillet over medium heat, add the olive oil. Once hot, cook the meatballs for about 4 to 5 minutes on each side or until they turn golden brown and are cooked through. Remove and set aside.

4. **To prepare the dipping sauce:** In a small saucepan, combine the ingredients for the dipping sauce. Warm over low heat, stirring until the ingredients are well combined and the sauce thickens slightly. Remove from heat.

5. Transfer the dipping sauce to a serving bowl and serve alongside the meatballs.

MAKES **16-20**

BURMESE KHAO SUEY

"But perhaps the most precious heirlooms are family recipes. Like a physical heirloom, they remind us from whom and where we came and give others, in a bite, the story of another people from another place and another time." —STANLEY TUCCI, *Taste: My Life Through Food*

Khao Suey, a cherished dish rooted in Burma, has seamlessly blended into the culinary landscape of Pakistan, with each household lending its unique flair to this rich, comforting noodle soup. My recipe is a heartwarming fusion of cherished family recipes, melding the authentic essence from my mother's Burmese friend, Hina's mom's exquisite Memon rendition, Fauzia's Bohri rendition, and Aunty Saira's unique spin, showcasing an amalgamation of individual takes on this classic recipe.

I like to serve my Khao Suey with the coconut curry on its own, allowing guests to personalize their bowls. The proteins such as beef, chicken, and tofu are also served individually, offering a choice to suit varied dietary preferences. Accompanying the dish is a variety of condiments like garlic chips, chili oil, cilantro, and sev, providing an opportunity for guests to customize their bowls to their liking. This approach not only caters to a spectrum of palates but also adds a communal and interactive aspect to the meal. —M.M.

MAKE AHEAD

Make Garlic Chips in advance and store them in an airtight container for up to a week. Enjoy your homemade garlic chips as a garnish for soups, salads, steaks, pastas, or even as a snack. The oil left in the pan is now infused with garlic and can be used for cooking other dishes.

The chili oil recipe yields approximately 1¼ cups of red chili oil. Once cooled, you can store the red chili oil in a clean, airtight glass jar. It should last for up to 1 month when stored in a cool, dark place. Always use a clean spoon when you are using the oil to prevent contamination.

Boil eggs up to 2 days in advance. Leave in shell and peel and chop just before serving.

EXTRAS

Sev/crunchy noodles

Potato sticks

Spaghetti

TIME SAVERS

Chili oil, ginger paste, and garlic paste can be purchased instead of making.

Styling Ideas

Use a blend of vintage and contemporary styles. Incorporate vintage bowls or dishes with modern tableware to create a unique and eclectic spread.

Make the meal interactive by setting up a serving station where guests can customize their Khao Suey. Arrange the proteins and condiments in an accessible manner, encouraging guests to build their own bowls.

KHAO SUEY

MARINADE
½ cup yogurt

2 tablespoons soy sauce

1 teaspoon ground cumin

½ teaspoon red chili powder

½ teaspoon ginger paste

½ teaspoon garlic paste

MEAT
1 pound chicken or beef
   tenderloin, finely chopped

½ cup oil

2 medium onions, finely
   chopped

4 fresh curry leaves (optional)

2 teaspoons red chili powder

1 teaspoon turmeric powder

1 teaspoon ground coriander

1 teaspoon ground cumin

½ teaspoon Garam Masala
   (page 53)

2 teaspoons ginger paste

2 teaspoons garlic paste

4 medium Roma tomatoes,
   pureed (you can use
   canned tomatoes too)

1 tablespoon tomato paste

½ lemon, juiced

COCONUT CURRY
½ cup olive oil

2 large onions, pureed

2 teaspoons red chili powder

1 teaspoon turmeric powder

½ teaspoon Garam Masala
   (page 53)

1 teaspoon kosher salt

1. **To marinate the meat:** In a medium-sized bowl, mix all the marinade ingredients using a fork until combined. Add the finely chopped chicken or beef to the marinade and mix until well coated. Marinate for 1 to 2 hours or overnight for best results.

2. **To prepare the meat:** In a medium-sized pan, heat oil over medium heat. Add the finely chopped onions and sauté until they turn golden brown. If using, add fresh curry leaves and sauté for an additional minute.

3. Add red chili powder, turmeric powder, ground coriander, ground cumin, Garam Masala, ginger paste, and garlic paste to the pan. Stir the spices together with the onions for about 5 to 7 minutes.

4. Pour in the pureed tomatoes and tomato paste, stirring continuously. Cook the mixture for another 10 minutes, then add the lemon juice and stir for an additional 2 minutes. Add the marinated meat to the pan and cook for 2 to 3 minutes while stirring. Cover the pan and let the mixture simmer on low heat for approximately 20 minutes or until the meat is fully cooked and tender.

5. **To Prepare the coconut curry:** While the meat simmers, start making the coconut curry. Heat oil over medium heat in a medium-sized pan and sauté the pureed onions until they turn golden brown. Add red chili powder, turmeric powder, ground coriander, ground cumin, Garam Masala, salt, ginger paste, and garlic paste to the pan. Stir the spices together with the onions for about 5 to 7 minutes.

6. Create a slurry in a small bowl by whisking chickpea flour into warm water. Add this slurry to the pan, whisking until fully combined with the spices. Incorporate the coconut milk and 2 cups of water into the mixture, stirring well.

7. Cover the pan, lower the heat, and allow the coconut curry to simmer gently for around 30 to 40 minutes. Stir at 10-minute intervals to prevent the curry from sticking to the bottom of the pan.

2 teaspoons ginger paste

2 teaspoons garlic paste

2 tablespoons chickpea flour

4 tablespoons warm water

3 cans coconut milk

2 cups water

GARLIC CHIPS

1 large head garlic

1 cup olive oil

Kosher salt to taste

RED CHILI OIL

½ cup red pepper flakes

1 tablespoon chili powder

1 cup oil (canola, vegetable, or sunflower)

GARNISH

Garlic chips

Red Chili Oil (above)

Finely chopped cilantro

Lemon wedges

Boiled eggs

Finely cut green chilies

Chili chips

1 box spaghetti or egg noodles

8. **To prepare the garlic chips:** Peel the garlic. Using a sharp knife or a mandolin, thinly slice each clove of garlic. Aim for consistency in the slice thickness as this ensures they will cook evenly.

9. In a small saucepan, add the olive oil and set it over medium-low heat. Once the oil is warm, add the sliced garlic. Cook them on medium-low heat, stirring occasionally. Cook slowly to avoid burning. Continue to cook until the garlic slices become golden brown and crispy. This may take around 15 to 20 minutes. Keep an eye on the heat and turn it down if the garlic starts to brown too quickly.

10. Use a slotted spoon to remove the garlic chips from the oil. Allow them to drain on a paper towel and sprinkle them lightly with salt while they're still warm. Let them cool completely.

11. **To prepare the red chili oil:** In a heatproof bowl, combine chili flakes and chili powder.

12. In a pan, heat 1 cup of oil until hot. Gradually pour the hot oil over the chili mixture. Stir carefully to combine. Allow the mixture to cool completely before using.

13. **To prepare the noodles:** In a separate pot, boil water with some salt. Cook the store-bought noodles according to the package instructions until they are al dente. Drain the water and set the cooked noodles aside.

14. To serve, place the cooked chicken in a serving dish and the coconut curry in a separate serving bowl. Arrange the noodles on a platter and transfer the garnishes into small bowls.

15. To assemble a serving, start with a portion of noodles in a bowl. Ladle the coconut curry over the noodles according to taste. Add the chicken or beef on top. Finish with a selection of garnishes as preferred.

VEGETARIAN OPTION: Replace meat with 1 pound tofu

SERVES **6**

PAKISTANI STREET FOOD

If you wish to understand Pakistan—its people, its history, and its cultural richness—there's no better place to start than with its street food. More than mere sustenance, it's a social connector, a shared language that binds the diverse nation together. It's an unfiltered experience that refuses to be toned down, revealing the authentic soul of Pakistan one bite, one sip, one shared smile at a time. As I reminisce about the roots of my culinary passion, the bustling, aroma-laden streets of Pakistan resonate with a melody of traditions and communal camaraderie. The journey began with each street food stall I encountered, every hearty laugh shared over a spicy plate of Chaat, and every impassioned debate over the authentic texture and taste of a Biryani recipe. They all unveiled a narrative of a culture deeply intertwined with its culinary traditions. The assortment of recipes in this chapter is a tribute to my homeland's vibrant street food culture, offering a glimpse into the heart of Pakistan. As we delve into the nuances of traditional recipes and the stories entwined with them, I invite you to taste, to experience, and to celebrate the unyielding spirit and rich culinary heritage of Pakistan. Through the bustling bazaars and cozy family gatherings, through the spicy, savory, and sweet concoctions, the tale of Pakistan's historic and cultural panorama unfolds, one delectable bite at a time. —M.M.

MAKE AHEAD

Both the chutneys can be made a week in advance and stored in airtight glass jars.

The spiced peanuts can be made a week in advance and stored in an airtight container.

The chickpea batter for the fritters can be made a day in advance and stored in an airtight container in the refrigerator until you are ready to use it.

The shredded chicken mixture for the Chicken and Potato Cutlets can be made a day in advance and stored in an airtight container in the refrigerator until you are ready to use it.

Make the Nankhatai the day before. Store in an airtight container. Garnish before serving.

EXTRAS

Pistachios

Dried Rose petals

Puffed Rice

Papri Chaat Crunch

Chili Garlic Sauce

TIME SAVERS

Use canned chickpeas for the Chaat Station.

Chutneys can be purchased.

You can use an already prepared rotisserie chicken for the Chicken and Potato Cutlets.

Styling Ideas

Create an assemble-yourself chaat station board.

Serve the pakoras on brown butcher paper or newspaper.

Use Pakistani-inspired linens and serveware.

RECIExPES

POTATO AND CHICKEN CUTLETS

These potato parcels of joy were a beloved fixture in my grandmother's house, where they were lovingly prepared and shared. Their practicality, ideal for freezing and serving on demand, made them a teatime staple during my upbringing. During my research, I was struck by how many countries have variations on these "potato puffs," as Laura fondly calls them. It's remarkable how such a simple yet flavorful dish can unite people across cultures. They were among the first Pakistani dishes Laura and her mother ever tried, becoming a frequent request during our cooking sessions. In this rendition, I've taken a traditional favorite and added a personal twist by incorporating shredded rotisserie chicken. —M.M.

POTATO LAYER

4 pounds potatoes, peeled and boiled

3 tablespoons melted butter

1 teaspoon kosher salt

2 teaspoons red chili powder

1 teaspoon Toasted Cumin Powder (page 54)

¼ cup cilantro, finely chopped

CHICKEN FILLING

2 cups shredded chicken

½ cup shredded cheddar cheese

3 tablespoons chopped cilantro

1 green chili, seeded and finely chopped

1 teaspoon Toasted Cumin Powder (page 54)

Kosher salt to taste

BREADCRUMB COATING

4 cups panko breadcrumbs

4–5 eggs

2 tablespoons water

¼ teaspoon black pepper

Kosher salt to taste

Oil to fry

1. **To make the potato layer:** In a medium bowl, mash potatoes. Add butter, salt, chili powder, Toasted Cumin Powder, and cilantro. Mix well and set aside.

2. **To make chicken filling:** In a medium bowl, add chicken, cheese, cilantro, green chili, cumin and salt. Mix well and set aside.

3. **To coat with bread crumbs:** Spread the breadcrumbs on a plate or in a shallow bowl. In a deep bowl, whisk the eggs with water, and season with salt and pepper.

4. **To assemble cutlets:** Line a baking sheet with parchment and set aside. Divide mashed potatoes evenly into 24 portions and form into balls. Press each ball on the palm of your hand to form a disk and add 1 tablespoon chicken filling in the center. Pull the edges of the potato together to form a patty. Dip each patty in egg wash then coat with breadcrumbs to complete the first coat. Coat each patty with eggs and then with breadcrumbs again for the second coat. Place on prepared baking sheet. When all cutlets have been coated, cover loosely with plastic wrap and allow them to firm up in the refrigerator for 30 minutes up to 4 hours.

5. Add 1½ inches oil to a medium frying pan and heat over medium high heat until oil reaches 350°F. Add 3 to 4 patties. Do not overcrowd the pan. Fry for 1 to 1½ minutes and flip using a flat spatula. Once golden brown on both sides, transfer to a serving platter. Serve hot with Mint Cilantro Chutney (page 51).

MAKES **24**

SPICED CHICKEN KEBABS

This recipe is an adaptation of my mother's "dum ka keema," which has been a treasured family dish for many years. These kebabs are highly popular at social gatherings, disappearing within minutes of being served. Given the persistent demand for this recipe, I am so excited to share it with you. —M.M.

1 pound ground chicken

⅓ cup plain yogurt

3 tablespoons low-sodium soy sauce

½ teaspoon turmeric

½ teaspoon red pepper flakes

1 teaspoon red chili powder

2 teaspoons Toasted Cumin Powder (page 54)

2 teaspoons roasted coriander powder

½ teaspoon Garam Masala (page 53)

1 tablespoon fresh ginger paste

2 cloves garlic, minced

⅓ cup ghee

⅓ cup finely sliced onions

⅓ cup chickpea flour

¼ cup chopped fresh cilantro

1 serrano pepper, seeded and finely diced

1 teaspoon vegetable oil

1 piece of coal for smoky flavor (optional)

1. In a large bowl, mix the ground chicken, yogurt, soy sauce, turmeric, red pepper flakes, red chili powder, cumin, coriander, Garam Masala, ginger, and garlic. Use your hands to thoroughly combine the ingredients. Cover the bowl with cling film and marinate the mixture in the refrigerator for 30 minutes or overnight.

2. Heat the ghee in a medium saucepan over medium heat. Add the sliced onions and cook until golden brown, stirring frequently.

3. Sift the chickpea flour into the ghee and onion mixture, stirring constantly for a few minutes until the flour is golden brown. Remove from heat and let cool.

4. Add the cooled flour mixture to the marinated chicken and stir until thoroughly combined. Add the chopped cilantro and diced serrano pepper.

5. Preheat the oven to 375°F and line a baking sheet with parchment paper.

6. Place a small metal bowl in the center of the chicken mixture. Heat a small piece of charcoal over an open flame until it is glowing hot. Place the hot charcoal in the metal bowl and drizzle with 1 teaspoon of vegetable oil. Immediately cover the bowl with a lid or foil, allowing the chicken to absorb the smoky flavor for 10 to 15 minutes. (This step is optional.)

7. Divide the chicken mixture into 15 equal portions and shape each portion into a small ball. Transfer the chicken balls to the prepared baking sheet and bake for 30 minutes or until fully cooked. Serve hot with your favorite dipping sauce or chutney.

MAKES **32**

PAPRI CHAAT

I can still feel the gentle jostle of my grandmother's Suzuki Swift, inching its way through the narrow lanes at 20 miles an hour. The vintage Bollywood tunes from the cassette player served as the soundtrack to our little adventures, even if the cassettes had a habit of malfunctioning. I'd fix them, of course, as we made our way to Bohri Bazar for her weekly shopping. There, the shopkeepers greeted us like family. We would invariably be offered stools to sit on and cups of tea, along with a serving of papri chaat. Those outings were more than shopping trips; they were a lesson in community. —M.M.

EQUIPMENT
2 or 2½ inch cookie cutters

PAPRI
⅔ cup all-purpose flour

¼ teaspoon kosher salt

¼ teaspoon red chili powder

¼ teaspoon carom seeds

1 teaspoon canola oil

4–6 tablespoons water

Peanut oil or other neutral oil for frying

CHAAT
2 medium-sized potatoes, peeled, diced, and boiled

1 (15-ounce) can chickpeas, drained

1 teaspoon Toasted Cumin Powder (page 54)

1 teaspoon Chaat Masala Blend (page 54)

½ teaspoon red chili powder

¼ teaspoon black salt (optional)

1 teaspoon kosher salt

½ cup plain yogurt

½ cup Tamarind and Date Chutney (page 50)

½ cup Mint Cilantro Chutney (page 51)

1. **To make the papri:** In a medium-sized bowl, sift the all-purpose flour. Add the salt, red chili powder, and carom seeds. Mix until combined. Add the canola oil and use your hands to mix it in. Gradually add water, 1 tablespoon at a time, until the dough comes together. Knead the dough for a few minutes. Cover the bowl with plastic wrap and set it aside for half an hour.

2. Add 3 to 4 inches of oil to a Dutch oven or heavy-bottomed pot. Clip a candy thermometer to the side of the pot or set an instant read thermometer near the stove. Preheat the oil to 375°F over medium-high heat.

3. Meanwhile, roll out the dough so that it is very thin. Use a 2- or 2½-inch cookie cutter and cut out thin circles. Fry in batches of 4 to 5 discs at a time for 2 to 3 minutes until golden brown. Transfer to the plate lined with the paper towel to drain and cool.

4. **To make and assemble chaat:** In a mixing bowl, add boiled potatoes and chickpeas. Add Toasted Cumin Powder, chaat masala, red chili powder, black salt, and kosher salt. Mix everything well.

5. In another bowl, whisk plain yogurt until smooth.

6. Arrange papri on a plate. Top the papri with the potato and chickpea mixture. Drizzle tamarind chutney, Mint Cilantro Chutney, and yogurt over the mixture.

7. Sprinkle sev over the chaat. Garnish with finely chopped coriander leaves and pomegranate seeds. Serve immediately.

8. Store unused papri in an airtight box for up to 2 to 3 weeks.

CONTINUED

GARNISH

¼ cup Sev (thin fried noodles made of chickpea flour)

¼ cup finely chopped coriander leaves

¼ cup pomegranate seeds

SERVE WITH

Yogurt Raita (below)

Mint Cilantro Chutney (page 51)

NOTES: You can purchase the papri from a local Indian/ ethnic store or online on Amazon.

You can purchase the date and tamarind chutney from a local Indian/ethnic store or online on Amazon. You can also use a regular tamarind chutney.

You can purchase the Mint Cilantro Chutney from a local Indian/ethnic store or online on Amazon, or make the recipe (page 51). You can also use any green chutney for this recipe.

SERVES **6–8**

YOGURT RAITA

MAKES 1½ CUPS

1 cup plain yogurt

¼ teaspoon Toasted Cumin Powder (page 54)

1 teaspoon Chaat Masala Blend (page 54)

¼ teaspoon salt

Pinch black pepper

1 teaspoon lemon juice

¼ cup finely chopped fresh coriander leaves

¼ cup finely chopped fresh mint leaves

1. In a mixing bowl, whisk together the plain yogurt, ground cumin, Chaat Masala Blend, salt, black pepper, and lemon juice.

2. Add the chopped fresh coriander and mint leaves. Mix well to combine. Cover the raita and refrigerate for at least 30 minutes to allow the flavors to meld.

BUN KEBAB

The enchanting charm of Pakistani street food lies in its ability to democratize cuisine. It erases the societal lines drawn between the suited businessmen and the day laborers, who, after a hard day's work, stand shoulder to shoulder, united by the tantalizing flavors offered on every corner. The bun kebab, often hailed as Pakistan's flavorful answer to the burger, encapsulates this essence quite perfectly. Whether made from lentils or meat, these delectable patties, slathered with chutney and enveloped in soft buns, are devoured with equal gusto across social strata. This recipe holds a special place in my heart, evoking cherished memories of relishing this delightful snack with my aunt and dear friend, Fauzia. Together, we'd navigate our way to Zainab Market, renowned for its bustling energy and unbeatable bun kebabs. —M.M.

2 medium potatoes

2 cups water

1 cup chana daal, soaked overnight

1 small onion

3 cloves garlic

½ piece ginger

2 tablespoons red pepper flakes

4 whole cloves

10 whole black peppercorns

2 teaspoons cumin seeds

1 teaspoon coriander seeds

¼ teaspoon cinnamon

½ teaspoon Garam Masala (page 53)

1 teaspoon Chaat Masala Blend (page 54) + more for serving

1½ teaspoons kosher salt

½ teaspoon white pepper

1 chopped serrano pepper

¼ cup chopped coriander leaves

¼ cup chopped mint leaves

1. **To make the kebabs:** Peel potatoes, boil with ½ teaspoon salt, mash, and set aside.

2. In a medium-sized pot, heat 2 cups of water over medium-high heat. Add daal, onion, garlic, ginger, red pepper, cloves, black peppercorns, cumin seeds, coriander seeds, and cinnamon to the pot. Reduce heat to low and cook until water evaporates and daal is fully cooked.

3. Allow the mixture to cool before transferring to a food processor. Pulse until ingredients are well-ground and combined.

4. In a large bowl, combine the daal mixture with boiled potatoes, Garam Masala, Chaat Masala, salt, white pepper, serrano pepper, coriander leaves, and mint leaves. Mix well using a wooden spoon or your hands.

5. Shape the mixture into round kebabs, approximately 2½ inches wide and 1 inch thick.

6. Crack eggs in a bowl. Add salt and pepper to taste and whip until soft peaks form.

7. Heat oil in a frying pan over medium heat. Coat kebabs generously in the egg mixture and add to the pan once heated. Shallow-fry until golden brown on both sides.

CONTINUED

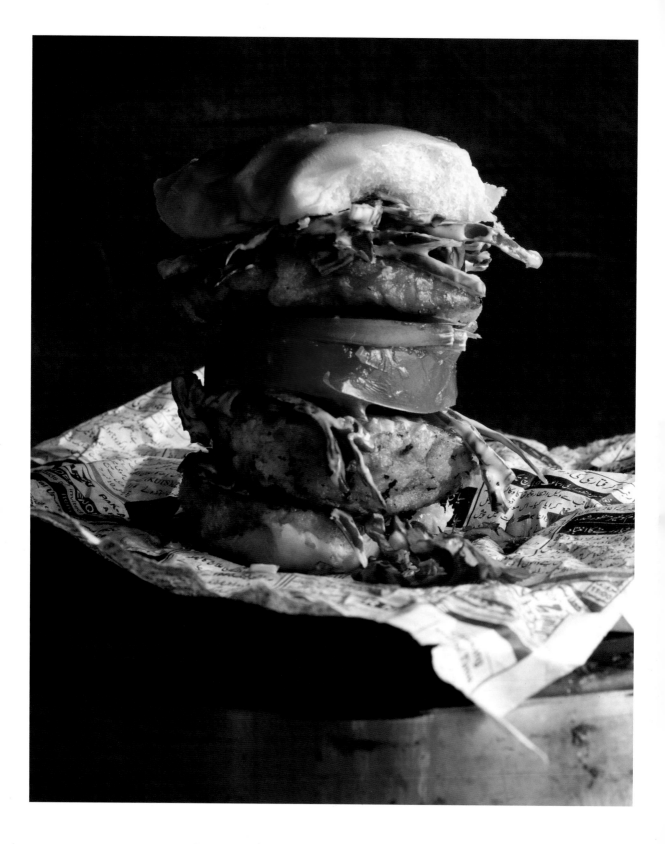

2 eggs

Oil for frying

12 slider buns

1 cup Mint Cilantro Chutney
(page 51)

1 cup Tamarind and Date
Chutney (page 50)

½ cup Yogurt Raita
(page 36)

Pickled Red Onions
(page 290)

2 sliced tomatoes

1 sliced red onion

8. In the same pan, add a bit more oil and lightly fry slider buns on both sides.

9. To assemble: Spread 1 tablespoon each of Mint Cilantro Chutney and Tamarind Chutney on the top and bottom of the slider buns. Place a kebab on the bottom half of the bun.

10. Drizzle with Yogurt Raita and top with Pickled Red Onions, a tomato slice, and an onion ring. Sprinkle with Chaat Masala.

11. In a heated frying pan, add 1 teaspoon of oil and cook the assembled bun kebab for an additional minute, pressing down gently with a spatula to lightly seal the bun halves together (like a grilled cheese).

SERVES **12**

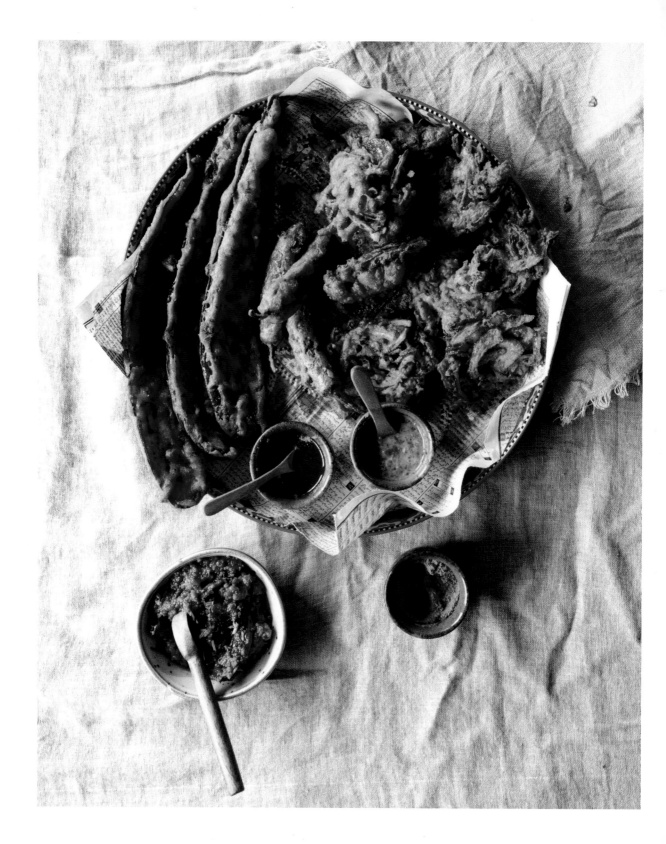

PAKORA MEDLEY

Hot, piping pakoras served on yesterday's news, dipped in a spicy cilantro chutney against the backdrop of the monsoon rains—served alongside the perfect cup of chai. This is what dreams are made of. They evoke a sense of comfort and nostalgia like no other street-side snack. —M.M.

BATTER

2 cups chickpea flour (also known as gram flour or besan)

½ teaspoon baking soda

1 teaspoon salt

1 teaspoon red chili powder

½ teaspoon turmeric powder

1 teaspoon cumin seeds

1 teaspoon ground coriander

1 teaspoon ground pomegranate seeds (optional)

¼ cup finely chopped fresh cilantro leaves

2 green chilis, finely chopped (adjust to your preferred spice level)

½ cup water (adjust as needed)

VEGETABLES

Oil, for deep frying

2 medium-sized Japanese eggplants (cut lengthwise into ¼-inch slices)

4–6 jalapeño peppers

2 medium potatoes, thinly sliced

1 onion, thinly sliced

1. In a large mixing bowl, combine the chickpea flour, baking soda, salt, red chili powder, turmeric powder, cumin seeds, ground coriander, and ground pomegranate seeds. Mix well to evenly distribute the spices. Add the cilantro and green chilies to the dry ingredients. Mix thoroughly and gradually add water to the mixture, stirring well to form a thick, smooth batter.

2. Heat oil in a deep-frying pan or wok over medium heat. To test if the oil is ready for frying, drop a small amount of batter into the oil. If it sizzles and rises to the surface immediately, the oil is hot enough.

3. Coat the eggplant slices in the batter and carefully drop them into the hot oil, making sure not to overcrowd the pan. Fry the pakoras in small batches, turning them occasionally to ensure even cooking and a golden-brown color on all sides. This should take about 4 to 5 minutes per batch. Use a slotted spoon to remove the cooked pakoras from the oil and place them on a plate lined with paper towels to drain any excess oil. Repeat the same process as the eggplant for the jalapeños and potatoes.

4. Once you have made the eggplant, jalapeños, and potato pakoras, add the onions to the leftover batter and mix well. Carefully drop spoonfuls of the batter into the hot oil and fry.

5. Serve the pakoras hot with your favorite chutney or sauce, such as Mint Cilantro Chutney (page 51), Tamarind and Date Chutney (page 50), and Tomato Chutney (page 55).

MAKES **8**–**10**

KARACHI-STYLE CHICKEN PARATHA ROLLS

Karachi's culinary narrative boasts the paratha roll as one of its cherished chapters. The tale began in 1971 with Hafiz Habib ur Rehman's creation at Silver Spoon. Over the decades, landmarks like Hot n Spicy and Red Apple have honed the recipe, each rendition echoing the city's spirit. For me, no trip back home feels complete without a couple of visits to this curbside eatery, immersing in the familiar allure of their rolls. Envision tender chicken, marinated in a symphony of spices, nestled within a flaky paratha, juxtaposed with the tangy crunch of pickled onions, and complemented by a refreshing green chutney raita. Comedian Akbar Chaudhry beautifully expressed its charm: "*Roll ek ehsaas hai, roll ek mohabbat hai*" (This isn't just a dish—it's an emotion, it's a love affair). —M.M.

1½ pounds boneless chicken

½ bunch fresh coriander leaves

3–4 green chilis

2 tablespoons lemon juice

½ teaspoon white pepper

3 tablespoons sour cream

2 tablespoons soy sauce

1 teaspoon ginger paste

1 teaspoon garlic paste

1 tablespoon Toasted Cumin Powder (page 54)

1 tablespoon red chili powder

¼ teaspoon Garam Masala (page 53)

1 teaspoon Chaat Masala Blend (page 54) (optional)

¼ cup vegetable oil

1 cup Yogurt Raita (page 36)

1 cup Pickled Onions (page 290)

10 Parathas (page 44)

1. Rinse the chicken thoroughly and freeze for 20 minutes. Then cut into 1-inch cubes.

2. In a food processor, blend the coriander leaves, green chilies, and lemon juice into a paste. Transfer the paste to a medium-sized bowl.

3. To the bowl, add the white pepper, sour cream, soy sauce, ginger paste, garlic paste, Toasted Cumin Powder, red chili powder, Garam Masala, and Chaat Masala Blend (if using). Stir until all ingredients are well combined. Add the chicken cubes to the mixture, ensuring they are evenly coated. Marinate for at least 1 hour or up to overnight.

4. In a large skillet, heat the vegetable oil over medium heat. Add the marinated chicken pieces and cook for 5 to 6 minutes, or until the chicken is cooked through and lightly browned. Remove the chicken from the skillet and set aside.

5. To assemble: Place a generous amount of the chicken onto the center of a warm paratha. Top with pickled onions. Drizzle with Yogurt Raita.

6. Roll the paratha tightly, folding one end to seal the roll. Wrap in parchment paper or foil to hold the roll together.

NOTE: You can also use store-bought frozen parathas.

MAKES **10**

PARATHAS

Parathas, a staple in South Asian cuisine, are flaky, buttery flatbreads that offer a multitude of culinary possibilities. Whether enjoyed with pickles, as a wrap for flavorful fillings, or as my personal favorite—dipped into a steaming cup of chai—these versatile delights have a special place in our hearts and tables. Growing up, our Bengali nanny introduced my sister and me to the comforting snack of "Maleeda," a blend of leftover parathas, rich desi ghee, and sweet jaggery. —M.M.

1 cup whole wheat flour

3½ cups all-purpose flour + more if needed

2 teaspoons fine kosher salt

1⅓ cups warm water

¼ vegetable oil

8 ounces ghee (clarified butter), divided

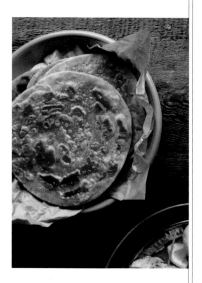

1. In the bowl of a stand mixer with the dough hook attachment, mix flours and salt. With the mixer on low, pour in water and oil. A soft dough should form. Knead on medium for 4 minutes. Form a ball with dough and wrap in plastic wrap. Refrigerate for 1 hour.

2. Melt 4 ounces of ghee in a medium bowl and set aside. Line a 9 × 13-inch airtight container with parchment and set aside.

3. Divide dough into 20 pieces. For even pieces, weigh dough ball and divide by 20 to get the ideal weight for each piece. Roll each piece into a ball and cover with a damp cloth or plastic wrap. Roll out the first ball as thin as you can in the shape of an oval. Brush melted ghee on the whole surface of the dough. Loosen the dough on one of the longer sides and roll it up to form a log. Flatten slightly and then roll the log into a spiral like a cinnamon roll. Place in prepared pan. Continue with the remaining dough balls. Brush any remaining ghee on the tops of the dough rolls. Cover and refrigerate for 4 to 24 hours.

4. When ready to cook, preheat a cast-iron skillet or griddle over medium heat. Set a plate and a clean towel near stove. On a lightly floured surface with a floured palm, flatten first dough roll. With a rolling pin, roll out to about a 6-inch round. Brush skillet with ghee and place rolled out paratha dough in skillet and cook for 2 to 4 minutes on each side. Paratha will bubble slightly when ready to flip. Place on plate and cover with towel to keep warm. Brush more ghee on skillet before cooking the next paratha.

MAKES **20**

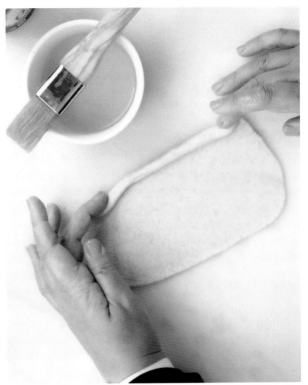

MINI GARLIC KULCHA

The Mini Garlic Kulcha is a petite wonder amidst the vast Indian-Pakistani culinary panorama. Its origin, rooted in the North Indian cuisine, has traveled across borders, narrating tales of shared heritage. Its simplicity complements the robust flavors of dishes it's paired with, be it at a high-end eatery like Indian Accent or a quaint dhaba. The blend of garlic-infused butter elevates its soft, pillowy texture, making each bite a modest, yet profound, culinary joy. —M.M.

3½ cups all-purpose flour + more if needed

1 teaspoon fine kosher salt

1 teaspoon baking powder

½ teaspoon baking soda

1½ cups warm whole milk

¼ cup full-fat plain yogurt

3 tablespoons vegetable oil

2 tablespoons sugar

3 tablespoons salted butter

2 cloves garlic

¼ cup chopped cilantro

1. In a medium bowl, whisk together flour, salt, baking powder, and baking soda and set aside.

2. In the bowl of a stand mixer with the paddle attachment, mix together milk, yogurt, oil, and sugar. Add about half of the flour mixture and beat until well combined. Switch to the dough hook. Add the remaining flour and mix until a soft shaggy dough forms. If dough is too sticky, add more flour 1 tablespoon at a time until dough holds together. Knead dough with dough hook for 2 more minutes. Cover bowl with a damp towel and allow to rest for 2 hours.

3. When ready to cook, melt butter in a small bowl. Mince garlic and stir into butter. Place butter mixture, cilantro, a medium platter, and a pastry brush near the stove.

4. Divide dough into 24 equal portions (about 50 grams each), form balls, cover and allow to reset 15 minutes. Preheat a cast-iron skillet or griddle over medium heat for 5 minutes. On a lighlty floured surface, roll out each dough ball into an oval about ¼ inch thick. Place on skillet and cook until dough browns slightly, about 3 to 4 minutes per side.

5. Transfer to platter. Brush each side with garlic butter and sprinkle with cilantro. Repeat with remaining dough. Serve immediately.

MAKES **24**

CHEDDAR CHEESE STRAWS

While not a traditional South Asian delicacy, Cheese Straws evoke a sense of nostalgia for many of us who grew up in Pakistan. These crispy, cheesy delights were a familiar sight in local bakeries, offering a unique twist on the vibrant tapestry of Pakistani street food. —M.M.

1 pound Rough Puff Pastry (page xxi) or packaged puff pastry

1 egg

1 tablespoon water

8 ounces freshly grated cheddar cheese

1. Allow frozen puff pastry to thaw in refrigerator for 4 hours or 45 minutes on counter in advance of baking the cheese straws. Preheat oven to 400°F. Line a baking sheet with parchment or a silicone mat.

2. Beat egg with 1 tablespoon water. Set aside.

3. Cut puff pastry in half. On a lightly floured surface, roll out first half of puff pastry so it is about 13 × 10 inches. Brush surface with egg wash. Sprinkle 2 ounces of cheese over pastry. Press cheese onto dough so it sticks. Flip pastry over and coat the backside with egg wash and cheese. Cut 1¼-inch-wide strips to create 1¼ × 10–inch pieces. Grasp each end and twist the dough strip 2 to 3 full rotations to form a straw shape with a hollow center. Place on prepared baking sheet. Leave about 1 inch between straws. Bake for 15 to 20 minutes or until pastry is golden brown. Repeat with second half of puff pastry.

4. Cheese straws are best served warm right from the oven or the same day. Store leftovers in an airtight container in the refrigerator for up to 1 day.

MAKES **20**

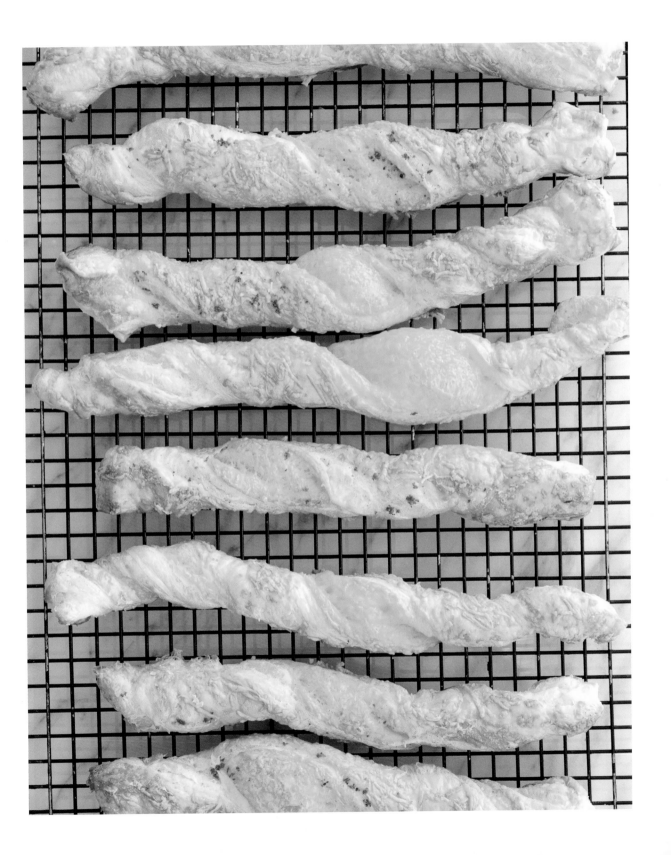

TAMARIND AND DATE CHUTNEY

This rich, tangy Tamarind and Date Chutney is the soul of Pakistani street food favorites like Papri Chaat and Bun Kebab. It bridges the various flavor realms with its sweet, sour, and mildly spiced demeanor, making every bite a harmonious melody of taste. The chutney's consistency drapes over the crispy papri and succulent kebab meat, tying the diverse textures together. Its traditional recipe has traveled through time, bringing along a legacy of the Pakistani culture's culinary richness. —M.M.

1 tablespoon canola oil

1 teaspoon cumin seeds

1 teaspoon ginger paste

½ teaspoon cayenne pepper

½ teaspoon Garam Masala

2 cups water

1 cup brown sugar

4 tablespoons tamarind concentrate

2 dates, pitted and finely diced

1. Combine the oil with cumin seeds, ginger paste, cayenne pepper, and Garam Masala in medium saucepan and cook, stirring for 2 minutes. Add the water, brown sugar, tamarind concentrate, and dates. Bring to a boil and turn down the heat and simmer for 30 minutes.

2. Allow to cool. Store in an airtight jar in the refrigerator for up to 2 weeks.

MAKES 1½ CUPS

MINT CILANTRO CHUTNEY

This chutney won me over the first time Mumtaz made it for me. I usually do my best to steer clear of condiments, so that's a strong endorsement. It is the perfect complement to just about everything in this chapter. If I'm lucky enough to have a leftover Chicken and Potato Cutlet, which is practically perfect on its own, I am genuinely disappointed if there isn't also some of this amazingness to accompany it. —L.K.

1¼ cups chopped cilantro

¾ cup chopped mint

2 cloves garlic

1 green chili

1 tablespoon Toasted Cumin Powder (page 54)

½ teaspoon salt

½ teaspoon jaggery or sugar

3 tablespoons roasted desiccated coconut

¼ cup water

2½ tablespoons lemon juice or lime juice

1. In a blender, puree all ingredients until smooth. Store in an airtight jar for up to 3 to 4 days.

NOTES: You can add half an avocado or ¼ cup cashews to make it creamier.

You can also add yogurt to make a raita once the chutney is ready.

MAKES **1** CUP

coriander seeds

cumin seeds

cardamom pods

black peppercorns

fennel seeds

whole cloves

cinnamon sticks

bay leaves

ground mace

GARAM MASALA

This aromatic spice blend encapsulates the essence of Indo-Pakistani cuisine. Dry roasting the mix of spices fills the kitchen with an irresistible aroma as it toasts. The resulting blend adds a wonderfully warm, earthy flavor and fragrance to curries, vegetables, meats, and more with just a dash or two.

4 tablespoons coriander seeds

3 tablespoons cumin seeds

4 tablespoons green cardamom pods

2 tablespoons black peppercorns

1 tablespoon fennel seeds

1 tablespoon whole cloves

2 large cinnamon sticks

2 bay leaves

1 teaspoon nutmeg powder

1. In a skillet over low heat, dry roast the whole spices (coriander seeds, cumin seeds, cardamom pods, peppercorns, fennel seeds, cloves, cinnamon sticks, bay leaves) for 2 to 3 minutes, stirring continuously.

2. Remove from heat and allow to cool completely before transferring to a dedicated spice grinder. Grind into a fine powder. Transfer the ground spices to a bowl and mix in the nutmeg powder until well blended. Pass final spice blend through a fine mesh sieve to remove any remaining coarse bits. Transfer sieved spice blend to an airtight container. Store at room temperature for up to 1 month.

MAKES ABOUT ¾ CUP

CHAAT MASALA BLEND

5 tablespoons ground cumin (jeera)

1 tablespoon peppercorns

2 tablespoon dried mango powder (amchur)

1 tablespoon Indian black salt (kala namak)

½ teaspoon ground asafetida (hing)

1. Heat a heavy-bottomed pan on medium-high and add all the ingredients. Toss them for 1 to 2 minutes until fragrant and slightly toasted. Once done, remove the mixture from the pan and let cool.

2. Blend the mixture in a grinder on high speed until it turns into a fine powder. Run the powder through a fine sieve to ensure a smooth texture. Store the Chaat Masala Blend in an airtight container for up to 3 months.

MAKES ABOUT ½ CUP

TOASTED CUMIN POWDER

Toasted cumin has become my secret weapon in the kitchen. I sprinkle it on everything from fish to guacamole for instant warmth and depth. Customizing the roast really brings out the spice's full earthy, aromatic potential. I make sure to keep a small jar on hand to elevate dishes as needed. —M.M.

¼ cup cumin seeds

1. Place the cumin seeds into a cold skillet and toast over medium heat for about 5 minutes. Shake the pan often to prevent burning until aromatic and darkened in color.

2. Remove from heat and allow the seeds to cool completely before transferring to a dedicated spice grinder. Grind into a fine powder. Transfer the ground cumin to an airtight container. Store at room temperature for up to 1 month.

MAKES ABOUT **6** TABLESPOONS

HYDERABADI TOMATO CHUTNEY

This flavorful tomato chutney recipe is inspired by my father's Hyderabadi heritage and is an adaptation of my mother's beloved version. The beauty of this chutney lies in the fact that every home takes pride in their unique rendition, adding their own personal touch to the dish. This has always been a huge hit at my gatherings. You can also use this as a base to make a variety of dishes. —M.M.

¼ cup vegetable oil

8–10 fresh curry leaves

1 teaspoon mustard seeds

¼ teaspoon nigella seeds

¼ teaspoon fenugreek seeds

2 teaspoons cumin seeds

3–4 whole dry red chilis

½ medium onion, finely minced

1 tablespoon roasted and ground sesame seeds

2 teaspoons Toasted Cumin Powder (page 54)

2 teaspoons coriander powder

1 teaspoon red chili powder

1 teaspoon turmeric powder

½ tablespoon ginger paste

½ tablespoon garlic paste

1 (28-ounce) can crushed tomatoes

2 tablespoons tomato paste

¼ cup finely chopped cilantro + extra for garnish

½ cup roasted shredded coconut

1. Heat the vegetable oil in a medium saucepan over medium heat. Add curry leaves, mustard seeds, nigella seeds, fenugreek seeds, cumin seeds, and dry red chilies. Stir for 2 to 3 minutes, or until fragrant.

2. Add the minced onions and sauté for 3 to 4 minutes, or until they turn light golden brown.

3. In a small bowl, combine ground sesame seeds, Toasted Cumin Powder, ground coriander, red chili powder, turmeric powder, ginger paste, and garlic paste. Add this spice mixture to the saucepan and stir for another 5 minutes.

4. Add crushed tomatoes and tomato paste to the saucepan. Stir for 2 to 3 minutes before adding chopped cilantro. Cover the saucepan, reduce the heat to low, and let it simmer for 30 minutes. Keep an eye on the mixture to prevent burning.

5. Add the roasted shredded coconut to the tomato mixture and stir until combined.

6. Garnish the tomato chutney with additional chopped cilantro before serving.

MAKES **2** CUPS

JALEBI

Burns Road is truly the heart of street food culture, lined with stalls that showcase culinary brilliance at every turn. Among these, the Halwais stand out with their art of making Jalebi: creating spirals from fermented batter, frying them in hot ghee, and then immersing them in fragrant sugar syrup. Tracing its roots back to ancient Persia, Jalebi holds a special place in Pakistan. It's a sought-after dessert during Ramadan, often gracing celebrations, and is particularly savored in the chilly months of winter. I've always had a preference for savoring them hot, accompanied by a dollop of fresh malai. Laura's take on this classic is commendable. Even without the firsthand experience from Burns Road, she brilliantly captures its essence. —M.M.

EQUIPMENT
Squeeze bottle
Funnel

SAFFRON SYRUP
2 cups sugar
1 cup water
1 teaspoon rosewater
1 teaspoon lemon juice
½ teaspoon turmeric
10 saffron threads

JALEBI BATTER
Peanut oil or other neutral oil
    for frying
2 tablespoons ghee
1¾ cups all-purpose flour
2 tablespoons chickpea flour
½ teaspoon turmeric
½ teaspoon cardamom
1 teaspoon baking powder
1¼ cups water
¼ cup yogurt
1 teaspoon lemon juice

1. To make saffron syrup: Cook all ingredients over medium-high heat, stirring constantly until sugar is completely dissolved and mixture starts to boil. Continue cooking until syrup reaches 225°F. Syrup will thicken when completely cool. Fry jalebi immediately after making syrup to avoid syrup being too thick to dip jalebi.

2. To make jalebi batter: Add 3 to 4 inches of oil to a Dutch oven or heavy-bottomed pot. Clip a candy thermometer to the side of pot or set an instant-read thermometer near stove. Add ghee and allow oil to preheat to 350°F over medium-high heat while mixing the jalebi batter.

3. Whisk together flours, turmeric, cardamom, and baking powder. Add water, yogurt, and lemon juice and whisk together until smooth. Using a funnel, pour batter into a squeeze bottle.

4. Line a baking sheet with a paper towel and set a cooling rack on top of baking sheet. Place baking sheet and syrup near stove. When oil reaches 350°F, squeeze batter in spirals about 3 inches wide. Create 2 to 3 more spirals depending on size of pot. Cook for 2 to 3 minutes per side. Remove jalebis from oil. Drain excess oil and immediately dip in syrup. Coat both sides in syrup and place on prepared cooling rack to dry.

5. Jalebi taste best when still warm. Serve immediately.

MAKES **20**

NANKHATAI

Nankhatai, a cherished delight, traces its origins back to the streets of Surat in the sixteenth century, where Dutch and Indian spice traders converged. As the Dutch departed India, a Parsi named Faramji Pestonji Dotivala assumed control of a local bakery. The story goes that Dutch-style bread didn't quite suit the local palate, inspiring Mr. Dotivala to embark on a flavorful experiment. By melding Dutch and Iranian baking techniques, he breathed life into Nankhatai—a treat that has since captured hearts worldwide. It's fitting that this cookie, inspired by the Dutch, finds a home in our book, where Laura's Dutch heritage and my South Asian roots come together to celebrate the fusion of culture and tradition. —M.M.

COOKIE
1 cup unsalted butter

1 cup sugar

1 teaspoon rose water

1 egg yolk

2 cups all-purpose flour

½ cup chickpea flour

½ teaspoon baking soda

¼ teaspoon salt

1 teaspoon ground cardamom

TOPPING
1 egg

½ cup pistachios, finely chopped

edible rose petals for garnish, (optional)

1. **To make the cookies:** Preheat oven to 350°F. Beat butter, sugar, and rose water for 3 minutes until light and fluffy. Add egg yolk to the butter mixture and beat until combined.

2. In a medium bowl, whisk together flours, baking soda, salt, and cardamom. Add to the butter mixture and beat until well combined.

3. Scoop dough, form into 1-inch balls, and place on a baking tray. Leave 1½ to 2 inches between dough balls. Lightly press down on each ball so it is about ¾ of its original height.

4. **To make the topping:** In a medium bowl, beat egg with a wire whisk until foamy. Using a pastry brush, coat the cookies with egg wash. Sprinkle with pistachios.

5. Bake for 14 to 16 minutes or until light golden brown. Allow to cool on the pan for 5 minutes before transferring to a cooling rack. Allow to cool completely and then store in an airtight container for up to 1 week.

6. Garnish with rose petals, if using, just before serving.

MAKES 36

PEANUT & SESAME CHIKKI

This recipe is a delightful blend of sweetness and nuttiness, perfect as a snack or dessert. It's golden-brown hue and jewel-like appearance evoke memories of the local street vendors who sold this beloved treat. As a child, I would save up my lunch money to buy my maternal grandmother her favorite Chikki, wrapped in cellophane. I still recall the joy on her face when I pulled out these little treasures from my uniform pocket. —M.M.

1 cup raw blanched peanuts
½ cup sesame seeds
1 tablespoon ghee
1 cup jaggery

1. In a pan, dry roast the peanuts on low heat until they turn golden brown. Remove from the pan and let them cool.

2. In the same pan, dry roast the sesame seeds on low heat until they start to turn golden brown. Remove from the pan and let them cool.

3. In a heavy-bottomed pan, heat the ghee on low heat. Add the jaggery and stir continuously until it melts completely. Once the jaggery has melted, increase the heat to medium-low and let the mixture boil for 3 to 4 minutes. To check the consistency of the jaggery syrup, drop a small amount into a bowl of water. It should form a hard ball.

4. Add the peanuts and roasted sesame seeds to the jaggery syrup and stir well. Pour the mixture into a greased tray and flatten it with the back of a spoon or a spatula.

5. Let it cool and harden for at least 15 minutes. Cut the chikki into 2 × 2-inch squares or diamond shapes using a sharp knife. Once completely cooled, store in an airtight container for up to one week.

NOTE: There are many ways to incorporate Peanut and Sesame Chikki into other desserts, so feel free to get creative and experiment with different ideas!

Crush the Peanut and Sesame Chikki and sprinkle it over ice cream or frozen yogurt for a crunchy topping.

Chop the chikki into small pieces and mix it into brownie batter for a unique and delicious twist on classic brownies.

MAKES **16** PIECES

DHABA CHAI

Doodh Patti Chai, or simply "Chai," is more than a drink; it's the keeper of stories and the glue that unites us. From local bazaars to homes, it's a daily ritual, transcending boundaries. Each home has its unique preparation method, but the intention remains sweet. In every rising swirl of steam from a teacup, there's a cherished story, a memory, and a moment of connection waiting to be shared. —M.M.

6 cups water

¼ teaspoon ground cardamom or 8 green cardamom pods

6 bags black tea or 6 teaspoons loose tea

1 cup whole milk

6 teaspoons sugar, or to taste

1. In a large pot, bring 6 cups of water to boil. Add the cardamon and tea.

2. Cover the pot and reduce the heat to low and simmer for 10 minutes.

3. Remove the lid, and add the milk and sugar. Stir to combine, and bring the pot to a simmer again. Simmer for another minute or so.

4. Strain and add to teapot or individual cups or glasses.

SERVES **6**

MANGO LASSI

Mango Lassi will always remind me of my dear friend, Vivek Rai. His fervor for mangoes is unmatched; he'll order this drink whenever he spots it on a menu, a testament to his unwavering devotion. Vivek's enthusiasm mirrors Pakistan's collective love affair with mangoes. In my homeland, mango isn't just a fruit; it's a season, a conversation starter, a bridge to countless memories. It's easy to see why: blend the rich, aromatic sweetness of mango with the cool tang of yogurt, and you've got a drink that's history, culture, and sheer indulgence in a glass. As Vivek scours New York's corners for the perfect mango, I'm reminded of the busy markets back home, where mangoes reign supreme and stories flow as freely as the lassi we treasure. —M.M.

2 cups ripe mangoes, peeled and chopped

½ cup canned mango pulp

1½ cups plain yogurt

½ cup milk

2–3 tablespoons sugar

¼ cup ice

½ teaspoon ground cardamom

Crushed pistachios, for garnish (optional)

1. Place the chopped mangoes, canned mango pulp, yogurt, milk, sugar, ice, and ground cardamom in a blender.

2. Blend the ingredients until smooth and creamy.

3. Pour the mango lassi into tall glasses. Garnish with a sprinkle of crushed pistachios. Serve immediately.

SERVES **4**

MIDDLE EASTERN TABLE

The diverse cuisines of the Middle East have been shaped over centuries by the region's strategic location at the crossroads of Asia, Europe, and Africa. This ancient junction has produced an amalgam of culinary influences seen through dishes, flavors, and ingredients. Hospitality and generosity around food form the core of Middle Eastern culture, evident in celebrations like Iftar feasts and meze spreads. Several staples that have gained global fame are deeply rooted in the Jewish and Arab food traditions of the Levant, including pita bread and hummus. Grilled lamb kebabs blend nomadic traditions with regional spices. Breadmaking retains cultural significance, from Armenian lavash to Turkish simit. Trade introduced treasured sweets like syrupy baklava pastries and sesame halva. From street food to fine dining, home cooking to festivities, Middle Eastern cuisine retains imprints of diverse cultures intertwining over history. The tradition of gathering for a meal remains central, making dining a communal experience. The recipes provide a window into the rich histories shaping the mosaic of culinary influences across the Middle East. —M.M.

MAKE AHEAD

Prepare the meat mixture for keftas a day in advance and store in an airtight container in the refrigerator.

Prepare the fillings for the Pide a day in advance. Store in an airtight container in the refrigerator.

Hummus and Muhammara can be prepared 2 to 3 days in advance. Store in an airtight container.

Za'atar Lavash Crackers can be made up to 3 days in advance. Store in an airtight container.

EXTRAS

Figs

Pomegranate

Pickled Red Onions (page 290)

TIME SAVERS

Purchase za'atar crackers.

Purchase hummus.

Purchase muhammara.

Purchase baklava and halva from a Middle Eastern bakery.

Styling Ideas

Use traditional Middle Eastern ingredients like pomegranates, figs, dates, nuts, and olives to embellish your table. Pick fresh flowers in jewel tones such as deep red, purple, and gold.

Use small bowls of spices like cumin, coriander, or sumac as both decor and seasonings for the food.

Opt for decorative and colorful Middle Eastern–style dinnerware with intricate patterns. Combine ceramic or mosaic serving platters and bowls with brass or copper trays. Add wooden boards or rustic breadbaskets for bread and flatbreads.

RECISPES

SAMBOUSEK

LEBANESE CHEESE ROLLS

Sambousek has long been a staple in Lebanese households, tracing its origins to the diverse communities of the Middle East. Traditionally filled with meats or spiced lentils, this feta and mozzarella version offers a contemporary twist. These cigar-shaped pastries are ubiquitous in Lebanese street markets, especially during festive occasions. Families often serve them during special gatherings or as a favored iftar treat during Ramadan. Whether purchased from a seasoned vendor in a bustling souk or freshly made in a grandmother's kitchen, Sambousek embodies the shared heritage and communal spirit of Lebanese culture.

8 ounces feta cheese

8 ounces shredded mozzarella

1 medium-sized potato, boiled, peeled, and mashed

1 tablespoon finely chopped flat-leaf parsley

1 teaspoon nigella seeds

18–20 spring roll wrappers

Frying-grade oil for frying

1. In a mixing bowl, crumble the feta cheese, add the mozzarella, mashed potato, parsley, and nigella seeds. Mix until well combined.

2. Lay out a spring roll wrapper on a clean, flat surface, keeping it in a diamond shape with one corner pointing toward you. Place about 1 tablespoon of the cheese mixture near the bottom corner of the wrapper. Begin to roll the wrapper tightly around the filling. Once you have rolled halfway, fold the left and right corners toward the center. Continue rolling until only the top corner remains. Dab a little water on the top corner and finish rolling to seal.

3. Heat frying-grade oil in a large pot until it reaches the appropriate frying temperature. Use a thermometer to accurately monitor the temperature. The oil should be about 3 inches deep. Carefully place a few Sambousek in the hot oil, ensuring they don't overcrowd the pan. Fry until they're golden brown, which should take about 2 to 3 minutes per side.

4. Using a slotted spoon, transfer the fried Sambousek to a plate lined with paper towels to drain any excess oil.

MAKES **18–20** ROLLS

KEFTA KEBABS

Kefta Kebab's heritage traces back to ancient Persia, epitomizing a long-standing culinary tradition of minced meat blended with herbs and spices, then grilled. The term "kefta" originates from the Persian "kuftan," meaning "to grind," mirroring the dish's preparation method.

1 pound ground lamb

1 pound ground beef

1 medium onion, finely chopped

3 large cloves garlic, crushed

¼ cup toasted pine nuts, coarsely chopped

½ cup finely chopped parsley

1 large jalapeño, seeded and finely chopped

1 teaspoon cinnamon powder

1½ teaspoons allspice powder

¾ teaspoon grated nutmeg

½ teaspoon paprika powder

½ teaspoon Toasted Cumin Powder (page 54)

1 teaspoon freshly ground black pepper

1 teaspoon kosher salt

4 tablespoons olive oil

LEMON TAHINI SAUCE

½ cup tahini paste

1 preserved lemon rind, finely chopped

2 cloves garlic, minced

3 tablespoons lemon juice

Kosher salt, to taste

½ teaspoon Toasted Cumin Powder (page 54)

6 tablespoons ice cold water

1. **To make the kebabs:** Preheat the oven to 375°F.

2. In a large bowl, combine the ground lamb, ground beef, onion, garlic, pine nuts, parsley, and jalapeño.

3. In another bowl, whisk together the cinnamon, allspice, nutmeg, paprika, cumin, pepper, and salt. Pour the spice mixture into the meat mixture, blending thoroughly.

4. Grab a heaped tablespoon of the meat mixture, molding it into a flattened oval about 3¼ inches long. Press firmly to ensure compactness. Repeat with the remaining meat mixture.

5. In a large pan, heat the olive oil over high heat. Sear the kebabs in batches, ensuring all sides are browned, for approximately 6 to 7 minutes. Make sure not to overcrowd the pan. Transfer the kebabs to the preheated oven and bake for an additional 5 minutes.

6. **To make the lemon tahini sauce:** In a bowl, combine the tahini paste and finely chopped preserved lemon rind. Add the minced garlic and fresh lemon juice to the tahini mixture and stir well. Season with a pinch of salt and cumin powder, stirring until well blended.

7. If the sauce is too thick, add water by the tablespoon to reach your preferred consistency. Store in an airtight container in the refrigerator until ready to serve.

TIPS: For a smoother sauce, you can blend all the ingredients in a food processor. Adjust the water and lemon juice as needed to get your preferred tanginess and thickness.

MAKES **25–30** KEFTAS

PIDE

TURKISH FLATBREAD PIZZAS

One of Turkey's most popular snacks, these boat-shaped baked flatbreads can be eaten for any meal, and like pizza, are filled in many different ways—from minced meat to vegetables, eggs, or cheese. This recipe makes 10 mini pides, half meat and half vegetarian, a variety that is great for party platters. If you want to make only one of the versions, simply double the filling ingredients on your favorite version.

DOUGH

1½ cups warm water

2 teaspoons active dry yeast

1 teaspoon sugar

2 cups all-purpose flour + more if needed

1¾ cups bread flour

1½ teaspoons fine kosher salt

¼ cup olive oil

MEAT FILLING

3 tablespoons olive oil

1 small red onion, diced

3 cloves garlic, minced

½ pound ground beef

1 teaspoon sumac spice

Kosher salt and pepper to taste

1 cup grape tomatoes, sliced

¼ cup chopped fresh cilantro

CHEESE FILLING

1 cup crumbled feta cheese

1 cup crumbled Piknik Turkish white cheese or mozzarella

2 scallions, sliced

2 cloves garlic, minced

Crushed red pepper

¼ cup fresh parsley, chopped

¼ cup salted butter, melted

1. **To make the dough:** In a small bowl, whisk together water, yeast, and sugar. Allow to stand until a thick foam has formed at the top, about 10 minutes.

2. In the bowl of a stand mixer, with the dough hook attachment, add flours and salt, and mix for 20 seconds to combine. Whisk olive oil into the foamy yeast mixture. With the mixer on low, slowly pour yeast mixture into the flour mixture. Mix on medium until a soft shaggy dough forms. Add more flour 1 tablespoon at a time until mixture comes together. Dough will be a little bit sticky. Knead on medium speed for 5 minutes.

3. Spray a large bowl with nonstick spray and place dough in bowl. Bowl-fold dough by stretching some dough from bottom to top, flip over dough ball. Cover bowl with plastic wrap or damp towel and allow dough to rise until it doubles in size, about 1 to 2 hours, depending on how warm your kitchen is.

4. Punch down dough and turn out onto a lightly floured surface. Divide dough into 10 equal portions. Form balls from each portion. Cover loosely and allow to rest 10 minutes.

5. **To make the meat filling:** Preheat oven to 450°F. Line two large baking sheets with parchment or silicone baking mats and set aside. In medium frying pan, add olive oil, onions, and garlic. Cook over medium heat for about 8 minutes. Add ground beef, sumac spice, salt, and pepper. Cook until meat has browned. Allow to cool. Stir in tomatoes and cilantro. Stir until all ingredients are incorporated. Divide into 5 portions.

CONTINUED

6. On lightly floured surface, roll out first dough ball into an oval shape. Transfer to prepared pan. Add the first portion of the ground beef mixture into the center of the dough oval. Fill to about 1 inch of each side. Fold over sides and pinch the short ends to create a boat shape. Brush folded over part of crust with butter. Assemble 4 more meat pides, reserving the rest of the dough for the cheese pides. Bake for 12 to 15 minutes or crust is lightly golden brown. Serve immediately.

7. To make the cheese filling: In a medium bowl, combine cheeses, scallions, and garlic. On lightly floured surface, roll out one dough ball into an oval shape. Transfer to prepared pan. Sprinkle with about ⅕ of cheese mixture to about 1 inch of each side. Fold over sides and pinch the short ends to create a boat shape. Brush folded over part of crust with butter. Assemble 4 more cheese pides. Bake for 12 to 15 minutes or until cheese is bubbly and crust is lightly golden brown. Serve immediately.

8. Store leftovers in an airtight container for up to 2 days. To revive pides, preheat oven to 300°F. Place pides on baking sheet and warm 8 to 10 minutes in oven.

MAKES **10**

SIMIT

TURKISH SESAME BREAD

Simit originated in Turkey during the Ottoman Empire. Now commonly served as a street food—these bagel-like, sesame-encrusted bread rings are dipped in water sweetened with grape molasses before baking. The end result is slightly sweeter than a bagel and not as dense and chewy. They are traditionally served with cheese, tomatoes, and olives—and will make a great accompaniment to the many dishes on our Middle Eastern table.

1¾ cups warm water

2 teaspoons active dry yeast

1 tablespoon honey

4 cups all-purpose flour + more if needed

½ cup semolina flour

1½ teaspoons fine kosher salt

2 tablespoons vegetable oil

COATING
¼ cup grape molasses

⅓ cup water

2 cups toasted sesame seeds

2 cups hot water for steaming

1. In a small bowl, whisk together water, yeast, and honey. Allow to stand until a thick foam has formed at the top, about 10 minutes.

2. In the bowl of a stand mixer, with the dough hook attachment, add flours and salt, mix for 20 seconds to combine. Whisk oil into the foamy yeast mixture. With the mixer on low, slowly pour yeast mixture into the flour mixture. Mix on medium until a soft shaggy dough forms. Add more flour 1 tablespoon at a time until mixture comes together into a smooth dough. Dough should make a slapping sound on the side of the bowl.

3. Knead on medium speed for 6 minutes. Line two large baking sheets with parchment or silicone baking mats and set aside.

4. Spray a large bowl with nonstick spray and place dough in bowl. Bowl-fold dough by stretching some dough from bottom to top, flip over dough ball. Cover bowl with plastic wrap or damp towel and allow dough to rise until it doubles in size, about 1 to 2 hours, depending on how warm your kitchen is.

5. Punch down dough and turn out onto a lightly floured surface. Divide dough into 12 equal portions. Form balls from each portion. Cover loosely and allow to rest 10 minutes.

CONTINUED

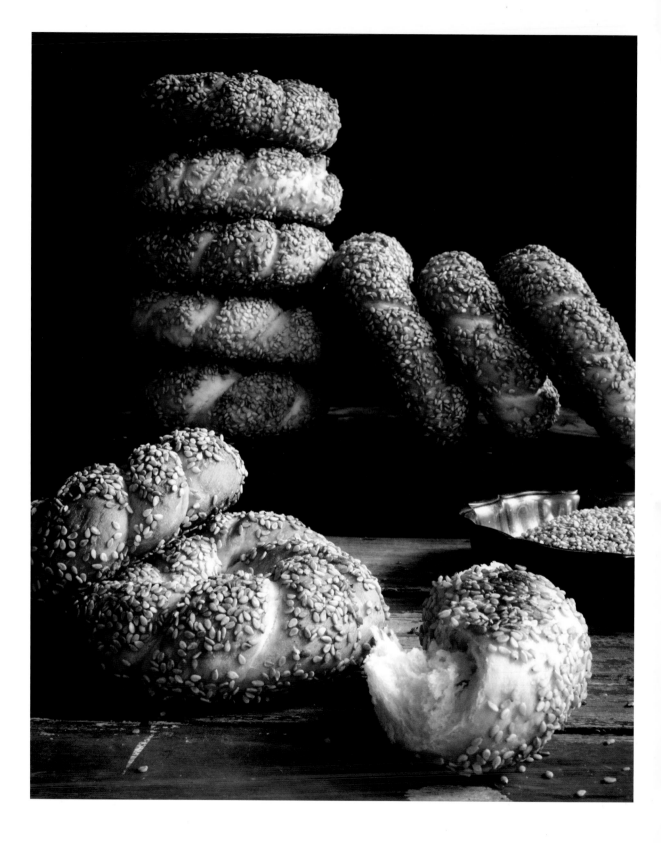

6. Prepare coating: in a medium bowl, whisk together water and molasses. Add sesame seeds to a shallow bowl. Line two baking sheets with parchment or silicone baking mats and set near coating bowls.

7. On a lightly floured surface, form a rope about 26 inches long. Fold rope in half. Twist folded rope and pinch ends together. Form a ring with the twisted dough and pinch ends together. Coat both sides of dough ring in molasses mixture, then coat both sides with sesame seeds. Place on prepared baking sheet, cover loosely, and allow to rise 30 more minutes.

8. Place one oven rack in center of oven. Place a second rack at the lowest level of oven. Place an empty 9 × 13–inch pan on the bottom rack. Preheat oven to 425°F. Set 1 cup of hot water near oven. Place first pan of simit on the center rack of oven. Pull out bottom rack and carefully pour water in pan. Return rack and close oven as quickly as possible so steam is trapped in oven.

9. Bake until golden, about 18 to 22 minutes. Fresh bread tastes best on the same day it is baked. Store leftovers in an airtight container in the freezer for up to a month. To revive frozen simit, preheat oven to 275°F. Place simit on a baking sheet and warm for 7 to 10 minutes.

MAKES **12**

ZA'ATAR LAVASH CRACKERS

Lavash is a common flatbread in Iran, Turkey, and Armenia. This version is made into a crisp, thin cracker and seasoned with the multifaceted Middle Eastern spice za'atar. These simple snacks make a perfect addition to any cheese board or party spread.

1 cup warm water

1 teaspoon active dry yeast

¼ cup plain yogurt

¼ cup olive oil + more for brushing

1 tablespoon honey

1½ teaspoons fine kosher salt

2 cups bread flour

2 cups all-purpose flour

3 tablespoons za'atar

1 tablespoon poppy seeds

1. Preheat oven to 400°F. In the bowl of a stand mixer fitted with the paddle attachment, mix water, yeast, yogurt, olive oil, honey, and salt until well combined. Switch to the dough hook and add flours 1 cup at a time. Knead on low for 10 minutes.

2. Turn out dough onto a lightly floured work surface, and divide into four equal portions. Form balls with each portion. Cover with a kitchen cloth and allow to rest for 30 minutes. Cut two pieces of parchment to the size of your baking sheet. Place one dough portion in the center of one piece of parchment. Top with second piece and roll out at thin as you can. Remove top parchment and place dough with parchment directly on a large baking sheet. Brush with olive oil and top with some za'atar and poppy seeds. Bake for 15 to 20 minutes or until flatbread has crisped.

3. Repeat with remaining dough. Allow flatbreads to cool and then break them up into smaller pieces and serve. Store in an airtight container for up to 1 week.

MAKES **4** LARGE FLATBREAD CRACKERS

ZA'ATAR SPICE BLEND

MAKES ABOUT ½ CUP

2 tablespoons sesame seeds

¼ cup dried thyme

2 tablespoons ground sumac

1 teaspoon dried marjoram (optional)

1 teaspoon dried oregano (optional)

½ teaspoon kosher salt

1. In a small skillet over medium-low heat, toast sesame seeds for 2 to 3 minutes, until fragrant and slightly golden. Transfer to a plate and let them cool.

2. In a small mixing bowl, combine dried thyme, ground sumac, cooled toasted sesame seeds, dried marjoram, dried oregano, and kosher salt. Mix well. Transfer the za'atar spice blend to an airtight container and store in a cool, dry place for up to 6 months.

CLASSIC HUMMUS

Hummus, a creamy dip made from mashed chickpeas, tahini, olive oil, lemon juice, salt, and garlic, has roots that stretch deep into the Middle Eastern antiquity. Its name, derived from the Arabic word for chickpeas, speaks to its primary ingredient, although its exact origins are often debated with claims from various countries including Lebanon, Israel, and Greece among others.

1 cup dried chickpeas

1 teaspoon baking soda

¼ cup well-stirred tahini (sesame paste)

¼ cup fresh lemon juice

1 small clove garlic, minced

½ teaspoon Toasted Cumin Powder (page 54)

Kosher salt to taste

3–4 ice cubes

1–2 tablespoons extra-virgin olive for drizzle

Dash of ground paprika or sumac, for serving

Freshly chopped parsley, for serving (optional)

1. Soak the chickpeas overnight in water that covers them by 3 to 4 inches. The next day, drain and rinse them, then transfer to a large pot. Add the baking soda and mix well. Allow them to sit for a few minutes before covering with water twice the amount of chickpeas. Bring to a boil and simmer for about 40 to 50 minutes or until they are very tender. During the boiling process, skim off any foam that floats to the surface. Drain.

2. In a food processor or blender, combine the tahini and lemon juice. Process for 1 minute. Add minced garlic, cumin, and a ½ teaspoon of salt to the whipped tahini and lemon juice mixture. Process for 30 seconds, scrape the sides and bottom of the bowl, then process another 30 seconds.

3. Add half of the chickpeas to the food processor, along with the ice cubes, and process for 1 minute. Scrape the sides and bottom of the bowl, then add the remaining chickpeas and process until thick and quite smooth, about 1 to 2 minutes.

4. If the hummus is too thick, or if there are still tiny bits of chickpea, you can slowly add a little water or extra olive oil until your desired consistency is achieved.

5. Transfer the hummus to a bowl, and create a shallow well in the center. Drizzle a small amount (1 to 2 tablespoons) of olive oil in the well. Sprinkle with paprika or sumac, and garnish with fresh parsley.

MAKES ABOUT **3** CUPS

MUHAMMARA

RED PEPPER AND WALNUT SPREAD

Muhammara, a vibrant red pepper and walnut spread, speaks to the heart of ancient Syrian culinary traditions, particularly from the city of Aleppo, famed for its rich gastronomic history. This dip, with its deep undertones of pomegranate molasses and toasted walnuts, was traditionally savored in local meze spreads and festive gatherings. Found in lively markets and intimate family gatherings alike, Muhammara has journeyed through time, symbolizing the resilient spirit of Syrian cuisine. Its earthy flavors and spicy kick are not just about taste; they narrate stories of trade routes, regional specialties, and age-old family recipes passed down through generations.

4 large red bell peppers

3 hot red chili peppers

1½ cups walnuts

1 vine tomato, finely chopped

2 scallions, finely chopped

1½ teaspoons Toasted Cumin Powder (page 54)

1 teaspoon red chili flakes

2 teaspoons kosher salt

2 tablespoons pomegranate molasses

1 teaspoon freshly squeezed lemon juice

4 tablespoons fresh breadcrumbs

4 tablespoons extra-virgin olive oil + extra for drizzling

Fresh parsley, for garnishing

1. Preheat your oven to 400°F. Place the red bell peppers and hot chili peppers on a baking sheet. Roast for about 20 minutes, or until their skins are blistered and slightly charred.

2. Transfer the peppers to a bowl and cover it (using a lid or plastic wrap). This will steam them and make peeling easier. After about 15 minutes, peel off the skins, discard the stems and seeds, and roughly chop the flesh.

3. Over medium heat in a dry skillet, toast the walnuts until lightly browned and fragrant, which should take about 3 to 4 minutes. Remove from heat and let cool.

4. In a food processor, add the chopped peppers, tomato, scallions, cumin, red chili flakes, kosher salt, pomegranate molasses, lemon juice, toasted walnuts, breadcrumbs, and olive oil. Blend until you achieve a smooth yet slightly chunky texture.

5. Transfer the Muhammara to a serving dish. Drizzle a little extra-virgin olive oil on top and garnish with chopped parsley.

MAKES ABOUT **2** CUPS

WALNUT AND PISTACHIO BAKLAVA

Baklava has its roots in the ancient Assyrian Empire and is a key pastry in the Middle East and Mediterranean cuisines. Though the dessert varies by region, its popularity has crossed cultures and religions. From an important part of Ramadan and Rosh Hashanah celebrations to Christians using 33 layers to represent the years Christ lived—baklava is a universally adored treat, rich in traditional sweetness and flavors.

BAKLAVA

3 cups walnuts

1 cup pistachios

¼ cup sugar

2 teaspoons ground cinnamon

¼ teaspoon ground cloves

1 cup salted butter, melted

1 pound phyllo dough, thawed

SYRUP

¾ cup water

¾ cup sugar

Peel of ½ lemon without pith

1 teaspoon vanilla extract

1 cup honey

2–3 tablespoons finely chopped pistachios for garnish

1. Preheat oven to 350°F.

2. Finely chop nuts in the bowl of a food processor. Add sugar, cinnamon, and ground cloves. Pulse to combine.

3. Brush a 9 × 13-inch pan with butter. Unroll phyllo dough. Trim dough to the size of your pan. Phyllo dough dries out quickly so keep it covered while you're working. Lay 2 sheets of phyllo dough in the pan. Brush the top of dough with butter and top with 2 to 3 tablespoons of nut mixture. Repeat these steps until you run out of nut mixture. For the top layer, add two sheets of phyllo, brush with butter, add two more sheets and brush with butter. With a sharp knife, cut baklava into diamonds. Make sure to cut all the way to the bottom of the pan. If you have any remaining butter, drizzle it over the top of the dough. Bake 35 to 40 minutes or until golden brown on top.

4. While baking, make the syrup. In a saucepan over medium-high heat, cook water, sugar, lemon peel, and vanilla extract to a boil. Reduce heat to medium. Add honey and continue cooking until mixture bubbles and liquid is a clear amber. You may have to move aside the foamy top to see if liquid is clear. Strain syrup.

5. After removing baklava from oven, immediately spoon syrup evenly over the top. The syrup will sizzle. Allow to cool completely. Cover and allow to rest at least 2 hours before serving so syrup has time to soak into all the layers of pastry. Store in an airtight container for up to 4 days.

SERVES **32**

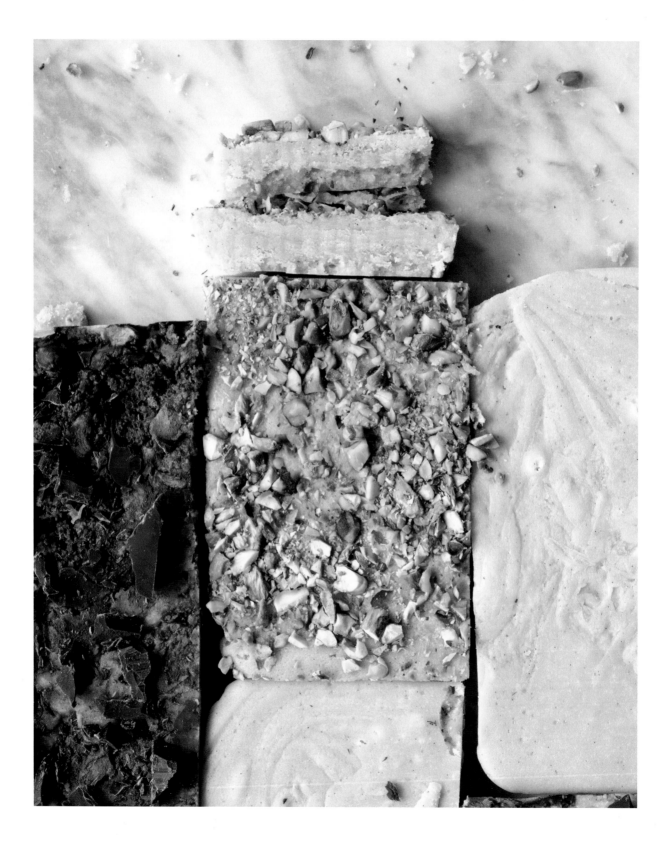

HALVA

The word halva comes from the Arabic word حلوة (halwa) meaning sweetness. This sesame-based confection is made in many varieties. It is fudge-like but not quite as sweet and has a slightly grainy texture. Halva originated in Iran, but is now popular all over the Middle East as well as in India, Pakistan, and Greece.

1½ cups tahini

1 teaspoon fine kosher salt

1½ teaspoons vanilla bean paste

2 cups sugar

½ cup water

PISTACHIO ROSE VARIATION

½ teaspoon rosewater

½ cup finely chopped pistachios

CHOCOLATE SWIRL VARIATION

2 ounces finely chopped semisweet chocolate + more for garnish

NOTE: When buying tahini, the only ingredient on the label should be sesame seeds.

1. In the bowl of a stand mixer fitted with the paddle attachment, add tahini, salt, and vanilla bean paste. Mix on low until combined. Line an 8 × 8–inch pan with parchment, leaving extra on sides. Set pan and a rubber spatula near mixer.

2. Fill a small bowl half full with water and set near stove with a pastry brush. Clip a candy thermometer to the side of a saucepan and add sugar and water. Whisk together sugar and water and cook over medium-high heat until a syrup forms. Continue cooking without stirring, swirling pan occasionally. If sugar starts to stick to the sides of saucepan, brush with a wet pastry brush. Cook until temperature reaches 245°F.

3. With mixer running on low, carefully pour syrup into tahini mixture. Mix just until everything is combined, about 1 minute. Be careful not to overmix. When overmixed, the texture becomes crumbly instead of fudgy. Work quickly to transfer the halva to prepared pan using heatproof rubber spatula. Cool completely. Lift halva from pan, set on a cutting board, and cut into 1-inch squares. Serve immediately or store in an airtight container for up to 5 days.

4. To make the Pistachio Rose variation: Add rosewater to tahini in step 1. Immediately after pouring halva in pan, top hot tahini with chopped pistachios. Using a piece of parchment, lightly press down on top of pistachios and halva to flatten the top and make sure pistachios stick.

5. To make Chocolate Swirl variation: Immediately after pouring halva in pan, sprinkle chocolate on top. The hot halva should melt the chocolate. Using a butter knife, swirl the chocolate into the halva. Garnish cooled halva with more chocolate.

MAKES **64** PIECES

GREEK MEZE BOARD

"We should look for someone to eat and drink with
before looking for something to eat and drink." —EPICURUS

Steeped in ancient history, Greek cuisine stands as a testament to the nation's rich cultural evolution. Its geographic positioning at the crossroads of Europe, Asia, and Africa brought diverse culinary influences, from the spices of the Silk Road to the grains of Northern Africa. The concept of Meze—a collection of small bites, dips, and appetizers—was brought to Greece during the Persian invasions in the third century B.C. The word comes from the Persian mazzeh: to relish. The concept was more than just culinary; it was a social notion that encouraged gathering, conversing, sharing, and savoring food as a way to sample a variety of dishes and connect with others. Meze is part of Greek culture to this day and is representative of the congeniality and hospitality of the Greek people. Festive celebrations center around food, underscoring the nation's deep-seated belief in "filoxenia" —the act of making a stranger a friend through food. The Meze was not just appetizers but an entire shared meal. Build this board with the many dips surrounded by a rainbow of fresh vegetables and plenty of drinks. The Greek table embraces the Mediterranean Triad: grapes, grains, and olives—the most important crops that are native to the region. Olives, pita, crackers, and wine are excellent Greek staples to make your board complete. Of course the gathering and conversation will be the most important part to relish.

RECIPES

Keftedes �֗ 87

Pita ✗ 88

Sesame Crackers ✗ 89

Mediterranean Feta and Roasted Pepper Dip ✗ 90

Tzatziki ✗ 91

Makedonitiki Skordalia ✗ 92

Beet Hummus ✗ 93

EXTRAS

Fresh fruit and vegetables

Red pepperazzi peppers

Good quality feta cheese

Marinated olives

Honey

Pita chips

TIME SAVERS

Purchase hummus.

Purchase tzatziki.

Purchase sesame seed crackers.

Purchase roasted beets.

Purchase packaged pita. Warm on a single layer in a preheated 250°F oven for 10 minutes before serving.

Styling Ideas

Use a large board to serve all the snacks. Organize items by color groupings to create a rainbow effect.

KEFTEDES

GREEK MEATBALLS

Across the vast culinary landscape of Greece, Keftedes stand out as a beloved dish. From the sun-kissed Aegean islands to the rugged terrains of the mainland, each area imparts its unique twist. Some regions highlight them with fresh mint, others infuse a hint of ouzo for an aniseed touch. A staple during local festivals and familial gatherings, Keftedes have found their place in daily Greek meals. Whether enjoyed in a local taverna or at a family's dinner table, they are a true testament to Greece's rich culinary heritage.

1 pound ground beef

1 pound ground lamb

½ cup crumbled feta cheese

1 large onion, finely grated

5 cloves garlic, minced

2 slices day-old bread, crusts removed, soaked in water and squeezed

1 large egg, beaten

½ cup finely chopped fresh mint

2 tablespoons finely chopped fresh parsley

2 teaspoons dried oregano

1 tablespoon lemon zest

1½ tablespoons red wine vinegar

2 teaspoons ground cumin

1 tablespoon dried basil

1 tablespoon olive oil + more for frying

Kosher salt and freshly ground black pepper, to taste

Pinch of ground nutmeg (optional)

Flour, for dusting

1. In a large mixing bowl, combine all ingredients through olive oil. Season generously with salt and freshly ground black pepper. If desired, add a pinch of ground nutmeg. Mix well until all the ingredients are evenly incorporated.

2. Using your hands, form the meat mixture into meatballs, about the size of a walnut.

3. Lightly dust each meatball in flour, ensuring they're evenly coated.

4. In a large skillet, heat enough olive oil to cover the base over medium heat. Once the oil is hot, add the meatballs in batches. Fry until they're golden brown and cooked through, roughly 4 to 5 minutes per side. Don't overcrowd the pan; this can reduce the temperature of the oil and result in soggy keftedes.

5. After frying, transfer the keftedes to a plate lined with paper towels. This will drain away any excess oil.

6. Serve your keftedes hot with Tzatziki sauce (page 91 or storebought).

SERVES **10–12**

PITA

Pita is one of the oldest bread varieties; its roots are in early prehistoric flatbreads that have been an essential part of Middle Eastern and Mediterranean meals for almost four thousand years. Like all bread, freshness is key, which is why homemade pita will always be better than something you find in a bag at the store. Getting the pitas to puff while baking is essential to getting the pocket in the center. Serve these with the many dips and sauces on this Greek board. They also go great on the Middle Eastern Table (page 62).

1 cup warm water

2 teaspoons active dry yeast

½ teaspoon sugar

2 cups bread flour

½ cup whole wheat flour

1 teaspoon fine kosher salt

2 tablespoons olive oil

1. Mix water, yeast, and sugar and allow to get foamy, about 5 minutes.

2. Combine flours and salt in bowl of a stand mixer with dough hook. Whisk olive oil into yeast mixture. Add to flour mixture and knead on medium speed for 5 minutes.

3. Cover bowl with plastic wrap or a damp kitchen towel. Allow to rise until doubled in size, about 2 hours.

4. Divide into 12 pieces (about 50 grams each) and roll into balls. Allow to rest covered for 15 minutes. Roll out to about ¼-inch thickness. Cover and allow to rest 30 minutes. Move oven rack to center. Preheat a baking stone or heavy-bottomed baking pan in oven to 500°F. (550°F if your oven goes that high.) Wait 5 minutes after oven reaches temperature so stone or pan is fully preheated.

5. Place 4 to 6 pitas on stone upside down. Stay close to oven—pitas bake quickly. When pitas have puffed and turned golden, they are ready, about 4–6 minutes. Remove from oven and place on a cooling rack. Allow stone to reheat in oven for 5 minutes before baking the next batch.

6. Store pitas in an airtight container for up to 1 day, or freeze for up to 1 month. To warm room-temperature pitas, lightly brush with olive oil and warm in a frying pan over medium heat for 2 minutes per side.

MAKES **12**

SESAME CRACKERS

These little bite-sized crackers are flakey and melt-in-your-mouth delicious all on their own, and they also go great with all the dips on this board.

2¼ cups flour
1 teaspoon fine kosher salt
½ cup unsalted butter
¼ cup olive oil
3–4 tablespoons cold water
1 egg, beaten with 1 tablespoon water (for egg wash)
½ cup black and white sesame seeds

1. In a medium bowl, mix the flour and salt. Slice the butter into small pats and toss into the flour. Cut the butter and flour with a pastry blender until you have a fine crumb. Add olive oil and blend again with pastry blender.

2. Sprinkle 2 tablespoons cold water over the crumb mixture. Combine with your hands, squeezing the crumbs together until a dough forms. If the dough doesn't come together, add more cold water 1 tablespoon at a time until you get the dough to form. Divide dough into 2 portions and flatten each into a disk. Cover with plastic wrap and refrigerate 2 hours, or overnight.

3. Preheat oven to 375°F and line a baking sheet with parchment or a silicone mat. On a lightly floured surface, roll out first disc of dough. Brush off any excess flour. Brush surface with egg wash and sprinkle with half of the sesame seeds. Press lightly on seeds to help them stick. With a fluted pastry wheel, cut 1-inch squares. Place on prepared baking sheet and bake 20 to 25 minutes or until slightly golden.

4. Serve immediately or store in an airtight container for up to 3 days.

MAKES ABOUT **100** CRACKERS

MEDITERRANEAN FETA AND ROASTED PEPPER DIP

In Greek culinary traditions, mezes are more than just appetizers; they are a reflection of the region's bountiful produce and ancient foodways. The Mediterranean Feta and Roasted Pepper Dip stands as a representation of this legacy. Feta, a cheese deeply woven into Greece's culinary fabric, pairs harmoniously with roasted red peppers, a staple in Mediterranean kitchens. This dip, with its vibrant colors and textures, encapsulates the region's penchant for combining simple ingredients to create bold, unforgettable flavors, making it a beloved choice in mezes spreads across the Aegean and beyond.

8-ounce block of authentic Greek feta

½ cup roasted red peppers, drained and finely diced

2 tablespoons red wine vinegar

1 clove garlic, minced

2 tablespoons Greek yogurt

Kosher salt and freshly ground black pepper to taste

3 tablespoons olive oil + additional for drizzling

Fresh parsley leaves, chopped (for garnish)

1. Break the feta into chunks and add to a food processor.

2. Add the diced red peppers, red wine vinegar, minced garlic, and yogurt to the processor. Season with salt and pepper. Pulse 2 to 3 times until ingredients are combined.

3. While the processor is running, slowly drizzle in the olive oil until the mixture becomes smooth.

4. Transfer the dip to a serving bowl. Garnish with chopped parsley and a touch more olive oil.

5. Serve with toasted pita, vegetables, and olives.

MAKES ABOUT **2** CUPS

TZATZIKI

Tzatziki is a staple in Greek cuisine, hailed for its simplicity and versatility. Originating from the culinary traditions of the ancient Greeks and the Middle East, its core ingredients—yogurt, cucumber, garlic, and olive oil—reflect the Mediterranean's fresh, wholesome produce. In Greece, Tzatziki is more than just a dip; it's a beloved companion to many dishes. It's traditionally served with grilled meats like souvlaki and gyros, providing a cool, tangy contrast to the savory flavors. It's also common to find Tzatziki alongside pita bread or as part of a meze spread, showcasing its role in the shared dining experience so central to Greek culture.

½ cup grated cucumber

1 cup Greek yogurt

2 cloves garlic, minced

1 tablespoon lemon juice

½ tablespoon lemon zest

1 tablespoon finely chopped fresh dill + extra for garnish

1 tablespoon finely chopped fresh mint + extra for garnish

½ teaspoon kosher salt

¼ teaspoon Toasted Cumin Powder (page 54)

¼ teaspoon ground black pepper

1 teaspoon extra-virgin olive oil

Pinch of crushed red pepper flakes

1. Using a paper towel, squeeze the grated cucumber to remove as much excess water as possible.

2. Transfer the drained cucumber to a medium-sized mixing bowl.

3. Add Greek yogurt, minced garlic, lemon juice, lemon zest, dill, mint, kosher salt, Toasted Cumin Powder, and black pepper to the mixing bowl.

4. Stir the ingredients together until they're thoroughly combined.

5. Transfer the tzatziki mixture to a serving bowl. Drizzle it with extra-virgin olive oil and sprinkle a pinch of crushed red pepper flakes on top.

6. Garnish with fresh sprigs of mint and dill.

MAKES ABOUT 1½ CUPS

MAKEDONITIKI SKORDALIA

MACEDONIAN GARLIC SAUCE

Skordalia is a beautifully balanced, creamy Macedonian garlic sauce. It is a harmonious blend of rustic bread, walnuts, garlic, vinegar, and extra virgin olive oil. When blended together, these ingredients create a symphony of flavor that's simply impossible to resist.

4–6 cloves garlic

Kosher salt, to taste

½ cup walnuts, coarsely chopped

4 slices stale rustic bread, crusts removed

¾ cup high quality extra-virgin olive oil

2–4 tablespoons red wine vinegar

1. Add the garlic cloves to a food processor and pulse until finely chopped. Season with salt according to your preference.

2. Continue by adding the coarsely chopped walnuts to the processor. Pulse until the mixture is similar in texture to a coarse meal.

3. Prepare your stale bread by briefly running the slices under tap water. Be diligent in squeezing out the excess moisture before breaking the bread into small, crumbled pieces. Merge the crumbled bread with the garlic-walnut mixture in the food processor. Process until the ingredients are well-incorporated.

4. With the food processor running, slowly add the olive oil and vinegar. It's essential to alternate between the two to ensure a balanced flavor profile. Continue blending until the skordalia reaches a smooth, creamy consistency. If the mixture seems too thick, add water to reach desired consistency.

5. Transfer to serving bowl. Serve with your choice of fresh, roasted, or grilled vegetables. For the most enjoyable experience, serve your skordalia right away.

NOTE: Walnuts could be substituted with pine nuts or almonds to experiment with different flavor profiles.

MAKES **2** CUPS

BEET HUMMUS

Beet Hummus, while not a traditional dish in the ancient Greek repertoire, showcases the innovative spirit of contemporary Greek cuisine. As mezes evolve with time, chefs have embraced the earthy sweetness of beets, blending them with the creamy richness of classic hummus. The result? A visually striking and palate-pleasing dip that marries the old with the new. This Beet Hummus not only stands out for its vibrant hue but also reflects the Mediterraneans' age-old practice of utilizing fresh, seasonal produce in inventive ways. It's a testament to the enduring adaptability and creativity of Greek culinary traditions.

1 medium-sized beet

1 cup Classic Hummus (page 78) or store bought

1 tablespoon extra-virgin olive oil + more for serving

¼ teaspoon kosher salt

Dash of ground paprika or sumac, for serving

Freshly chopped parsley, for serving (optional)

1. Preheat your oven to 400°F.

2. Wash the beets and wrap each in foil. Place them on a baking sheet. Roast for about 45 minutes to 1 hour, or until the beets are tender and can be easily pierced with a fork.

3. Once roasted, remove from the oven and let them cool. Once cooled, peel the skin off the beets and roughly chop.

4. In a food processor or blender, combine hummus, chopped roasted beets, and olive oil and blend until the mixture is smooth and well-integrated.

5. Transfer the beet hummus to a serving bowl. Create a shallow well in the center, and drizzle with some more olive oil. Sprinkle with paprika or sumac, and garnish with freshly chopped parsley, if desired.

MAKES 1½ CUPS

ITALIAN TABLE

"The name of Italy has magic in its very syllables." —MARY SHELLEY

It's difficult to decide what to love more about Italy—the sights and atmosphere, the beautiful history on the facades of the buildings, the art in every vista, the color-rich stacks of the buildings of Portofino, the slender-columned rows of cypress in Tuscany, the grandeur of the past at every turn—or the food. Is there any cuisine more universally loved than Italian? Italy has a rich and complex culinary history. The Roman Empire spanned from the Middle East to North Africa, which brought many new spices and ingredients to Rome. In the Middle Ages, Arabs from North Africa brought lemons, durum wheat, sugar, artichokes, and eggplants to Sicily. During the Renaissance, feasting was popular and wealth abounded with new merchandise coming in through trade. Though it's now difficult to separate tomatoes from Italian cuisine, it wasn't until the sixteenth century that tomatoes first arrived in Italy from the new world. The recipes on this spread represent the diverse history of Italian food and celebrate the simple classic flavors, from pesto to burrata, olives to asiago, and a little bit of cannoli and biscotti sweetness to accompany an after-dinner cappuccino. This table covers some of the best of Italy in small bites and will delight all those who gather around it. —L.K.

MAKE AHEAD

Form and bread Arancini Rice Balls the day before and store in an airtight container in the refrigerator. Fry just before serving.

Make Caponata the day before and store in refrigerator.

Because biscotti is baked twice, it tastes great much longer than a normal cookie. Make biscotti up to 5 days in advance and store in an airtight container.

Amaretti Cookies can be made a day in advance. Store in an airtight container.

Make Peach Cookies a day before and store in refrigerator. Add mint garnish just before serving.

EXTRAS

Kalamata olives

Fresh basil

Tarallini

Italian cheese crackers

TIME SAVERS

Purchase ready-made pesto.

Purchase ready-made polenta for the Polenta Squares.

Purchase marinara sauce for the Arancini Rice Balls.

Styling Ideas

Use a rustic bread board or cutting board to serve.

Embellish with rustic flowers for added color.

Add fresh vegetables for color and texture.

RECISES

CROSTINIS 3 WAYS

1 baguette, sliced into ½-inch thick rounds

Olive oil, for brushing

1. Preheat your oven to 375°F. Arrange baguette slices on a baking sheet and brush each slice lightly with olive oil on both sides. Bake in the oven for about 5 to 7 minutes, or until the slices turn golden and crisp. Once done, remove from the oven and allow to cool. Season each crostini with sea salt and freshly ground black pepper. Drizzle with a generous amount of extra virgin olive oil. Top each crostini with one of the three toppings below.

CROSTINI WITH ROASTED TOMATO WITH BURRATA AND CHILI

Tri-color cherry tomatoes, roasted for the jam

Extra virgin olive oil, for drizzling

Sea salt and freshly ground black pepper, to taste

2 (12-oz.) packages burrata

1 tablespoon deseeded, finely chopped Calabrian chili pepper

1. Preheat oven to 400°F. Place the tri-color cherry tomatoes on a baking tray, drizzle with olive oil, sprinkle with salt and pepper. Roast for 20 to 25 minutes or until tomatoes burst and slightly char. Let them cool and blend to a chunky jam consistency. Set aside.

2. Tear burrata into four equal parts. Place a piece on each crostini. Sprinkle the finely chopped Calabrian chili over the burrata. Season with salt and pepper.

CROSTINI WITH WHIPPED RICOTTA, BROWN BUTTER & SAGE

1 cup Whipped Ricotta with Brown Butter and Sage (page 100)

Sea salt, to taste

Lemon zest, for garnish

Crushed red pepper, for garnish

Honey, for drizzling

1. Generously spread each crostini with the whipped ricotta. Place a fried sage leaf on each crostini. Drizzle a bit of the remaining brown butter over each crostini. Sprinkle with sea salt, lemon zest, and a touch of crushed red pepper if using. Finish each one with a light drizzle of honey.

CROSTINI WITH WHIPPED RICOTTA AND CAPONATA

1 cup Caponata (page 101)

2 tablespoons pine nuts

1 tablespoon fresh parsley, chopped

1. Generously spread each crostini with the Caponata. Sprinkle with pine nuts and parsley.

EACH VERSION MAKES **12**

WHIPPED RICOTTA WITH BROWN BUTTER AND SAGE

This recipe for Whipped Ricotta with Brown Butter and Sage was inspired by a dish I enjoyed at a local Brooklyn restaurant, Ms. Ada. I was impressed by the simple yet flavorful combination of creamy whipped ricotta with the nutty accent of brown butter and the aromatic touch of sage. Motivated to recreate this dish in my own kitchen, I experimented with the ingredients until I captured the essence of that delightful dining experience. —M.M.

½ cup unsalted butter + 1 tablespoon

3–4 tablespoons minced fresh sage + a few leaves for garnish

2 cups (16 ounces) whole milk ricotta cheese

1 tablespoon lemon juice + zest of 1 lemon

3 tablespoons honey

Sea salt

Crushed red pepper (optional for garnish)

1. Prepare the Brown Butter: In a small saucepan, melt the ½ cup butter over medium heat. Keep an eye on it, stirring occasionally. As it cooks, it will begin to foam and then subside. Watch closely as lightly browned specks begin to form at the bottom of the pan. Once the specks are amber brown and the butter has a nutty aroma, remove from heat and pour into a separate bowl to avoid burning the butter.

2. Using the same saucepan with the brown butter, add the sage leaves and fry them for about 30 seconds on each side, or until they're crisp but not browned. Remove the sage leaves and place them on a paper towel to remove any excess butter.

3. In a separate bowl, whip the ricotta cheese and lemon juice until it becomes smooth and creamy. Add the honey and 1 tablespoon of melted butter to the ricotta cheese and mix them together. Sprinkle some sea salt, lemon zest, and minced fresh sage on top of the ricotta cheese.

4. Garnish with crushed red pepper, if using. Serve with crackers, bread, or vegetables for dipping. Or use to make Crostinis (page 99).

MAKES **2** CUPS

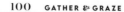

CAPONATA

SICILIAN EGGPLANT DIP

The journey of Caponata, an esteemed Sicilian dish, narrates a tale of culinary adaptation originating from historical circumstances. The term "Caponata" is believed to be derived from the Spanish word *caponada*, which is further linked to *capone*, a term for the lampuga fish in certain Sicilian regions. This fish, associated with the aristocracy, was traditionally served with a sweet and sour sauce. However, due to economic constraints, the common populace sought a more affordable alternative. Thus, eggplant replaced the aristocratic fish, while the distinctive sweet and sour sauce was retained, giving birth to the Caponata we recognize today.

3 large purple eggplants, cut into large chunks

2 tablespoons olive oil

1 large yellow onion, finely chopped

5 large tomatoes, roughly chopped

2 cloves garlic, peeled and finely sliced

1 bay leaf

1 teaspoon dried oregano

Sea salt and black pepper, to taste

2 tablespoons capers, rinsed and drained

1 cup green olives, pitted and sliced

2–3 tablespoons herb vinegar

6 tablespoons olive oil

3 tablespoons sugar

3 tablespoons vinegar

Small bunch of flat parsley, finely chopped

Grated zest of 1 lemon

Crushed chili flakes, to garnish

2 tablespoons slivered almonds, finely chopped

1. Sprinkle the eggplant chunks with 2 tablespoons of salt and let them drain in a colander for 30 minutes.

2. In a pan, heat the olive oil over medium heat. Add the onions and cook until they are tender and golden. Add the tomatoes, garlic, bay leaf, oregano, salt, and pepper, and cook until the mixture thickens into a sauce. Add the capers, olives, and herb vinegar, and stir for another 1 to 2 minutes.

3. Rinse the eggplant chunks and dry them with a kitchen towel. Heat 6 tablespoons of olive oil in a separate saucepan and add the eggplant chunks. Cook until the eggplant is tender and cooked through, adding extra oil if needed.

4. Add the cooked eggplant to the tomato mixture and stir to combine.

5. In a small bowl, mix the sugar and vinegar together until the sugar is dissolved. Add the mixture to the pan and stir to combine.

6. Garnish with parsley, lemon zest, crushed chili flakes, and almonds. Drizzle with additional olive oil if desired.

7. Serve the caponata as a dip or spread or on Crostinis (page 99). It can also be used as a topping for pasta or grilled meats.

SERVES **12**

PAN-FRIED POLENTA SQUARES

Polenta is a cherished staple in Northern Italy, often gracing family tables as a rustic side or appetizer. Topped with pesto, they beautifully merge the northern regions with the fresh, herbal flavors of Liguria.

4 cups water or chicken/vegetable broth

1 cup yellow cornmeal (polenta)

1 teaspoon salt (adjust based on preference and if using salted broth)

1 tablespoon olive oil or unsalted butter

½ cup freshly grated Parmesan cheese

2 tablespoons olive oil (for pan-frying)

1 cup pesto (page 102)

Fresh basil leaves for garnish (optional)

1. In a large saucepan, bring the water or broth to a boil. Gradually whisk in the cornmeal, ensuring to avoid any lumps. Reduce the heat to low and continue to cook, stirring often, until the mixture thickens and the cornmeal is tender, about 20 to 25 minutes. Once the polenta is cooked and thick, stir in the salt, 1 tablespoon of olive oil or butter, and Parmesan cheese. Mix until all ingredients are well combined.

2. Pour the hot polenta into a greased 9 × 13-inch pan. Smooth the top with a spatula. Allow it to cool at room temperature, then place in the refrigerator to set for at least 2 hours, or overnight for best results. Once set, turn the polenta out onto a cutting board. Cut the polenta into 3-inch squares using a sharp knife.

3. Heat olive oil in a large skillet over medium-high heat. Once hot, add the polenta squares (working in batches if necessary) and cook until golden brown and crispy on both sides, about 3 to 4 minutes per side. Place the fried polenta squares on a serving plate. Top each square with a generous dollop of pesto. Garnish with fresh Parmesan and basil leaves.

MAKES **12**

PESTO

MAKES 1 CUP

¼ cup pine nuts

2 cloves garlic

¼ teaspoon salt

¼ teaspoon freshly ground black pepper

2 packed cups fresh basil leaves

⅓ cup extra virgin olive oil

½ cup freshly grated Parmesan cheese

1. In the bowl of a food processor, coarsely chop pine nuts, garlic, salt, and pepper. Add basil leaves and pulse until basil is finely chopped. Pour in olive oil while food processor is running. Process until smooth. Add cheese and pulse to combine.

2. Serve immediately or store in an airtight container in the refrigerator for up to 2 days.

ARANCINI RICE BALLS

Arancini, meaning "little oranges" for their shape and color, are Italy's celebrated rice balls, with roots tracing back to tenth-century Sicily during Arabic rule. Born from the tradition of repurposing leftover risotto, Arancini epitomizes Italian culinary creativity. These crispy, golden orbs encase a variety of fillings, from gooey cheese to savory meat ragù, demonstrating the versatility of this humble yet delightful dish. Over time, regions and families have crafted their unique Arancini recipes, showcasing a spectrum of Italy's local produce and culinary inclinations. Whether opting for a gooey mozzarella core or a hearty meat sauce, each variant reflects a slice of Italy's rich and diverse food culture.

2 tablespoons unsalted butter

¼ cup minced shallots

1½ cups (10½ ounces) arborio rice

5 cups chicken stock or canned low-sodium broth

½ cup (2 ounces) freshly grated Parmesan cheese

2 teaspoons kosher salt

1 teaspoon freshly ground pepper

2 tablespoons finely chopped parsley

4 large eggs, divided

½ cup all-purpose flour

1 cup fine dry breadcrumbs

1½ ounces mozzarella, cut into 18 (½-inch dice) pieces

18 fresh or frozen peas

Vegetable oil, for frying

1. In a medium saucepan, melt the butter. Add the shallots and cook over moderate heat, stirring occasionally, until softened for about 3 minutes. Add the arborio rice and cook, stirring, for 4 minutes. Add 1 cup of the chicken stock to the pan and cook, stirring gently, until all the stock is absorbed. Add the remaining stock, ½ cup at a time, and cook, stirring gently, until the rice is al dente, about 25 minutes. Stir in the Parmesan, 2 teaspoons of salt and a teaspoon of pepper.

2. Transfer the risotto to a heatproof bowl and let cool for 10 minutes. Stir in the parsley and 1 egg. Press a piece of plastic wrap directly onto the rice and refrigerate the risotto for at least 4 hours or, preferably, overnight.

3. Line a baking sheet with parchment paper.

4. In a shallow bowl, beat the remaining 3 eggs. Put the flour and breadcrumbs on separate plates. Season the breadcrumbs with salt.

5. Using moistened hands, form ¼-cup portions of the rice into 2-inch balls. Tuck a piece of mozzarella and a pea in the center of each rice ball and seal any holes. Set the balls on the prepared baking sheet.

6. Dredge the rice balls in the flour, tapping off any excess. Working with 1 at a time, dip each ball in the egg, then coat

CONTINUED

with breadcrumbs, rolling in the crumbs to help them adhere. Place the coated rice balls back on the prepared baking sheet.

7. In a large, heavy saucepan, pour vegetable oil to a depth of about 3 inches. Heat the oil over medium heat until it reaches 350°F on a deep-fry thermometer.

8. Carefully add the rice balls to the hot oil in batches, taking care not to overcrowd the pan. Fry until golden brown and crispy, about 4 to 5 minutes, turning them occasionally for even browning. Using a slotted spoon, transfer the arancini to a plate lined with paper towels to drain.

9. Serve with marinara sauce or your preferred dipping sauce on the side for added flavor.

MAKES ABOUT **18** BALLS

HOMEMADE MARINARA SAUCE

MAKES ABOUT 2 CUPS

2 tablespoons olive oil

1 small onion, finely chopped

3 cloves garlic, minced

1 (28-ounce) can crushed tomatoes

1 teaspoon dried oregano

1 teaspoon dried basil

½ teaspoon sugar

Salt and freshly ground black pepper, to taste

½ teaspoon red pepper flakes (optional for a little heat)

2 tablespoons fresh basil, chopped (optional for garnish)

1. Sauté onion and garlic: In a large saucepan, heat the olive oil over medium heat. Add the chopped onion and sauté until translucent, about 2 to 3 minutes. Add the minced garlic and sauté for another 30 seconds, ensuring it doesn't burn.

2. Pour the crushed tomatoes into the saucepan with the onion and garlic. Add the dried oregano, dried basil, sugar, salt, and black pepper. Add red pepper flakes, if using. Stir well to combine.

3. Reduce the heat to low and let the sauce simmer for about 20 to 25 minutes. Stir occasionally. The sauce will thicken and the flavors will meld together. Serve warm with Arancini Rice Balls garnished with basil, if using.

BALSAMIC AND PARMESAN DIPPING OIL

Dipping oils hold a quintessential spot on the Italian table, embodying a tradition of enjoying bread with simple yet flavor-packed olive oil blends. This Balsamic and Parmesan Dipping Oil recipe celebrates this age-old practice. The sweet, tangy essence of balsamic vinegar harmoniously melds with the salty, umami-rich Parmesan, creating a dipping oil that's both authentic and inviting. Historically, olive oil has been a staple in Italian cuisine for centuries, and its fusion with locally sourced ingredients like balsamic vinegar and Parmesan cheese reflects Italy's culinary tradition of melding simplicity with robust flavors. This dipping oil transports you to an Italian gathering, where food is a bond, shared and enjoyed in its wholesome essence.

⅔ cup high-quality extra-virgin olive oil

5–6 cloves garlic, crushed and minced

1½ tablespoons oregano or Italian seasoning

⅓ cup fresh, finely grated Parmesan cheese

¼ teaspoon crushed red pepper or crushed Calabrian chili paste

⅓ cup balsamic vinegar, or to taste

Freshly ground black pepper, to taste

1. In a small saucepan, combine the olive oil and minced garlic. Gently heat the mixture over medium-low heat until the garlic becomes fragrant but not browned. Remove the saucepan from the heat and let the garlic-infused oil cool for a few minutes.

2. Pour the cooled garlic-infused olive oil into a deep plate or wide, shallow bowl. Sprinkle the oregano (or Italian seasoning), finely grated Parmesan cheese, and crushed red pepper over the oil.

3. Drizzle the balsamic vinegar over the oil and cheese mixture, creating a marbled effect. Top with freshly ground pepper. Serve with crusty bread.

MAKES ABOUT **1** CUP

RED ONION AND OLIVE FOCACCIA

Focaccia gets its name from *panis focacius*, which is Latin for hearth bread. During Roman times flat bread was cooked by fire. Over time, the bread spread throughout Europe and eventually was baked in ovens. It evolved to its current airy, soft-on-the-inside and crisp-on-the-outside form. Fresh-from-the-oven focaccia is always a hit at gatherings and is perfect accompaniment with an Italian meal or party spread.

2 cups warm water

1½ teaspoons sugar

1 tablespoon yeast

2 cups all-purpose flour + more if needed

2 cups bread flour

2 teaspoons kosher salt

¼ cup olive oil + more for the pan

TOPPING

¼ cup olive oil

2 cloves garlic, minced

1 teaspoon crushed red pepper

½ medium red onion, sliced

½ cup kalamata olives, quartered

Coarse sea salt to taste

1. In a small bowl, mix water, sugar, and yeast. Allow to stand until a thick foam has formed at the top, about 10 minutes.

2. In the bowl of a stand mixer with the dough hook attachment, stir together flours and salt. Whisk olive oil into yeast mixture. With the mixer on low, slowly pour in yeast mixture. Mix until a soft shaggy dough forms. Dough should be sticky. If dough is too sticky, add more all-purpose flour 1 tablespoon at a time until dough comes together.

3. Knead dough on medium speed for 6 minutes. Cover bowl with plastic wrap and allow to rest 30 minutes.

4. Generously oil a 9 × 13-inch pan and place dough in pan. With oiled fingers, stretch dough to cover the bottom of the pan evenly. Cover with oiled plastic wrap and allow to rise until dough has doubled in bulk, about 1 to 2 hours. When ready, preheat oven to 425°F.

5. To make the topping: Mix olive oil, garlic, and crushed red pepper. Remove plastic wrap from dough and add dimples across the surface by pushing your fingers all the way into the dough. Evenly brush oil mixture over top. Evenly layer onion slices and olives. Sprinkle with coarse sea salt. Bake for 25 to 30 minutes or until golden brown on top.

6. When cool enough to handle but still warm, remove focaccia from pan and place on a cutting board. Cut into rectangles with a pizza cutter. Serve immediately. Focaccia tastes best on the same day it is baked. Store leftovers in an airtight container in the freezer for up to a month.

MAKES **20** PIECES

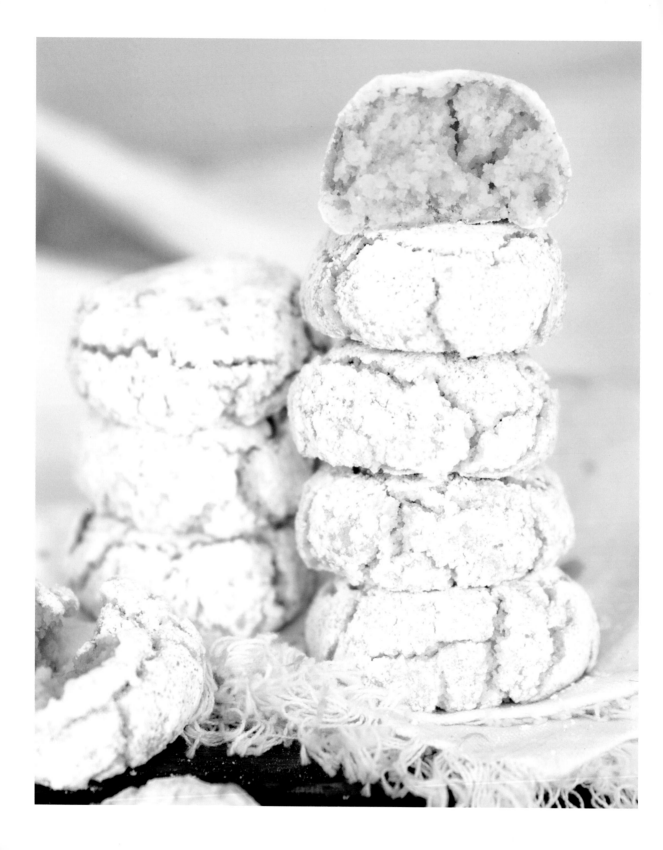

AMARETTI COOKIES

Amaretti translates to "little bitter things," referring to the almonds in the recipe. However, these soft, chewy bites of sweetness are the opposite of bitter. They have been popular in Italy for hundreds of years, and are a great treat to go with cappuccinos or on a party spread as a gluten-free sweet.

2⅔ cups almond flour

1 cup sugar, divided

½ teaspoon fine kosher salt

Zest of 1 lemon

3 egg whites

¼ teaspoon cream of tartar

1 teaspoon vanilla extract

1 teaspoon almond extract

FOR COATING

½ cup sugar

½ cup confectioners' sugar

1. Preheat oven to 350°F. In a medium bowl, whisk together almond flour, ½ cup of the sugar, salt, and lemon zest. Set aside.

2. In the bowl of a stand mixer with the whisk attachment, beat egg whites at medium-low speed until foamy. Add cream of tartar. Increase speed to medium and add remaining sugar slowly, 1 teaspoon at a time. Increase speed to medium-high for 2 minutes. Increase again to high speed and continue to beat until stiff peaks form, about 2 to 4 additional minutes. Add vanilla and almond extracts and turn mixer on low just until incorporated.

3. Add the egg mixture to the dry ingredients, and mix with a rubber spatula until fully incorporated. Place each of the coating sugars in two separate bowls. Scoop dough with a 1 ounce cookie scoop and roll into a ball. Coat the ball in sugar, and then generously coat it with confectioners' sugar.

4. Place coated dough ball on a cookie sheet and repeat, placing dough balls about 2 inches apart. Bake for about 11 to 13 minutes. Allow the cookies to cool for about 5 minutes before transferring them to a cooling rack. Store in a sealed container for up to 3 days.

MAKES **22**

MINI ALMOND CHOCOLATE CHIP BISCOTTI

Originating in Tuscany, these twice-baked cookies are now popular worldwide and make the prefect accompaniment to cappaccino. They also come in many varieties. I love how the chocolate in this version melts when dipped in hot coffee, and the almonds are a classic addition.

5 tablespoons unsalted butter, softened

1 cup sugar

3 eggs, room temperature

1½ teaspoons almond extract

2¾ cups flour

½ teaspoon fine kosher salt

1 tablespoon baking powder

1 cup mini chocolate chips

½ cup almonds, coarsely chopped

12 ounces white chocolate

1 teaspoon coconut oil

1. Preheat oven to 375°F. Line a half-sheet baking tray with parchment paper or a baking mat.

2. In a medium mixing bowl, beat butter and sugar with a mixer for 3 minutes, until light and fluffy. Add eggs and almond extract and beat until combined.

3. In a small mixing bowl, combine flour, salt, and baking powder. Add to the butter mixture and beat until combined. Stir in chocolate chips and almonds. Refrigerate dough for about 45 minutes.

4. Divide dough in three equal portions. With floured hands, form each portion into a log that is about the length of the baking sheet. Place logs on the prepared pan. Bake 16 to 18 minutes.

5. Remove from oven and let rest for 5 to 10 minutes. Reduce oven temperature to 325°F. Prepare a second baking pan by placing a cooling rack on top of the baking pan. Slice biscotti logs on an angle into ½-inch to ¾-inch slices. Place slices on their side on cooling rack. Biscotti will not expand on second baking, so you can place them close together.

6. Bake a second time for 18 to 20 minutes. Allow to cool.

7. Lay out 2 to 3 feet of parchment paper on counter. Melt white chocolate with coconut oil in a heatproof container. Dip bottoms of each biscotti in chocolate and set on parchment to dry. After chocolate has set completely, store in an airtight container for up to 3 weeks.

MAKES **65**

MINI CANNOLI

I had my first cannoli in Boston's North End. My friend Allison introduced me to Mike's Pastry—a long-standing, neighborhood staple started by a first generation Italian immigrant. The smell of a thousand delicious delicate sweets hits your nose the moment you walk in. The glass cases of beauties make it hard to choose, but cannoli was our favorite to take home in white boxes tied with baker's twine. The ricotta-filled sweet treats were a perfect afternoon pick-me-up with coffee. —L.K.

EQUIPMENT
2¾-inch round cookie cutter

Mini cannoli forms

Cheesecloth

Pastry bag with large round or star tip

CANNOLI SHELLS
2 cups all-purpose flour + more for rolling

2 tablespoons sugar

½ teaspoon fine kosher salt

¼ cup unsalted butter, cold

1 egg

⅓ cup Marsala wine or water + more if needed

Peanut oil or other neutral oil for frying

1 egg white, beaten

CANNOLI FILLING
1 cup whole-milk ricotta

½ cup mascarpone

¾ cup confectioners' sugar

½ teaspoon ground cinnamon

½ cup mini semisweet chocolate chips

½ cup pistachios, finely chopped

1. **Make cannoli shells:** In the bowl of a food processor, add flour, sugar, and salt. Pulse to combine. Slice butter into pats and toss into flour mixture. Pulse until butter is in small pieces. Add egg and wine or water. Process just until combined. If dough is not holding together, add more wine or water 1 teaspoon at a time until it starts to hold together. Turn out dough onto a work surface and form a ball, flatten into a disk, and cover with plastic wrap. Refrigerate for 1 hour or overnight.

2. Add 3 to 4 inches of oil to a Dutch oven or heavy-bottomed pot. Clip a candy thermometer to the side of pot or set an instant read thermometer near stove. Preheat to 350°F over medium-high heat while rolling out the cannoli dough on a lightly floured surface. Roll half of the dough out thin, to about ⅛ thickness or less. Make 2¾-inch rounds with cookie cutter. Wrap around a cannoli form. Brush egg white where dough overlaps to securely connect the dough.

3. Line a baking sheet with paper towel and set a cooling rack on top of baking sheet. Place baking sheet near stove. Using tongs, carefully lower dough on form into preheated oil. Add up to 4 cannoli shells at a time. Turn shells after 1 minute. Continue moving shells until they are golden brown on all sides, about 2 to 3 additional minutes. Remove from oil and place on prepared pan to drain. Continue frying shells until all the dough has been used. Monitor oil temperature throughout frying process, keeping temperature close to 350°F. Allow fried shells to cool and remove forms.

4. **Make cannoli filling:** Place ricotta cheese in cheesecloth and squeeze out as much extra liquid as possible. Place

NOTE: It is important to get as much liquid out of the ricotta as possible to keep the filling from being runny. To drain more liquid from the ricotta, wrap ricotta in several layers of paper towel and press down. Allow to rest for 15 minutes. Discard paper towels.

drained ricotta cheese in the bowl of a stand mixer with the whisk attachment. Add mascarpone, confectioners' sugar, and cinnamon and beat on high for 5 minutes. Transfer to a pastry bag. Pipe filling into cooled cannoli shells. Dip ends in mini chocolate chips or pistachios. Serve immediately.

5. Cannoli are best served right after filling or on the same day that the shells were fried. If you will not serve all cannoli on the day you made them, store unfilled shells in an airtight container in the freezer. Store filling separately in refrigerator in an airtight container for up to 5 days. To serve after freezing, warm cannoli shells on baking sheet in 250°F oven for 8 minutes. Allow to cool completely before filling.

MAKES **36**

PEACH COOKIES

Though the name leads one to believe that these treats taste like peaches, they are actually traditionally flavored with Alkermes—a sweet, spiced Italian liqueur. Since Alkermes is difficult to find in the States, I created a spiced simple syrup to use as an alternate. If you want your peach cookies to actually taste like peaches, try using a peach syrup. No matter your flavor preference, they will look sweet on your spread, garnished with mint leaves for the perfect peachy effect. —L.K.

SPICED SIMPLE SYRUP

1 cup water

1 cup sugar

1 star anise

1 cinnamon stick

⅛ teaspoon coriander

⅛ teaspoon mace

⅛ teaspoon nutmeg

Peel of ½ orange without pith

1 tablespoon vanilla extract

3 drops orange gel food coloring

1 drop red gel food coloring

COOKIES

½ cup unsalted butter, softened

1 cup sugar

2 large eggs, room temperature

1 teaspoon vanilla extract

3½ cups all-purpose flour

½ teaspoon fine kosher salt

1 tablespoon baking powder

⅓ cup buttermilk

1. **To make the spiced simple syrup:** Add all syrup ingredients except gel food coloring to a medium saucepan. Cook over medium-high heat until mixture starts to bubble. Reduce heat to medium and allow to simmer for 10 minutes. Stir in gel food coloring and whisk until evenly distributed. Strain syrup and allow to cool before using on cookies.

2. **To make cookies:** Preheat oven to 350°F.

3. In the bowl of a stand mixer, beat butter and sugar for 3 minutes, until light and fluffy. Add eggs and vanilla and beat until combined.

4. In a small mixing bowl, combine flour, salt, and baking powder. Add to the butter mixture and beat until combined. Add the buttermilk and beat until combined. Using a rubber spatula, scrape the sides and bottom of bowl to ensure dough is evenly mixed.

5. Scoop ½ tablespoon of dough and form ball. Place ball onto a cookie sheet and flatten slightly. Fill baking sheet, leaving 2 inches of space around each dough ball.

6. Bake just until cookies are lightly golden, about 10 minutes. Transfer cookies to a cooling rack and cool just until you can handle them. With a knife with a sharp point, hollow out some of the bottom center of each cookie. Take out just enough to allow some room for the pastry cream. Allow to cool completely.

CONTINUED

ASSEMBLY

¾ cup Spiced Simple Syrup or Torani Peach Syrup

½ cup sugar + more if needed

¾ cup Vanilla Bean Pastry Cream (page 119)

1 bunch fresh mint

7. To assemble cookies: Place 2 to 3 feet of parchment on counter. Add sugar to a small shallow bowl. With a pastry brush, coat top and sides of cookie with syrup. Immediately roll top and sides of cookie in sugar. Set on parchment and allow to dry for 30 minutes.

8. If cookies vary in size, match cookies into pairs of similar sizes. With an offset spatula, spread pastry cream into the hollowed-out section of each cookie and twist together. Be careful not to add too much pastry cream. Pastry cream should just reach the edge of cookies when assembled. Just before serving, top each peach with mint leaves by inserting a small section of a stem between cookie halves.

9. Store in an airtight container in refrigerator for up to 3 days or freeze for up to 3 months.

MAKES **36**

VANILLA BEAN PASTRY CREAM

Pastry cream, also called creme patissiere, is a versatile silky custard perfect for filling desserts like eclairs and Peach Cookies (page 117). It is also used to make diplomat cream, which is a lighter cream and pairs amazingly with fruit, especially strawberries. Try it in Tarte Aux Fraises (page 174). The vanilla bean really amps up the flavors in this delicious, baker's-essential cream.

1 cup whole milk

1 cup heavy cream

¼ teaspoon kosher salt

⅔ cup sugar, divided

4 egg yolks

2 tablespoons cornstarch

1 vanilla bean

3 tablespoons unsalted butter

1. In a medium saucepan, add milk, cream, salt, and ⅓ cup sugar. Whisk together and cook over medium heat until mixture reaches a simmer.

2. In the bowl of a stand mixer with the whisk attachment, mix egg yolks, cornstarch, and remaining sugar on low. With a sharp knife, cut open vanilla bean lengthwise. Scrape the seeds and add to yolk mixture. With mixer still running, carefully pour hot milk mixture. Once fully combined, pour mixture back into saucepan and cook over medium-high heat, whisking constantly. Cook until mixture thickens and reaches 160°F, about 2 to 3 minutes.

3. Transfer back to stand mixer bowl. With paddle attachment, mix on low. Add butter 1 teaspoon at a time, waiting until each addition is fully incorporated before adding the next. Continue to run mixer on low for 6 to 7 minutes to allow cream to cool. Running the mixer prevents a skin from forming on pastry cream while cooling.

4. Transfer pastry cream to a medium bowl. Cover with plastic wrap by pressing directly onto the surface of cream. Refrigerate for at least 2 hours or up to 3 days. Whisk pastry cream before using.

MAKES **2½** CUPS

DUTCH TABLE

"Good food is very often, even most often, simple food." —ANTHONY BOURDAIN

I grew up in a community of third and fourth generation Dutch immigrants which influenced the foods I ate and the traditions of my family. As many do, we changed our food over generations to become more American than Dutch, but the basis of foods we love still rests in the rich fields of the Netherlands where produce, meat, and dairy abound. Dutch cuisine is solidly based on these ingredients—with cheese, butter, meats, vegetables, and bread all important parts of the daily menu. In the twentieth century, households valued efficiency over complicated cuisine, which led to a reputation of Dutch food being bland, but it was also an efficiency that made this small country into the second largest exporter of agricultural goods in the world. The Dutch table may seem simple, but to me there is so much comfort in freshly baked bread with butter or cheese, and there is beauty in the fields of produce and the work and craftsmanship that it takes to bring this basic nourishment to the table. My ancestors brought their love of farm-to-table with them across the Atlantic. Most likely my appreciation and joy in good, fresh, simple foods is part of my DNA. —L.K.

MAKE AHEAD

Saucijzenbroodjes can be prepared up to 4 hours in advance and baked just before serving. Cover and refrigerate until ready to bake.

Make Bitterballen and Aardappelkroketten a day in advance and fry just before serving. Or make them up to a week in advance and freeze them in an airtight container. Move from freezer to refrigerator about 8 hours before frying.

Speculaas can be baked a day in advance.

Make caramel for Stroopwafels up to a week in advance. Store in refrigerator and warm to room temperature before assembling Stroopwafels.

EXTRAS

Gouda, Edam, and Leyden cheese

Butter

Mustard to go with Bitterballen

TIME SAVERS

Purchase jarred caramel for the Stroopwafels or already prepared Stroopwafels from a bakery.

Purchase frozen puff pastry for Saucijzenbroodjes.

Styling Ideas

Delft pottery has been handpainted in the Netherlands since the 1600s. The traditional blue and white dishes are perfect for this board. The originals may be cost-prohibitive, but you can find machine-made replicas. Antique shops can also be an excellent source for similar dishes.

The Netherlands is one of the largest exporters of flowers in the world. They are known for tulips, but they also grow most other floral varieties. Fill your table with fresh cut flowers. Yellow looks especially nice with the blue and white china.

RECIPES

SAUCIJZENBROODJES

DUTCH SAUSAGE ROLLS

My mom, aunts, and grandmother used to get together to make homemade pigs in a blanket—a tradition among the mostly Dutch community where I grew up. Their version used ground pork wrapped in homemade pie dough. The recipe was likely brought over with our ancestors from the Netherlands and based on Saucijzenbroodjes. This more traditional version has a bit of spice added to the meat and is wrapped in puff pastry. —L.K.

MEAT
2 pound ground beef or
　　ground pork or a 50/50
　　mixture

1 egg

⅓ cup breadcrumbs

1 tablespoon Oelek chili paste

1 clove garlic

2 tablespoons chopped fresh
　　parsley

¼ cup finely chopped white
　　onion

PASTRY
1 egg, beaten with
　　1 tablespoon water (for
　　egg wash)

1 pound Rough Puff Pastry
　　(page xxi) or packaged
　　puff pastry, thawed

1. Line a baking sheet with parchment or a silicone baking mat. Set 2 feet of parchment on counter.

2. In a medium bowl, mix all meat ingredients with your hands until all ingredients are completely incorporated. Divide into 16 portions and form log shapes that are about 3½ inches long and place on parchment.

3. In a small bowl, whisk egg until foamy. Set aside. Divide puff pastry into 16 pieces. On a lightly-floured surface roll out each piece to about 5 × 4 inches. Brush off excess flour. Set one meat log on each portion of puff pastry. With a pastry brush, coat the edges of the puff pastry with egg wash. Fold pastry over sausage. Using a fork, crimp edges of the pasty to seal. Place on prepared baking sheet. Repeat with remaining pastry and sausage. With a sharp knife, cut three vents in top of each roll. Brush tops with more egg wash. Place baking sheet in refrigerator for 30 minutes so puff pastry can firm up.

4. Preheat oven to 400°F. Bake 20 to 25 minutes or until pastry is golden brown and meat is cooked through. Serve immediately. Store leftovers in an airtight container in refrigerator for up to 3 days.

5. To revive cold Saucijzenbroodjes, preheat oven to 325°F. Place on a baking sheet and warm for 8 to 10 minutes in oven.

MAKES **16**

BITTERBALLEN

DUTCH MEATBALLS

Bitterballen—small breaded and fried balls of beef ragout—is one of the Netherlands' most popular snacks. Contrary to the name, they are not bitter—they got their name from bittertje, the alcoholic beverage they most frequently accompanied. Now you're more likely to see them served up in pubs alongside pints of beer with mustard for dipping.

BEEF

1¾ pound beef roast

Water

¼ white onion

1 bay leaf

1 clove garlic

4 sprigs fresh thyme

1 teaspoon kosher salt

ROUX

6 tablespoons unsalted butter

1 clove garlic, minced

1 cup all-purpose flour

2 cups whole milk

1½ cups beef stock

¼ cup finely chopped fresh parsley

Kosher salt and pepper to taste

1. **To cook the meat:** With a sharp knife or kitchen scissors, cut beef into cubes. Place in a pot or slow cooker and add enough water to cover beef by 1 inch. Cook over medium-high heat on stove or on high heat in slow cooker. Coarsely chop onion and add to pot. Add bay leaf, garlic, thyme, and salt. Stir to combine. If cooking on stove, when water starts to boil, reduce temperature to a simmer and cook uncovered until meat is cooked through and tender, 2 to 3 hours. If using the slow cooker, place on lid and allow to cook for 4 to 5 hours.

2. When meat has finished cooking, remove meat from pot with a slotted spoon and place on a cutting board. Strain cooking liquid into a large measuring cup or medium bowl and reserve 1½ cups. With a sharp knife, cut meat into small pieces, place in a bowl, and set aside.

3. **To make the roux:** Melt butter in a large frying pan or braiser over medium heat. Add garlic and cook until fragrant, about 3 minutes. Add flour and whisk until a paste forms. Carefully pour milk into pan and whisk until it fully combines with butter mixture. Add beef stock reserved from cooking beef; whisk until completely smooth. It will take a couple of minutes to get all the lumps out. Increase heat to medium high. Bring mixture to a boil. Reduce heat so mixture is at a simmer and continue to cook for 30 minutes, stirring occasionally. When finished cooking, add fresh parsley and salt and pepper to taste. Allow to cool.

BREADING

3 eggs

2 tablespoons water

½ cup all-purpose flour

1 cup panko breadcrumbs

1½ cups plain bread crumbs

Peanut (or other neutral) oil
for frying

4. In a medium bowl or airtight container, combine meat with cooled roux; stir until completely incorporated. Cover with plastic wrap or lid. Refrigerate for 4 hours or overnight.

5. To bread the bitterballen: In a medium bowl, whisk eggs until foamy, add water, and whisk to combine. Add flour to a small plate. Mix breadcrumbs in a shallow bowl. Line a baking sheet with parchment and set near breading ingredients. Scoop 1½ tablespoons of cold beef ragout. Form a ball and set on baking sheet. Continue making balls until ragout is gone.

6. Roll a ball in flour. Dip it in the egg mixture, and coat ball completely. Roll ball in breadcrumbs. Then add back to the egg mixture and again in the breadcrumbs for a second coat. Set on baking sheet. Coat remainder of bitterballen. Cover bitterballen with plastic wrap and place in refrigerator for 30 minutes to firm up.

7. To fry the bitterballen: Clip a candy thermometer to a heavy-bottomed pot or Dutch oven, pour in 3 to 4 inches oil, and preheat to 350°F. Line another baking sheet with paper towels and set a cooling rack on top. Using a metal skimmer, carefully lower 4 to 5 bitterballen into oil, one at a time. Fry until golden brown, about 3 minutes per side. Remove with metal skimmer and place on prepared cooling rack to drain. Serve hot with a side of mustard or your favorite condiments.

8. Bitterballen are best freshly fried. Only fry what you expect to serve. Store extras in an airtight container in freezer for up to 1 month. Move from freezer to refrigerator about 3 hours before frying.

MAKES ABOUT **40**

AARDAPPELKROKETTEN

DUTCH POTATO CROQUETTES

Potatoes have been a staple in the Dutch diet, so much so that farmers and villagers often ate them as their main course. Van Gogh's famous painting "The Potato Eaters" features this very common meal among Dutch working-class people. Aardappelkroketten takes mashed potatoes flavored with aged Gouda and chives and packages it into the-much-loved kroketten. These are the perfect addition to a snack board or party spread. These simple savory treats are sure to be a favorite. —L.K.

POTATOES

2½ pounds potatoes

6 tablespoons salted butter, melted

¼ cup half-and-half

½ cup grated aged gouda

Salt and pepper to taste

¼ cup chopped chives

1 tablespoon chopped fresh parsley + more for garnish

⅛ teaspoon nutmeg

BREADING

3 eggs

2 tablespoons water

¼ cup flour

3 cups panko breadcrumbs

Peanut (or other neutral) oil for frying

1. Peel potatoes and boil over medium-high heat until tender. Drain potatoes. With a ricer, rice potatoes back into pot. Add butter, half-and-half, cheese, salt, and pepper. Mix over low heat with a wooden spoon until cheese is melted and all ingredients are fully incorporated. Turn off heat and stir in chives, parsley, and nutmeg. Allow to cool, cover, and refrigerate 30 minutes.

2. In a medium bowl, whisk eggs until foamy, add water, and whisk to combine. Add flour to a small plate. Pour breadcrumbs into a shallow bowl. Line a baking sheet with parchment. Scoop 3 tablespoons of potato mixture and form into logs. Place on prepared baking sheet.

3. Roll a log in flour. Dip it in the egg mixture; coat log completely. Roll log in breadcrumbs. Then add back to the egg mixture and again in the breadcrumbs for a second coat. Set on baking sheet. Coat remainder of aardappelkroketten. Cover with plastic wrap and place in refrigerator for 30 minutes to firm up.

4. To fry the aardappelkroketten: Clip a candy thermometer to a heavy-bottomed pot or Dutch oven, pour in 3 to 4 inches oil and preheat to 350°F. Line another baking sheet with paper towels and set a cooling rack on top. Using a metal skimmer, carefully lower 3 to 4 aardappelkroketten into oil, one at a time. Fry until golden brown, about 3 minutes per side. Remove with metal skimmer and place on prepared cooling rack to drain. Serve hot with your favorite condiments and garnish with more fresh parsley.

MAKES ABOUT 20

TIJGERBOL

MOTTLED CRUST ROLLS

Tijgerbol (or Tijgerbrood when it's baked as a bread loaf) gets its name from the crisp, cracked pattern that forms on the top crust of the bread as it bakes. These rolls have all the delicious perfection of European breads, soft on the inside with a dense crumb and a crisp slightly chewy crust all around.

DOUGH

1½ cups warm water

1 teaspoon sugar

1 tablespoon active dry yeast

4 cups bread flour

2 teaspoons salt

1 tablespoon unsalted butter, softened

TOPPING

½ cup rice flour

1 teaspoon active dry yeast

1 tablespoon sugar

½ teaspoon salt

1 tablespoon olive oil

¼ cup water

2 cups of water for steaming rolls

1. **Make the dough:** In a small bowl, mix water, sugar, and yeast. Allow to stand until a thick foam has formed at the top, about 10 minutes.

2. In the bowl of a stand mixer, with the dough hook attachment, stir together flour and salt. With the mixer on low, slowly pour in yeast mixture. Mix until a soft shaggy dough forms. If dough is too sticky, add more flour 1 tablespoon at a time until dough comes together. With mixer running, add butter in 2 portions. Allow butter to fully incorporate before adding the next portion.

3. Knead on medium speed for 5 minutes.

4. Lightly butter a large bowl and place dough in bowl. Cover bowl with plastic wrap or damp towel and allow dough to rise until it doubles in size. Bowl-fold dough by stretching from bottom to top. Allow to rise again for 30 minutes.

5. **Make the topping:** During second rise, whisk together rice flour, yeast, sugar, and salt. Add oil and water and mix until a paste forms. Cover with plastic wrap and allow to rest.

6. Divide dough into 16 even portions (about 50 grams each). Form balls from each portion. Line 2 large baking sheets with parchment or a silicone baking mat. Place a dough ball on baking sheet and flatten slightly with palm of hand. Fill both sheets. Allow to rest 30 minutes.

CONTINUED

7. Place one oven rack in center of oven. Place a second rack at the lowest level of oven. Place an empty 9 × 13-inch pan on the bottom rack. Preheat oven to 425°F.

8. Add about 1 tablespoon topping to the top of each roll. With the back of a spoon, smooth topping over tops and sides of dough rolls. Set 1 cup of hot water near oven. Place first pan of rolls on the center rack of oven. Pull out bottom rack and carefully pour water in pan. Return rack and close oven as quickly as possible so steam is trapped in oven.

9. Bake until golden, about 13 to 15 minutes. Serve warm. Fresh bread tastes best on the same day it is baked. Store leftovers in an airtight container in the freezer for up to a month.

10. To revive frozen rolls, preheat oven to 275°F. Place rolls on a baking sheet and warm for 7 to 10 minutes.

MAKES **16**

DUTCH CHEESES

With its abundant fields filled with grazing cows, goats, and sheep and long-history of dairy-rich diets, its no wonder the Netherlands is one of the top exporters of cheese in the world. The three most popular cheeses are named after the Dutch cities where they originated. You can build a cheese board with these classic varieties to add to your Dutch table. Serve with rusk crackers, rye bread, and your favorite fruits and vegetables.

Aged Gouda

Gouda

Edam

Leyden

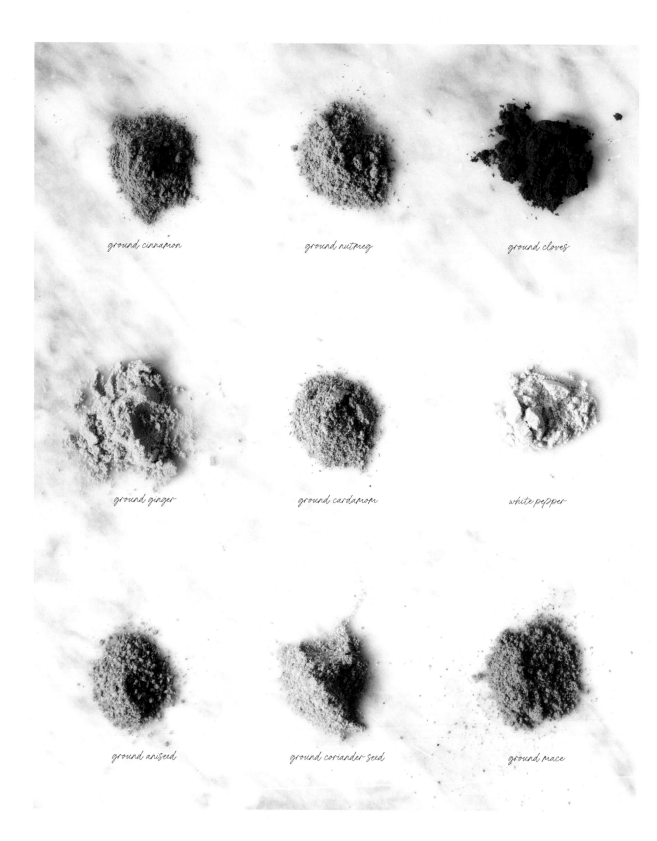

ground cinnamon

ground nutmeg

ground cloves

ground ginger

ground cardamon

white pepper

ground aniseed

ground coriander seed

ground mace

SPECULAAS SPICE MIX

Making this spice mix in advance will save time and effort when baking your speculaas. You can also try a little in your hot chocolate, latte, or cappuccinos. Mix it with chocolate sauce for ice cream or add to your French toast recipe.

5 tablespoons cinnamon
1 teaspoon ground nutmeg
1 teaspoon ground cloves
1 teaspoon ground ginger
1 teaspoon ground cardamom
½ teaspoon white pepper
½ teaspoon ground aniseed
½ teaspoon ground coriander
   seed
½ teaspoon ground mace

1. In a small bowl, whisk together all ingredients. Pour into a spice jar and seal and store with your spices.

MAKES ABOUT ½ CUP

SPECULAAS

Speculaas were traditionally given to well-behaved children for Saint Nicholas Day on December 6 in the Netherlands, Belgium, and Germany. The slightly crisp, spiced cookies became popular in the sixteenth century when more spices became available in the Netherlands due to the success of the spice trade of the Dutch East India Company. Speculaas were traditionally formed in a wooden mold in the shape of Saint Nicholas, but are now more often formed into windmill shapes—earning them their other moniker: windmill cookies.

EQUIPMENT
Speculaas mold

½ cup almonds

3 cups all-purpose flour

1 teaspoon baking soda

1 teaspoon salt

2½ tablespoons Speculaas
   Spice Mix (page 135)

1 cup unsalted butter

1½ cups dark brown sugar

1 teaspoon vanilla extract

2 large egg yolks

1. Preheat oven to 350°F. Place almonds on a single layer on a baking sheet, bake 7 minutes, and allow to cool.

2. In a food processor, process cooled almonds until fine. Add flour, baking soda, salt, and speculaas spice. Pulse until well combined.

3. In the bowl of a stand mixer, beat butter, brown sugar, vanilla, and egg yolks until light and fluffy, about 3 minutes.

4. Add almond mixture to the butter mixture. Beat just until combined.

5. Divide the dough into two portions. Wrap in plastic and refrigerate for 1 hour or overnight.

6. When ready to bake cookies, preheat oven to 350°F. Line a baking sheet with parchment or a baking mat. Lightly flour speculaas mold. Press cold dough firmly into mold. Cut off any extra dough. Peel back one edge of dough and carefully pull out of mold. Place on baking sheet. Leave about 1 inch of space between cookies. Bake for 12 to 15 minutes. Allow cookies to cool on the pan for 5 minutes before transferring them to a cooling rack. Store in an airtight container for up to 3 days or freeze for up to 3 months.

MAKES ABOUT **30**

STROOPWAFELS

Stroopwafels are said to have been invented in Gouda in the late eighteenth century. They became popular locally and eventually spread around the world. You can now find them packaged in most stores. The packaged variety really can't compare to a freshly made stroopwafel—the gooey warm caramel and fresh-from-the-iron waffle layers are buttery, sweet, crisp deliciousness. They may seem like they will be challenging to make, but they come together easily as long as you have a waffle cone maker.

EQUIPMENT
Nonstick electric waffle cone maker

3½-inch round cookie cutter

3 large eggs, room temperature

1 cup light brown sugar

½ cup unsalted butter, melted and cooled

1 tablespoon vanilla extract

1¾ cups all-purpose flour

½ teaspoon fine kosher salt

2 teaspoons baking powder

Caramel (page 149)

NOTE: For firmer caramel reduce heavy cream in caramel recipe (page 149) to ¾ cup.

1. In the bowl of a stand mixer with the whisk attachment, beat eggs on medium speed for 1 minute. Add sugar and beat until combined. Pour in melted butter and vanilla extract and beat until combined.

2. In a small bowl, combine flour, salt, and baking powder. Add flour mixture to egg mixture. Mix on low just until combined. Scrape the sides and bottom of bowl to ensure even mixing.

3. Preheat waffle cone maker. Ladle 1½ tablespoons of batter in center of bottom iron. Close lid and lock. Cook until golden brown, or about 2 minutes. Transfer to a flat plate or cutting board. While still hot, cut with a 3½-inch cookie cutter. Transfer to a wire rack to cool completely. Continue cooking until all batter is gone.

4. Warm caramel enough so it is at an easily spreadable consistency. Spread a thin layer on one waffle cookie. Cover with a second layer and lightly press together to attach. Serve immediately or store in an airtight container for up to 4 days.

MAKES **12**

LIEGE WAFFLE BOARD

"Take me to the land of chocolate and waffles." —ANONYMOUS

The light, crisp, deeply grooved Brussels waffle is usually what we think of when we say "Belgium waffles" in the United States. The Brussels waffle was introduced at an exposition in Seattle in the 1960s and has been popular ever since. Though more common in the United States, the Brussels waffle isn't Belgium's most popular waffle. Sweeter and denser, the Liege waffle can be found all over Belgium and is legendary in its Middle Ages origins. Liege waffles have long been served as a street snack and are usually eaten on their own. The sweet bits of caramelized sugar pearls and buttery crisp exterior make them fabulous fresh from the hot iron all by themselves. I also love them with a drizzle of chocolate or caramel, and they are fabulous with fruit. Build this board for a breakfast, brunch, or dessert and your guests will have fun making their own waffle masterpieces. —L.K.

RECIPES

Liege Waffles ✖ 143

Warm Cinnamon Apples ✖ 144

Toffee Pecans ✖ 144

Raspberry Sauce ✖ 146

Apple Cinnamon Glaze ✖ 147

Dark Chocolate Sauce ✖ 148

Caramel ✖ 149

EXTRAS

Mixed berries

Cream Cheese Whipped Cream (page 353)

Coffee or cappaccino

Orange and apple juice

MAKE AHEAD

Dough for Liege Waffles can be made the night before and stored covered in the refrigerator.

Toffee Pecans can be made up to 3 days in advance.

Make sauces up to 3 days in advance and store in jars in refrigerator.

Styling Ideas

Use a large food-grade tray with sides for your waffle board. The sides will keep berries from falling off. Set out plates and forks and encourage your guests to create their favorite flavor combinations.

LIEGE WAFFLES

These brioche-like waffles take their name from the Belgian city of Liege, where legend says that a Prince-Bishop in the Middle Ages requested an extra sweet dessert, and his pastry chef created this recipe to please him. Pearl sugar is an essential component that gives the waffles spots of sweet crunch and a caramelized exterior. After trying these rich, buttery, soft-on-the-inside, crisp-on-the-outside beauties, you will likely have a new favorite waffle.

¾ cup warm milk

2½ teaspoons yeast

2 tablespoons brown sugar

3 large eggs, room temperature

¾ cup unsalted butter, softened

1 tablespoon vanilla

4¼ cups flour

1 teaspoon salt

1 cup pearl sugar

Cold salted butter for waffle iron

NOTE: Pearl sugar can be found in larger grocery stores or smaller shops that cater to baking. If you have trouble finding it, it's easy to order online.

1. In a medium bowl, whisk together milk, yeast, and brown sugar. Allow to set for 5 to 10 minutes, or until foamy.

2. In the bowl of a stand mixer with the paddle attachment, beat eggs, butter, and vanilla. It is important to use room temperature eggs to avoid the butter stiffening. Beat until well combined, then add milk mixture and 1 cup of flour. Beat on medium speed for 2 minutes. Add second cup of flour and beat on medium for 1 minute. Scrape the sides and bottom of bowl with a rubber spatula to ensure even mixing. Switch to the dough hook attachment. Add remaining flour and knead for 2 minutes on medium speed.

3. Cover bowl with plastic wrap or a damp towel and allow to rise in a warm place until doubled in size, about 1 to 2 hours. Turn out dough and knead in pearl sugar. Divide into 16 even pieces and form balls. Place balls on a pan and cover. Refrigerate 30 minutes.

4. Preheat waffle iron. Butter iron and place one ball per square in iron. If you have a small waffle iron, cook waffles one at a time. Cook for 3 to 5 minutes, or until golden brown. The pearl sugar will caramelize, and some will stick to the iron. Remove waffles with care; the sugar will be extremely hot. Serve hot or allow to cool and store in an airtight container for up to 1 day in refrigerator or 2 months in the freezer.

5. To revive frozen waffles, preheat oven to 275°F. Place waffles on baking sheet and reheat in oven for 8 to 10 minutes.

MAKES **16**

WARM CINNAMON APPLES

This versatile and easy recipe goes great on waffles, pancakes, or French toast. It makes an especially comforting topping for crisp autumn mornings.

4 medium apples
¼ cup brown sugar
1½ teaspoons cinnamon
1 teaspoon vanilla bean paste
¼ cup unsalted butter

1. Core, peel, and slice apples. In a medium bowl, combine apples, brown sugar, cinnamon, and vanilla bean paste. Stir until apples are coated. In a skillet over medium-high heat, melt butter. Add apple mixture to skillet and cook for 4 to 5 minutes or until apples are soft. Serve warm.

2. Store any extra apples in an airtight container in refrigerator for up to 4 days. To revive refrigerated apples, add to skillet and cook over medium heat, just until warm.

MAKES ABOUT **2** CUPS

TOFFEE PECANS

Sprinkle this topping on anything that goes great with a salty sweet crunch like ice cream, cakes, brownies, and of course waffles.

1 cup whole pecans
5 tablespoons salted butter
½ cup firmly packed brown sugar
1 tablespoon pure vanilla extract
¼ teaspoon salt (optional)

1. Chop pecans and set aside. Line a baking sheet with parchment paper and set near stove.

2. In a cast-iron braiser or nonstick skillet, melt butter over medium-high heat. As butter starts to melt, add brown sugar, vanilla, and salt if using. Stir constantly until fully combined. Allow mixture to bubble for about 2 minutes. Add chopped pecans. Stir constantly for about 2 minutes. Pour mixture onto prepared baking sheet.

3. Allow to cool completely. Transfer cool pecans to a cutting board and chop to desired size for snacking or for a topping.

MAKES ABOUT **1** CUP

RASPBERRY SAUCE

1 tablespoon water

1 tablespoon cornstarch

3 cups raspberries

⅓ cup sugar

1 teaspoon vanilla extract

1. In a small bowl or cup, mix cornstarch with water until smooth. In a medium saucepan over medium-high heat, cook raspberries and sugar, stirring constantly until berries break down and liquify. Add cornstarch mixture and vanilla and continue to cook until thickened, about 4 to 5 minutes.

2. Strain with a fine mesh sieve. Use a rubber spatula to push as much of the sauce through the sieve as possible. Pour into a glass jar and allow to cool completely. Cover and store in refrigerator for up to 1 week.

MAKES **1** CUP

APPLE CINNAMON GLAZE

¼ cup apple juice or apple cider

1 teaspoon vanilla extract

1 cup confectioners' sugar

2 teaspoons cinnamon

1. In a medium bowl, whisk together ingredients until smooth and fluid. At first, the mixture will be difficult to whisk but will come together and become easy to stir. If it's too thick, add more apple juice, ½ teaspoon at a time. Serve immediately. Leftovers can be stored in a glass jar in the refrigerator for up to 1 week. Before using, microwave glaze in jar for 15 seconds and stir.

MAKES ¾ CUP

DARK CHOCOLATE SAUCE

This versatile chocolate sauce is easy to make in advance. The deep, bittersweet flavor is a perfect topping to balance sweet desserts. Store it in glass jars in your refrigerator, and warm up just the portion you need for churros, waffles, ice cream, or to add to a cappuccino to create a rich mocha.

2½ cups half-and-half

1 cup sugar

⅛ teaspoon fine salt

1 cup unsweetened cocoa

8 ounces high-quality bittersweet (70% cacao) chocolate, chopped

1 vanilla bean or 2 teaspoons vanilla bean paste

1. Whisk together half-and-half, sugar, and salt in a medium saucepan. Cook over medium-high heat until it starts to boil. Reduce temperature to medium and add cocoa. Whisk continuously until completely incorporated. Reduce temperature to low and add chocolate. Whisk until chocolate is completely melted and there are no lumps. Scrape the seeds from vanilla bean and add to mixture (or add vanilla bean paste, if using) and stir until combined.

2. Pour chocolate sauce into 2 pint-sized glass jars and allow to cool uncovered for a half hour. Cover and refrigerate for up to 3 weeks. Sauce will become thick in refrigerator. To use, scoop portion needed and warm on stove or in microwave.

MAKES **2** PINTS

CARAMEL

Homemade caramel is a joy to drizzle over all kinds of desserts. Try this on Tres Leches Cake Cups (page 293) and in Stroopwafels (page 139). Warm before serving on this board or for any table spread with sweets.

⅓ cup water + more for brushing

1¾ cups sugar

¼ teaspoon salt

1 cup heavy cream

1 vanilla bean or 2 teaspoons vanilla bean paste

1. Fill a small bowl half full with water and set near stove with a pastry brush. In a medium Dutch oven or heavy-bottomed pot, add ⅓ cup water and sugar. Whisk together sugar and water and cook over medium-high heat until sugar starts to melt. Continue cooking without stirring, swirling pan occasionally. If sugar starts to stick to the sides of pot, brush with wet pastry brush. Cook until sugar turns a deep amber, about 10 minutes.

2. Turn off heat and pour heavy cream slowly down the side of pot. Mixture will bubble and spatter. Scrape the seeds from vanilla bean and add to mixture (or add vanilla bean paste, if using).

3. Whisk continuously until fully incorporated. Serve warm. Pour any leftovers into a glass jar. Allow to cool completely, cover, and refrigerate for up to 3 weeks. To serve after refrigerating, scoop amount needed into a small heatproof bowl and microwave in 15-second intervals—stirring in between—until smooth and warm.

NOTE: If you prefer salted caramel, use 1 teaspoon salt.

MAKES **1½** CUPS

FRENCH TABLE

My mother's training at the prestigious French culinary institute instilled in her a mastery of the mother sauces, which she happily passed on to me starting at a young age. As a child, I felt I had special powers knowing her "secret sauce"—the versatile béchamel that could transform everything from vol-au-vents to cauliflower gratin. From her lessons emerged a lifelong adoration for French cuisine. The recipes she taught me over the years, many featured here, combine skill with joy—Beef Wellington Bites, Smoked Salmon Blinis, Chicken and Mushroom Vol-Au-Vents. Classic French techniques come sized for passing around with ease. Savory, sweet, simple, and decadent—this collection encapsulates my mother's wealth of knowledge along with the flavors of France we came to cherish together. Though her academy training was formal, our food memories are filled with warmth, laughter, and a pinch of French flair. —M.M.

MAKE AHEAD

Make the crème fraîche in advance. Once prepared, this can be stored in the refrigerator for up to 3 weeks.

Make the filling a day in advance and store in the refrigerator in an airtight container.

Bake tart crusts and make filling a day in advance for Petite Tarte Aux Fraises. Assemble just before serving.

Make macaron shells up to 2 weeks in advance. Freeze in an airtight container. Remove from freezer 2 hours before serving. Add fillings just before serving.

Make crust dough for Frangipan Blueberry Mini Galettes the day before baking.

EXTRAS

Fresh fruit and vegetables

Baguettes

Mini brie

Fig jam

Rosemary for garnish

TIME SAVERS

Crème fraîche can be purchased.

Vol-Au-Vents can be purchased.

Mini Blinis can be purchased.

Styling Ideas

Create a custom butter board.

Use a mini skillet to bake and serve your baked camembert.

Use a combination of wood and marble boards and platters. Add colorful glassware.

Add color with fresh fruits, vegetables, and flowers.

RECIPES

BEEF WELLINGTON BITES

Though Beef Wellington traces its origins to nineteeth-century England, the lavish dish of tenderloin wrapped in pastry encapsulates the decadence and richness that exemplifies French haute cuisine. The extravagance pays homage to French culinary culture, much like Beef á la Mode. Over the years, my father would request my mother prepare this French-inspired dish. These miniature Wellington Bites offer a taste of the flavors of a French classic in individual handheld form. Tender beef and d'uxelles wrapped in puff pastry distill this lavish yet cozy dish into nostalgic bites ready for passing and sharing. —M.M.

2 tablespoons olive oil

1 pound beef tenderloin or filet mignon, cut into 20 (1-inch) cubes

1–2 tablespoons Dijon mustard

2 tablespoons butter

2 shallots, finely chopped

2 cups white cremini mushrooms, finely diced

1 sprig Italian parsley, finely chopped

2–3 sprigs fresh thyme + some for garnish

¼ teaspoon salt

¼ teaspoon fresh ground pepper

1 pound Rough Puff Pastry (page xxi) or packaged puff pastry, thawed but still cold

1 egg, beaten with 1 tablespoon water (for egg wash)

1. Preheat the oven to 400°F.

2. In a skillet or cast-iron pan over medium heat, add 2 tablespoons of olive oil. Season the beef cubes with salt and pepper and sear all sides. Transfer to a plate.

3. Brush the seared beef cubes generously with Dijon mustard and set aside.

4. In a medium saucepan over medium heat, melt the butter and sweat the shallots for 2 to 3 minutes. Add the mushrooms and cook for 5 minutes, stirring, until the mixture becomes dry. Incorporate the finely chopped parsley, leaves from the thyme sprigs, salt, and pepper.

5. Unroll the puff pastry sheet and cut it into 20 squares. Press one square into the bottom and up the sides of each well in a mini muffin pan, leaving a slight overhang.

6. Spoon a piece of the seared beef into each pastry-lined well and top with mushroom mixture. Fold the overhanging pastry over the filling.

7. Brush the top of each bite with egg wash and sprinkle with additional thyme leaves.

8. Bake for 15 to 20 minutes, or until the pastry turns golden brown. Serve immediately.

MAKES **20** BITES

SMOKED SALMON AND CRÈME FRAÎCHE BLINIS

In France, blinis exemplify sophistication through simplicity. Though originally Slavic, these miniature buckwheat pancakes came to epitomize French brunch fare when topped with smoked salmon and crème fraîche. The leavened batter produces a subtle tang and browned edges, providing a sturdy yet tender base. With options from lemon to caviar, blinis encapsulate the French philosophy of art de vivre—creating the art of living by savoring life's simple pleasures.

BLINIS

1 cup all-purpose flour

1 teaspoon baking powder

1 pinch salt

1 large egg

2 tablespoons olive oil + additional for frying

1 cup whole milk

Unsalted butter, for frying

CRÈME FRAÎCHE

2 cups heavy cream

2 tablespoons buttermilk

TOPPINGS

7 ounces smoked salmon slices

1 cup crème fraîche

Fresh dill sprigs, for garnish

1 lemon, cut into wedges (optional)

Freshly ground black pepper

Caviar (optional)

Blanched asparagus tips (optional)

1. To prepare the blinis: In a mixing bowl, combine the all-purpose flour, baking powder, and salt. Make a well in the center of the dry mixture. Crack the egg into the well, add the 2 tablespoons of olive oil, and mix the wet ingredients into the dry. Gradually add the milk, stirring continuously, until you achieve a smooth, lump-free batter.

2. Heat a nonstick skillet over medium heat. Add a slice of unsalted butter and allow it to melt, ensuring it covers the pan's surface.

3. Pour tablespoons of the batter into the pan, ensuring enough space between each.

4. Cook each blini for approximately 1 minute or until it's golden brown on the underside and bubbles appear on the surface. Flip each one and cook for an additional minute on the other side. Adjust heat if needed.

5. Transfer the blinis to a plate and continue with the process until all the batter is used.

6. To prepare the crème fraîche: In a saucepan, heat the heavy cream until very hot, ensuring it doesn't reach a boil. Transfer the hot cream into a container and mix in the buttermilk. Cover the container and allow it to stand at room temperature for 24 hours or until the mixture becomes thick. Once thickened, refrigerate the crème fraîche. It can be stored for up to 3 weeks.

CONTINUED

7. To prepare the smoked salmon: If the smoked salmon is very cold or has just come out of the refrigerator, let it sit for a few minutes. This makes it more pliable and easier to work with.

8. Using a sharp knife, cut the smoked salmon slices into strips, approximately 1 inch wide and the entire length. Begin at one end of the strip and tightly roll the salmon. This forms the center of the rose. As you roll, twist or ruffle the upper edge outward slightly to mimic the delicate, layered appearance of rose petals. For a simpler approach, you can slice the salmon in small bite-sized pieces.

9. For the assembly: Once the blinis have cooled slightly, place a small dollop of crème fraîche on each one. You can also use a pastry bag to pipe for a more elevated presentation.

10. Add the prepared salmon rose or the cut salmon slice on top of the crème fraîche. Garnish with a sprig of fresh dill and freshly ground black pepper.

11. You can also top with a spoonful of caviar and a blanched asparagus tip. Serve immediately with lemon wedges on the side, allowing guests to add a squeeze of lemon juice if they desire.

MAKES **20–24**

BAKED CAMEMBERT
WTH HERBS AND HONEY

Camembert has epitomized French cheese since the eighteenth century, dubbed "the cheese of kings" by Talleyrand. Its soft, earthy interior and edible rind come wrapped in a charming wooden box perfect for conveying French hospitality. Baked briefly and adorned with slivers of garlic, rosemary, and chili flakes, the hot cheese becomes an irresistible, gooey spread for crusty bread among friends.

1 Camembert cheese wheel
    (about 9 ounces/
    250 grams)

1 clove garlic, thinly sliced
1 sprig fresh rosemary
1 pinch dried red chili flakes
Sea salt flakes, to taste
Freshly cracked black pepper,
    to taste
1 tablespoon honey

1. Preheat your oven to 375°F.

2. Unwrap the Camembert and place it back in its wooden box or in a small baking dish. Use a knife to make small slits on the top surface of the cheese. Insert slivers of garlic and pieces of rosemary sprig into these slits.

3. Sprinkle the dried red chili flakes, sea salt flakes, and freshly cracked black pepper over the top. Place the dish in the preheated oven for about 15 to 20 minutes, or until the cheese is soft and gooey.

4. Drizzle the tablespoon of honey over the top right after you take it out of the oven. Serve with slices of baguette.

SERVES **4 – 6**

CHICKEN AND MUSHROOM VOL-AU-VENTS

These petite puff pastry shells provide the perfect vessel for creamy chicken and mushrooms in classic French style. Inspired by rural French cooking elevated through the generations, these miniature pot pies put farmhouse flavors into an elegant finger food.

1 pound Rough Puff Pastry (page xxi) or packaged puff pastry, thawed but still cold

1 egg yolk, beaten for glazing

FILLING

2 cups chicken stock

8 ounces chicken breast

8 ounces white mushrooms, chopped

3 tablespoons butter

¼ cup all-purpose flour

½ cup heavy cream

½ teaspoon Dijon mustard

1 teaspoon kosher salt

Freshly ground pepper, to taste

¼ teaspoon ground nutmeg

¼ cup cheddar cheese, grated

Red chili flakes (for garnish)

Chopped parsley (for garnish)

TIPS: The chill step is crucial, as it helps maintain the pastry's shape during baking and ensures a flakier end result.

If the pastry puffs up too much in the center during baking, you can gently press it down while it's still warm to create more space for the filling.

1. **To make the puff pastry shells:** Preheat the oven to 390°F. Line a baking sheet with parchment paper.

2. On a lightly floured surface, roll out the puff pastry to a thickness of about ⅛ inch. Using a cookie cutter, cut out four 4-inch discs. Transfer these discs to your prepared baking sheet. Cut out 8 additional 4-inch discs. From these 8 discs, use a 2-inch cookie cutter to remove the center, forming rings.

3. Brush the 4-inch discs lightly with beaten egg yolk. Carefully position one ring on top of each base disc, pressing gently to adhere. Give this ring a light brush with the yolk. Place another ring on top, ensuring you align it well with the first ring, and gently press it down. After assembling the two rings, set the 2-inch "cap" piece (the center you cut out earlier) atop the second ring without pressing down; this will be removed later to allow filling. Finish by giving the entire assembly, including the cap, a brush with the yolk.

4. Place the pastry shells in the refrigerator for 20 to 30 minutes, ensuring they firm up. Bake for 10 minutes, then reduce the temperature to 320°F and continue to bake for an additional 10 minutes, or until the pastry is golden brown and has risen significantly.

5. **To make the filling:** In a medium saucepan, bring the chicken stock to a simmer over medium heat. Add the chicken breast, ensuring it's submerged, and let simmer for 25 minutes.

6. Add the chopped mushrooms to the simmering stock and cook for an additional 5 minutes. Using a slotted spoon, transfer the chicken and mushrooms from the stock, setting them aside. Retain the stock for the roux-based sauce.

7. In a separate saucepan over medium heat, melt the butter. Once melted, quickly stir in the flour to form a smooth roux. Maintain a low heat, continuing to whisk until the mixture takes on a light, bubbly texture. Gradually pour the reserved stock into the roux, whisking constantly to prevent any lumps. Add the heavy cream, then allow the mixture to simmer while continuously whisking for 10 minutes. Season the sauce with mustard, salt, pepper, and nutmeg. Dice the poached chicken into bite-sized pieces. Add the chicken and cooked mushrooms back into the sauce, stirring to combine.

8. Preheat your oven to 375°F for the final baking. Carefully lift the top cap off each pastry shell using a paring knife, ensuring you don't pierce the base. Spoon the creamy chicken and mushroom filling into each pastry shell. Sprinkle the top of each filled shell with grated cheddar cheese, a touch of red chili flakes, and a dash of chopped parsley.

9. Place the filled vol-au-vents back into the oven and bake for an additional 5 to 7 minutes or until the cheese is slightly melted and golden.

MAKES **4**

FILET MIGNON BITES WITH ROQUEFORT AND WALNUT

In this bite, seared filet mignon finds balance with creamy Roquefort and the crunch of walnuts. A careful composition brings out the best in each high-quality ingredient.

1 (1.5-pound) filet mignon or tenderloin, cut into bite-sized pieces

Fine sea salt, to taste

Freshly ground white pepper, to taste

2 tablespoons olive oil

3 tablespoons walnut oil

1 tablespoon red wine vinegar

20 thin radish slices

¼ pound Roquefort cheese, cut into ½-inch cubes

20 walnut halves, toasted

1. Season the filet mignon pieces to taste with fine sea salt and freshly ground white pepper.

2. In a heavy pan, heat olive oil over high heat until it starts to shimmer. Carefully place the meat in the pan, ensuring the pieces are not overcrowded. Sear on all sides until they reach a medium-rare doneness.

3. Remove the meat from the pan and let it rest on a cutting board for 5 minutes.

4. In a small bowl, whisk together walnut oil and red wine vinegar until emulsified. Set aside.

5. Cut the rested meat into ½-inch cubes.

6. On each bamboo skewer, layer a piece of meat, followed by a thin slice of radish, then top with a cube of Roquefort cheese and a walnut half. Arrange the skewers on a serving platter. Drizzle each skewer lightly with the walnut vinaigrette.

SERVING SUGGESTIONS: These bites can be presented atop a mini puff pastry circle or a blini for a more substantial appetizer. If serving with puff pastry or blini, place the skewer atop the pastry, allowing guests to remove the skewer before eating. Consider adding a fresh herb, like chervil or tarragon, for added flavor and a touch of green.

TIP: For best results, ensure your pan is very hot before searing the meat to achieve a beautiful crust.

MAKES **20** BITES

MAÎTRE D'HÔTEL BUTTER

Maître d'Hôtel Butter is a quintessential component in French cuisine, epitomizing the nation's commitment to enhancing the flavors of staple dishes with nuanced, aromatic touches. Originating from the bustling kitchens of grand hotels, this preparation pays homage to the maître d'hôtel, the esteemed steward of guest experience. This butter is the perfect companion to grilled meats, fish, and vegetables. Given its ability to elevate the simplest of dishes to gourmet status, Maître d'Hôtel Butter stands as a testament to the elegance and sophistication inherent in French culinary arts. Its versatility and storability further underscore its timeless appeal, making it a treasured recipe in kitchens worldwide.

½ small bunch fresh parsley, finely minced

1 teaspoon lemon juice, freshly squeezed

½ cup unsalted butter, at room temperature

½ teaspoon fine sea salt

Freshly ground black pepper, to taste

NOTES: This butter pairs wonderfully with grilled steaks, fish, or vegetables.

For an added zest, add a small amount of minced garlic or zest from the lemon.

1. In a mixing bowl, combine the finely minced parsley with the fresh lemon juice. Stir to blend. With a silicone spatula, fold the softened butter into the parsley mixture. Continue mixing, ensuring the parsley and lemon juice are well-integrated with the butter.

2. Season the butter blend with fine sea salt and a touch of freshly ground black pepper. Mix again to ensure the seasonings are distributed throughout.

3. Place a sheet of waxed paper on a flat surface. Transfer the butter mixture onto the center of the waxed paper, shaping it into a rough log.

4. Roll the butter mixture inside the waxed paper, forming a tight cylinder. Twist the ends to seal.

5. Refrigerate the butter log for at least 2 hours, or until firm. When ready to serve, unwrap the butter and slice into rounds. The butter can be stored in the refrigerator for up to a week or in the freezer for up to a month. If freezing, simply slice off rounds as needed.

MAKES ABOUT ½ CUP

ANCHOVY BUTTER

Anchovy Butter is a classic preparation deeply rooted in French cuisine, reflecting the country's penchant for combining simple ingredients to create profound flavors. Typically served with rustic bread or as a finishing touch on grilled meats, this butter showcases the balance and depth characteristic of French culinary techniques.

1 medium shallot, peeled and quartered

1 clove garlic, minced

2 (2-ounce) cans anchovies in oil, drained

1 tablespoon freshly squeezed lemon juice

11 tablespoons (just under ¾ cup) butter, softened and cut into small chunks

¼ cup almond meal, toasted

½ teaspoon hot paprika

Kosher salt, to taste

1. Using a food processor fitted with a blade attachment, combine the quartered shallot, minced garlic, drained anchovies, and lemon juice.

2. Pulse the mixture several times until it forms a consistent purée. Add the softened butter chunks to the food processor. Continue to pulse until the mixture is smooth and creamy.

3. Add in the almond meal and hot paprika. Season with kosher salt according to your preference. Pulse a few more times to ensure all ingredients are well-blended and the mixture has a uniform consistency.

4. Place a sheet of waxed paper on a flat surface. Transfer the butter mixture onto the center of the waxed paper, shaping it into a rough log.

5. Roll the butter mixture inside the waxed paper, forming a tight cylinder. Twist the ends to seal.

6. Chill in the refrigerator for at least 2 hours, allowing it to firm up. Once chilled, slice the butter into rounds for serving.

MAKES ABOUT 1½ CUPS

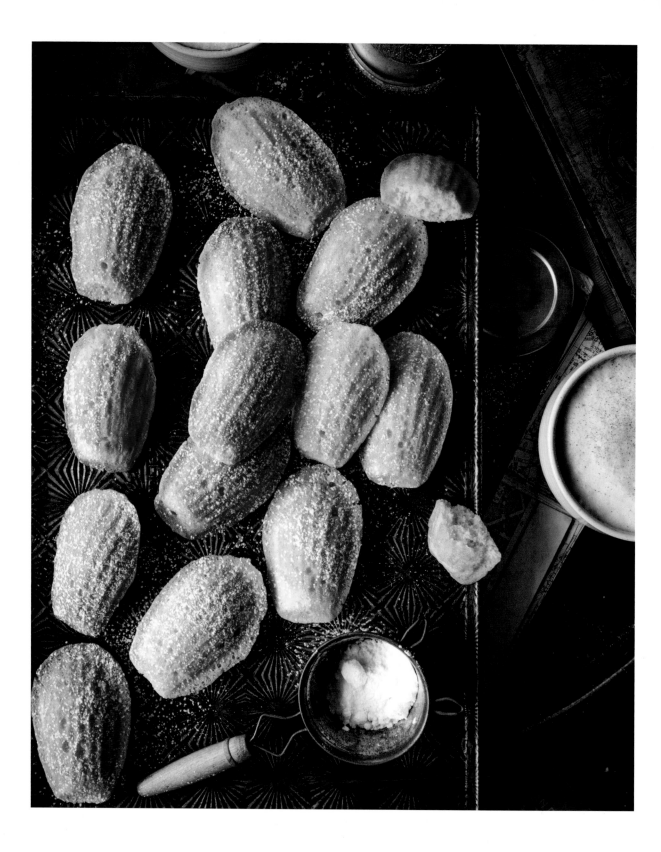

BROWNED BUTTER MADELEINES

These classic shell-shaped mini cakes originated in the Lorraine region of France. This browned butter version is a favorite in our house and they never last long. —L.K.

1 cup butter, unsalted

1 tablespoon brown sugar

4 eggs

1 cup sugar

1 vanilla bean

2 cups flour

1 teaspoon baking powder

½ teaspoon salt

1 tablespoon butter for pan

Confectioners' sugar, for dusting (optional)

1. Set out a medium heatproof bowl near the stove. Melt butter in a medium saucepan over medium-high heat. Whisk butter and continue to cook until small brown specks appear near the bottom of pan. Butter should have a nutty aroma. Pour into the bowl to prevent further cooking and possibly burning butter. Stir in brown sugar and allow to cool.

2. In the bowl of a stand mixer fitted with the whisk attachment, beat eggs and sugar on medium speed for 1 minute. Increase speed to high and beat mixture for an additional 5 minutes.

3. With a sharp knife, slice vanilla bean open and scrape the seeds into the egg mixture. Mix until combined.

4. In a small bowl combine flour, baking powder, and salt. Switch to the paddle attachment. Add to egg mixture and mix just until combined. Add cooled butter and mix until combined. Scrape the bowl, including the bottom, and mix again to ensure even mixture. Cover dough with plastic wrap and refrigerate for 2 hours or up to 12 hours.

5. When ready to bake, preheat oven to 350°F. Melt 1 tablespoon butter and brush in the wells of a madeleine pan. Place the pan in the refrigerator for about 5 minutes until the butter solidifies on the pan. Press about 2 tablespoons of chilled dough in each well. Bake 8 to 11 minutes or until the dough is domed and a cake tester inserted comes out clean.

6. Allow madeleines to set in pan for 2 to 3 minutes, then carefully remove from pan and place on a cooling rack. Dust with confectioners' sugar, if using. Madeleines are best on the day they are baked, but you can also store them in an airtight container for 2 to 3 days.

MAKES **30**

VANILLA BEAN MACARONS

These almond-based macaron shells are said to have originated in Italy and were brought to France with Catherine de Medici in the 1500s. The macaron in its modern sandwich form was invented in the bakeries of Paris. There are endless combinations to try. I love to mix things up with different flavors and colors. The process takes care and attention, but the creation of these delicate beauties will show love and sweet, thoughtful affection. —L.K.

SHELLS
2/3 cup almond flour

1 cup confectioners' sugar

1/4 teaspoon salt

2 large egg whites

1/4 cup sugar

1 1/2 teaspoons vanilla bean paste

FILLING
2 tablespoons unsalted butter

4 ounces cream cheese

1/2 teaspoon vanilla extract

1 1/4 cups confectioners' sugar

Milk (optional)

1. Line a half-sheet baking pan with parchment paper or nonstick baking mat and set aside. Prepare a large piping bag with a medium round tip and prop in a tall glass. Fold over the top 2 to 3 inches of the opening so it is ready to be filled.

2. Sift almond flour and confectioners' sugar into a medium mixing bowl. Whisk in salt and mix until incorporated. Set aside.

3. In the bowl of a stand mixer with the whisk attachment, beat egg whites at medium-low speed until foamy. Increase speed to medium and add sugar slowly, 1 teaspoon at a time. Increase speed to medium-high for 2 minutes. Increase again to high speed and continue to beat until stiff peaks form, about 2 to 4 additional minutes. Add vanilla bean paste and turn mixer on low just until vanilla is incorporated.

4. Add the dry ingredients to the meringue. Fold together with a rubber spatula. The longer the ingredients are mixed, the more deflated the egg whites will get, and the batter will become runnier. This step is one of the most crucial aspects of getting your macaron shells to come out right. When the batter falls off the spatula in ribbons, it is ready. One way to check is to try to draw a figure eight with the batter without the batter breaking. Once you're able to do this, stop mixing and pour into the prepared piping bag.

5. Pipe discs onto the prepared baking sheet. Hold the piping bag vertical and the tip close to the baking sheet. Create rounds about 1 3/4 inches wide; these will spread to about 2 inches. Make 5 rows of 4 for a total of 20. Tap the pan on the counter several times to release air bubbles.

CONTINUED

6. Allow the pan to rest for 30 to 60 minutes until the outside of macaron shells have dried. You should be able to lightly touch the shell without it sticking to your finger. It's tempting to skip this step, but it is essential to getting the macaron shells to rise properly.

7. Preheat oven to 300°F. Bake shells for 17 minutes. Don't open the oven door while baking. After removing from oven, allow the shells to rest on the pan for 30 minutes before removing them from the sheet. This will allow the bottoms to dry completely and make them easy to lift off the parchment or baking mat.

8. To make the filling: While macarons are cooling, using a stand mixer with the paddle attachment, beat the butter, cream cheese, and vanilla until fluffy. Sift the confectioners' sugar into the butter mixture and beat until combined. Scrape the bowl, including the bottom, to make sure all ingredients are incorporated. If filling is too thick, you can add milk 1 teaspoon at a time until you reach your desired consistency.

9. Prepare a medium piping bag with a medium round tip and prop in a tall glass. Fold over the top 2 to 3 inches of the opening and fill with cream cheese frosting. Once macaron shells are completely cooled, pipe frosting onto one shell and top with another to form a sandwich. Continue with remaining shells. Store macarons in an airtight container for up to 3 days.

ROSEWATER AND PISTACHIO VARIATION

SHELL ADDITIONS
2–3 drops pink food coloring gel
¼ teaspoon rosewater

FILLING
2 tablespoons unsalted butter
4 ounces cream cheese
1¼ cups confectioners' sugar
Milk (optional)
¼ cup pistachios, shelled and chopped

1. For shells, replace vanilla with ½ teaspoon rosewater and add 2 to 3 drops pink food coloring gel.

2. To make the filling: Using a stand mixer with the paddle attachment, beat the butter, cream cheese, and vanilla until fluffy. Sift the confectioners' sugar into the butter mixture and beat until combined. Scrape the bowl, including the bottom, to make sure all ingredients are incorporated. If filling is too thick, you can add milk 1 teaspoon at a time until you reach your desired consistency.

3. After assembling macarons, roll sides in pistachios.

MINT CHOCOLATE VARIATION

SHELL ADDITIONS
½ teaspoon pure peppermint extract
2–3 drops green food coloring gel
2 tablespoons chocolate cookie crumbs

FILLING
2 tablespoons unsalted butter
4 ounces cream cheese
¼ cup Dutch-processed cocoa
1 cup confectioners' sugar
Milk (optional)

1. For shells, replace vanilla with ½ teaspoon pure peppermint extract and add 2 to 3 drops green food coloring gel. Sprinkle chocolate cookie crumbs on shells immediately after piping onto pan.

2. To make the filling: Using a stand mixer with the paddle attachment, beat the butter, cream cheese, and vanilla until fluffy. Sift the confectioners' sugar and cocoa into the butter mixture and beat until combined. Scrape the bowl, including the bottom, to make sure all ingredients are incorporated. If filling is too thick, you can add milk 1 teaspoon at a time until you reach your desired consistency.

MAKES **10**

FRANGIPANE BLUEBERRY MINI GALETTES

Frangipane is a sweet almond filling commonly found in French pastries. I especially love to use it in galettes and tarts. It is named for an Italian, Marquis Muzio Frangipani, who was said to have been its originator during his time living in France. —L.K.

CRUST

1¾ cups flour

½ teaspoon salt

¾ cup unsalted butter

3 tablespoons ice water + more if needed

FILLING

⅓ cup unsalted butter, softened

⅓ cup sugar

1 egg

½ teaspoon almond extract

1 teaspoon vanilla extract

⅔ cup almond flour

¼ teaspoon salt

10 ounces blueberries

ASSEMBLY

1 egg

2 tablespoons turbinado sugar

1. **To make the crust:** In a medium bowl, mix the flour and salt. Slice the butter into small pats and toss into the flour-salt mixture. Cut the butter and flour mixture with a pastry blender until you have a fine crumb. Sprinkle the ice water over the crumb mixture and cut into mixture. Combine with your hands, squeezing the crumbs together until a dough forms. If the dough doesn't come together, add more ice water 1 teaspoon at a time until you get the dough to form. Wrap in plastic wrap and refrigerate for at least 1 hour.

2. When ready to bake, preheat oven to 400°F. Line two baking sheets with parchment or silicone baking mats.

3. **To make the frangipane:** In a medium bowl, beat butter, sugar, egg, and almond and vanilla extracts until smooth. Mix salt into almond flour. Add to butter mixture. Beat until smooth.

4. **To assemble:** Divide crust dough into 8 equal pieces. Roll out to a rough 7-inch round. Place onto one of the prepared pans. Repeat with remaining dough, for 4 rounds per pan. Divide the frangipane evenly between the 8 crusts. Spread it out in the center, leaving 1 inch of crust plain around the edge. Cover the frangipane with a layer of blueberries. Fold over the extra crust and pinch seams.

5. Beat egg and brush on top crust. Sprinkle crust with turbinado sugar. Bake about 25 minutes or until golden brown. While first pan bakes, store second pan in refrigerator until ready to bake. If any frangipane leaked out while baking, cut away and discard. Allow to cool on pan and serve immediately or store in an airtight container for up to 2 days.

MAKES **8**

PETITE TARTE AUX FRAISES

MINI STRAWBERRY TARTS

A French classic—this tart combines a buttery crust, crème pâtissière (pastry cream) mixed with whipped cream, and fresh strawberries. I love to make these when berries are in season—for the prefect combination of early summer flavors. —L.K.

EQUIPMENT
6 (3½-inch) mini tart pans

CRUST
11 tablespoons unsalted butter

½ teaspoon salt

2 teaspoons vanilla extract

½ cup confectioners' sugar

1½ cups all-purpose flour

FILLING
⅔ cup heavy cream

⅔ cup Vanilla Bean Pastry Cream (page 119)

10 ounces strawberries

Confectioners' sugar, for dusting

1. Preheat oven to 350°F.

2. To make the crust: In a medium heatproof bowl, melt butter. Stir in salt, vanilla, and confectioners' sugar. Add flour and combine until dough forms. Press dough into prepared pan going up the sides of pan. If dough is too loose to work with, refrigerate 10 to 15 minutes before pressing into pan. Line each crust with parchment and fill pans with pie weights. Bake for 18 minutes. Remove pie weights and bake for an additional 5 to 7 minutes, or until golden brown. Allow to cool completely before filling.

3. To make the filling: In the bowl of a stand mixer, using the whisk attachment, beat heavy cream on high until stiff peaks form. With a rubber spatula, fold in pastry cream and stir by hand just until combined. Fill each tart crust with filling.

4. Wash and hull strawberries. Cut each in half. Top cream mixture with strawberries, cut-side down. Dust with confectioners' sugar and serve immediately, or cover with plastic wrap and refrigerate for up to 1 day.

MAKES **6**

ENGLISH HIGH TEA

The intersection of British and Indo-Pakistani culinary traditions during the colonial era significantly impacted British cuisine. As trade routes flourished, returning expatriates brought with them a taste for spices like turmeric, cumin, and coriander, enlivening the British palate. The enduring love for spicy foods resulted in the creation of iconic dishes like Chicken Tikka Masala, often hailed as a British national dish, and the incorporation of spicy samosas and Thai curry in local pubs. Growing up, London held a magical charm for my sister and me, courtesy of our father. Our excursions ranged from exploring the toy aisles of Hamleys to enjoying the savory salt beef sandwiches at Selfridges, each experience embedding itself in our memory. A standout among these was the tradition of High Tea, especially the one at the Langham Hotel, which epitomized the elegance of this British culinary practice. Originating in the 1840s to address the working class's afternoon hunger, High Tea evolved into a refined social event. The beautifully laid tables, adorned with delicate china, presented an array of sandwiches, scones, pastries, and cakes, offering a moment to feel like we had been invited by the Queen herself. —M.M.

MAKE AHEAD

You can prepare all the sandwich fillings (for Coronation Chicken, Smoked Salmon and Cream Cheese, Cucumber and Cream Cheese) up to 2 days in advance. Store them in airtight containers in the refrigerator.

Freeze the bread slices ahead of time, then cut them into shapes when needed. Freezing preserves the bread's freshness, and cutting in advance saves time on the day of serving.

Make the mashed potatoes a day ahead. Once prepared, store them in an airtight container in the refrigerator. Reheat gently when ready to use.

Prepare the ground beef mixture for the Shepherd's Pie in advance. After cooling it to room temperature, store it in an airtight container in the refrigerator. Reheat it before assembling the mini ramekins on the day of serving.

Make crust for Spinach Cheddar Mini Quiches the night before.

Make Lemon Curd and Raspberry Jam up to 2 days in advance. Store in jars in the refrigerator.

EXTRAS

Vanilla Bean Macarons (page 168)

Shortbread

Cadbury fingers

Clotted cream

Apricot jam

Petit fours

Tea

TIME SAVERS

Use rotisserie chicken instead of cooking and shredding chicken breasts.

Lemon curd and raspberry jam can be purchased.

Purchase baked beans as a ready-made filling to make baked beans on toast.

Styling Ideas

Serve food on vintage silver trays and antique English plates.

Use a three-tiered tray to serve desserts to conserve space and for a quintessential British tea look.

RECISES

CORONATION CHICKEN SANDWICHES

Dainty tea sandwiches have long stood as icons of the English afternoon tea tradition. Classics like cucumber slices on buttered brown bread, smoked salmon and cream cheese on petite toasts, and Coronation chicken salad in soft bread encapsulate the delicacy and refinement that high tea is known for. When the Duchess of Bedford pioneered afternoon teatime in 1840, petite sandwiches emerged as the perfect light fare for staving off hunger until dinner. Though small, they formed the heart of the three-tiered spread, preceding scones, jam, and cakes. Beyond sustenance, these tidily crafted bites represented national custom. Passed between loved ones at long oak tables, their flavors came to represent comfort and connection. More than a snack, the nostalgic tea sandwich connects us to generations of rituals and refinement.

⅓ cup heavy whipping cream

3 cooked chicken breasts, shredded

¾ cup full-fat Greek yogurt

½ teaspoon curry powder

2 tablespoons sweet mango chutney

Juice of ½ lime

¼ cup golden raisins or sultanas

½ teaspoon kosher salt

Freshly ground black pepper

8 slices white bread

1 stick (½ cup) butter, softened

½ cup pickled onions, drained

Fresh cilantro leaves, for garnish

1. In a medium mixing bowl, lightly whip the heavy cream using a whisk attachment until it forms soft peaks. To this, add the shredded chicken, Greek yogurt, curry powder, mango chutney, lime juice, raisins/sultanas, and salt. Season with black pepper, then gently fold to combine the ingredients.

2. Lay the bread slices on a flat work surface. Spread a thin layer of softened butter on each slice, ensuring edge-to-edge coverage. On 4 of the buttered bread slices, evenly distribute the chicken mixture. Top each with a few pickled onions and a sprinkle of fresh cilantro leaves. Cover with the remaining 4 slices of bread, buttered side down. Using a sharp knife, cut each sandwich into 4 triangles.

MAKES **24** SANDWICH TRIANGLES

SMOKED SALMON AND WHIPPED CREAM CHEESE CANAPÉS

8 ounces cream cheese, softened

1 teaspoon lemon zest

1 teaspoon lemon juice

1 teaspoon capers, finely chopped

Pinch of freshly ground black pepper

8 thin slices whole wheat bread, previously frozen for 3–4 hours

14 ounces smoked salmon, sliced

Kosher salt and pepper, to taste

Fresh dill, for garnish

Whole capers, for garnish

1. In a medium mixing bowl, whisk the cream cheese on high speed until fluffy, about 3 minutes. Gently fold in the lemon zest, lemon juice, chopped capers, and black pepper. Set aside.

2. On a flat work surface, arrange the partially frozen bread slices. Using a 2½-inch round cutter, cut out 2 rounds from each bread slice, resulting in 16 rounds total.

3. Spread half of the cream cheese mixture evenly among 8 bread rounds. Place a second bread round on top of each cream cheese–covered piece, pressing gently. Spread the remaining cream cheese mixture on these top rounds.

4. Layer smoked salmon slices atop the double-layered bread rounds. Finish each canapé with a sprinkle of fresh dill, a few whole capers, a dash of black pepper, and a light squeeze of lemon juice.

MAKES **8**

CUCUMBER & CREAM CHEESE TEA SANDWICHES

1 English cucumber, peeled and thinly sliced

8 ounces cream cheese, softened

Zest from 1 lemon

2 teaspoons finely chopped fresh dill

1 teaspoon finely chopped fresh chives

¼ teaspoon garlic powder

Kosher salt, to taste

Freshly ground black pepper (optional, to taste)

16 thin slices of soft white sandwich bread

Unsalted butter, at room temperature

1. After slicing the English cucumber, lay out the slices on a couple of layers of paper towels. Place another layer of paper towels on top and press gently. Allow the cucumber slices to rest for about 10 minutes. This process helps in removing excess moisture to ensure your sandwiches stay crisp.

2. In a medium bowl, combine the softened cream cheese, lemon zest, chopped dill, chopped chives, and garlic powder. Mix thoroughly until well-integrated. Season with salt and freshly ground pepper and stir again.

3. Using a 2½-inch cookie cutter, cut out circles from each slice of bread. Then, spread a thin layer of unsalted butter on one side of each bread circle. Lay out half of the buttered bread circles. Spread a generous layer of the seasoned cream cheese mixture onto them.

4. Place a single layer of cucumber slices over the cream cheese mixture on each bread circle. Top each with another buttered bread circle, creating a two-tier sandwich. Place a cucumber slice on the top of each two-tier sandwich, ensuring it aligns with the circular shape.

TIPS: Freeze the bread before cutting into round shapes.

MAKES **16**

FISH AND CHIPS BITES

Fish and chips stand as icons of British cuisine, with origins tracing back to the 1860s when the dish was a staple of London's East End. These crispy fish bites served atop waffle fries encapsulate the spirit of the beloved pub classic in miniature form. From the light beer batter encasing tender white fish to the crunchy "chips," each component pays homage to the hot, salty flavors that define this national staple. Pop one of these special bites, and memories of cozy chippies come flooding back. —M.M.

FISH
2 pounds white fish filets (preferably cod, halibut, or mahi-mahi)

Kosher salt and freshly ground black pepper, to taste

Juice of 1 lime

BATTER
1½ cups all-purpose flour

½ cup rice flour

1 teaspoon baking powder

½ teaspoon kosher salt

½ teaspoon freshly ground black pepper

½ teaspoon ground cumin

½ teaspoon paprika

2 cups very cold club soda or beer

Frying-grade oil, for frying

FOR SERVING
¼ cup tartar sauce

30 waffle fries, cooked according to package instructions

30 small pickles

30 bamboo skewers

¼ cup malt vinegar

1. **To prepare the fish:** Slice the fish filets lengthwise, then cut diagonally into 2-inch cubes. Season with salt, pepper, and lime juice. Let the fish marinate for 30 minutes in the refrigerator.

2. **To make the batter:** In a mixing bowl, combine the all-purpose flour, rice flour, baking powder, salt, black pepper, cumin, and paprika.

3. Gradually whisk in the club soda or beer, ensuring there are no lumps. The batter should be thick but pourable. Let it rest for 5 minutes.

4. Heat frying-grade oil in a large pot until it reaches the appropriate frying temperature. Use a thermometer to accurately monitor the temperature. The oil should be about 3 inches deep. Dredge the marinated fish pieces in the batter, shaking off any excess, then carefully lower the fish into the hot oil. Fry the fish in small batches to prevent overcrowding. Once the fish is cooked and crispy, transfer it to a wire rack.

5. **To assemble:** On each bamboo skewer, thread a waffle fry, followed by a piece of fried fish, and top with a small pickle.

6. Serve immediately with the tartar sauce and a side of vinegar.

MAKES ABOUT **30** BITES

SPINACH CHEDDAR MINI QUICHES

My dad, who was endlessly fond of quirky jokes and puns, always loved to quote the 1980s quip, "real men don't eat quiche," while helping himself to a large slice of whatever quiche my mom had just served. A crowd favorite, this small, bite-size version is the perfect addition to a party spread. —L.K.

CRUST
2¾ cups flour

1 teaspoon fine kosher salt

1 cup + 2 tablespoons unsalted butter

⅓ cup ice water + more if needed

FILLING
3 eggs

¾ cup whole milk

½ teaspoon fine kosher salt

½ teaspoon black pepper

1 cup chopped spinach

½ cup scallions, sliced

4 ounces white cheddar, shredded

1. To make the crust: In a medium bowl, mix the flour and salt. Slice the butter into small pats and toss into the flour-salt mixture. Cut the butter and flour mixture with a pastry blender until you have a fine crumb. Sprinkle about half of the ice water over the crumb mixture. Combine with your hands, squeezing the crumbs together until a dough forms. If the dough doesn't come together, add more ice water 1 tablespoon at a time until you get the dough to form.

2. Divide dough in half and form two discs. Wrap each in plastic wrap and refrigerate for 1 hour or up 24 hours.

3. To make the mini quiches: Preheat oven to 375°F.

4. In a medium bowl, beat eggs with a whisk until yolks and whites are completely incorporated. Add milk, salt, and pepper. Whisk until combined. Set aside.

5. Roll out first disc of dough to about ⅛-inch thickness. Cut out rounds with a 3-inch round cookie cutter. Add crust to one well of a 24-well mini muffin pan. Press crust into well with a tart tamper or by hand. Fill each crust with spinach, scallions, and cheese. Pour egg mixture on top of filling until each crust is almost full. Repeat process for second pan. Bake 22 to 25 minutes.

6. Serve immediately or store in an airtight container and refrigerate up to 2 days. To reheat just before building your spread, preheat oven to 300°F. Place mini quiches on a baking tray and place in the oven for 8 minutes.

MAKES **48**

SHEPHERD'S PIE IN MINI RAMEKINS

My mother would bake her rendition of Shepherd's Pie regularly, inspired by the traditional version she tasted during the years she lived in London, eventually perfecting it. Flavorful tender meat and vegetables enveloped in a blanket of creamy mashed potatoes scented with rosemary and thyme. Though "perfect" is subjective, my nostalgia insists no iteration has surpassed my mother's. Now, I portion her iconic recipe into individual ramekins to share for this high tea spread. —M.M.

POTATO TOPPING

6 medium russet potatoes, peeled and quartered

6 tablespoons unsalted butter

⅓ cup half-and-half

¾ cup shredded aged white cheddar

Kosher salt and freshly ground black pepper, to taste

FILLING

1 tablespoon olive oil

1 medium yellow onion, diced

2 medium carrots, peeled and diced

4 cloves garlic, minced

2 sprigs fresh thyme, leaves removed and chopped

1 sprig fresh rosemary, leaves removed and chopped

1 pound ground beef

2 teaspoons kosher salt

¼ cup tomato paste

1 teaspoon Worcestershire sauce

1 teaspoon Dijon mustard

½ cup frozen peas

1 cup beef stock

¾ cup fresh parsley, chopped

½ cup shredded aged white cheddar (for topping)

¼ cup breadcrumbs

1. **To make the potato topping:** In a large pot, cover potatoes with water and add a pinch of salt. Bring to boil and cook until tender, about 15 minutes.

2. Drain potatoes and return to the pot. Mash the potatoes with butter, half-and-half, and cheese. Season with salt and pepper. Set aside.

3. **To make the filling:** In a large skillet over medium heat, heat the olive oil. Add onions and carrots and sauté until softened. Add garlic, thyme, and rosemary, and sauté for another minute until fragrant.

4. Increase the heat to medium-high and add the ground beef. Season with salt and cook until browned. Add tomato paste, Worcestershire sauce and mustard, and stir until well-combined. Add peas and pour in the beef stock, reduce the heat to low, and simmer for about 10 minutes. Remove from heat and stir in the parsley. Check seasoning and adjust as necessary.

5. **To assemble:** Preheat the oven to 400°F. Spoon the meat filling into the 6 ramekins, pressing down slightly to make an even layer. Top with the mashed potato mixture, spreading it to the edges. Sprinkle a generous layer of the shredded white cheddar on top of each ramekin. Lightly sprinkle breadcrumbs over the cheese. Place the ramekins on a baking sheet to catch any overflow. Bake in the preheated oven for about 20 to 25 minutes, or until the tops are golden brown and bubbly.

6. Let the mini pies cool slightly before serving. Garnish with additional fresh parsley if desired.

MAKES 6

BRITISH SCONES

Traditional British Scones have a simple flavor profile and are not sweet. They are closer to a biscuit from the American South than they are to an American scone. The sweetness comes in the form of the toppings. They are amazing with clotted cream and jam or lemon curd. To get the best rise and layered, flaky results be sure to use a soft wheat flour and don't overmix the butter. —L.K.

4 cups self-rising flour (for best results use a soft wheat flour, such as White Lily)

2 tablespoons sugar

½ teaspoon fine kosher salt

2 teaspoons baking powder

½ cup unsalted butter

2 cups heavy cream

1 egg, beaten

1. Preheat oven to 350°F.

2. In a medium bowl, combine flour, sugar, salt, and baking powder. Slice the butter into small pats and toss into the flour mixture. Cut the butter and flour mixture with a pastry blender until you have a coarse crumb. This step can also be achieved with a food processor. Be careful not to overprocess.

3. Stir in cream. When liquid is mostly worked into the crumb, turn out onto a pastry board or countertop. Finish combining with hands just until the dough holds together. Roll out betweem ¾ and 1-inch thick with a lightly floured rolling pin. Create cut outs with 2½-inch round biscuit cutter. Place scones on cookie sheet, leaving 1 inch between scones. Brush tops of scones with egg wash. Bake 20 to 25 minutes. Scones will be lightly browned when ready.

4. Serve immediately. If preparing in advance, freeze scones in an airtight container. To serve after freezing, preheat oven to 275°F. Bake for 10 to 12 minutes or until scones are warm all the way through.

MAKES ABOUT **20**

LEMON CURD

Lemon curd is delightful on scones or between layers of vanilla cake. It is a lovely, tart, flavorful addition to your board. If you've seen lemon curd in a variety of places, you may have noticed that it varies in color from a very pale yellow—almost cream color—to a vibrant yellow. Though we relate lemons with yellow, it is not the lemon juice or zest that makes lemon curd yellow—it's the egg yolks. A more vibrantly yellow lemon curd was made with pasture-raised eggs. The paler variety comes from factory-farmed eggs. The yolks of pasture-raised eggs are naturally more vibrant from all the variation in the hens' diets and the beta carotene from the green plants the hens eat. —L.K

8 egg yolks

Zest of 2 lemons

2/3 cup lemon juice

1 cup sugar

10 tablespoons salted butter

1. Whisk together egg yolks, zest, lemon juice, and sugar in a saucepan. Cook over medium-high heat, stirring constantly, until mixture becomes thick and coats the back of the spoon—8 to 10 minutes. Temperature should reach 160°F. Transfer to the bowl of a stand mixer with the paddle attachment. Mix on low. Add butter 1 tablespoon at a time, mixing until fully combined before adding the next tablespoon of butter. Strain through a sieve into a medium bowl.

2. Cover with plastic wrap, pressing plastic directly onto the surface to prevent a skin from forming on curd. Refrigerate for at least 2 hours or up to 3 days.

MAKES ABOUT 1¾ CUPS

RASPBERRY JAM

So easy to make and so much tastier than store-bought—homemade raspberry jam is a staple in my refrigerator. It is especially amazing when local berries are in season, but fresh raspberries are delicious all year round and this is a sweet and beautiful bright red addition to your scone board.

3 cups raspberries
1¼ cups sugar
2 tablespoons lemon juice
½ teaspoon lemon zest
1 tablespoon cornstarch

1. Cook raspberries, sugar, lemon juice, lemon zest, and cornstarch in a medium saucepan over medium-high heat. As you stir, raspberries will break down and turn to liquid. Bring mixture to a boil. Reduce temperature to medium. Cook and stir until the mixture coats the back of the spoon, about 8 to 9 minutes. Keep in mind jam will thicken more when it has cooled.

2. Pour into a glass pint jar and store in the refrigerator for up to 2 weeks.

MAKES ABOUT **2** CUPS

SPANISH TAPAS

"Any reasonable, sentient person who looks at Spain, comes to Spain, eats in Spain, drinks in Spain, they're going to fall in love. Otherwise, there's something deeply wrong with you. This is the dream of all the world." —ANTHONY BOURDAIN

Spanish tapas are small plates packed with big flavor meant for sharing and sampling. While origins are disputed, tapas culture likely began centuries ago when sherry drinkers in Andalusia were given snacks, or "tapas," to accompany their drinks. Today, bars and restaurants across Spain put their unique spin on tapas, blending regional ingenuity with traditional ingredients like olive oil, garlic, and tomato. From churros sprinkled with sugar to crispy fried croquetas de pollo, tapas run the gamut from iconic bites to regional specialties. Seafood, meat and vegetables are elevated into tasty tapas for passing around the table. Tapas dining encourages exploration and discovery; moving from bar to bar trying new combinations captures Spanish conviviality. More than just appetizers, tapas are an eating style that embodies community, celebration and savoring life's little pleasures. Shared with good drink and company, tapas offer a quintessential Spanish experience. —M.M.

MAKE AHEAD

Boil and peel your eggs for Spanish-Style Deviled Eggs one day in advance and store in a ziplock bag in the refrigerator.

For the Croquetas de Pollo, prepare the chicken mixture and shape the croquettes a day ahead.

Prepare Garlic Aioli, Romesco Sauce, and Mojo Verde de Cilantro sauces 2 days in advance, and store in airtight jars in the refrigerator.

Polvoróns can be made a day in advance.

Churro batter can be made up to a week in advance. Pipe batter on a parchment lined cookie sheet. Freeze for 1 hour and then move into an airtight container. Fry just before serving.

EXTRAS

Membrillo (Sweet Quince Paste)

Queso Manchego

Marinated Spanish Olives

Marcona Nuts

Jamón serrano

TIME SAVERS

Boiled eggs can be purchased.

Garlic aioli can be purchased.

Purchase peeled garlic to speed up prep time.

Styling Ideas

Use a large board with a few smaller ones as the base to display the tapas.

Combine colors (a bright base) and textures (vintage dishes) to create a rich narrative.

Incorporate ceramic platters, bowls, and terracotta dishes in different shapes and sizes to hold the various tapas.

RECIPES

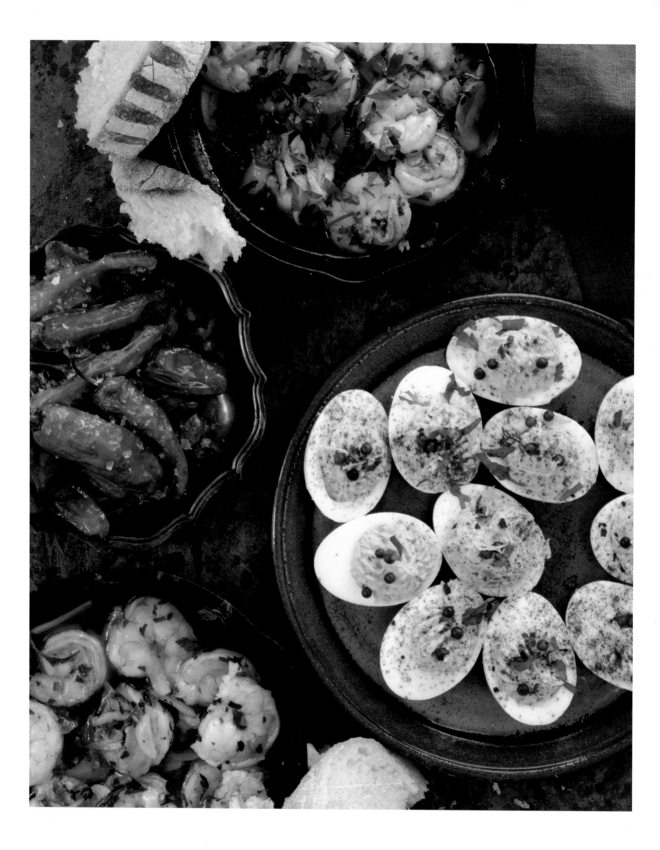

GAMBAS AL AJILLO

SIZZLING SHRIMP WITH GARLIC AND CHILI

Gambas al Ajillo epitomizes the unpretentious beauty of Spanish tapas. Succulent shrimp, aromatic garlic, and a hint of red chili sizzle in rich olive oil, crafting a flavor that's nothing short of transcendent. Each time I prepare it, I am transported to a sun-kissed terrace in Spain, reaching for crusty bread to dip into that liquid gold. —м.м.

¼ cup extra-virgin olive oil

6–7 cloves garlic, sliced

1 pound medium or large shrimp, peeled, deveined, and washed

Kosher salt, to taste

1 teaspoon crushed red chili flakes

½ teaspoon finely grated lemon zest

1 teaspoon fresh lemon juice

¼ cup parsley, minced + extra for garnish

Pan de Cristal or any other crusty bread of your choice for serving

1. In a large skillet, heat the olive oil over medium-high heat.

2. Add the garlic and let sizzle for about 2 minutes, until the garlic is golden in color.

3. Add the shrimp to the skillet. Then add salt and chili pepper and cook and stir for about 2 to 3 minutes.

4. Add lemon zest, lemon juice, and chopped parsley to the shrimp and cook for another minute. Remove from heat.

5. Transfer to serving dish and sprinkle with chopped parsley set aside for garnish. Serve immediately with crusty bread.

SERVES 4

PIMIENTOS DE PADRON

BLISTERED GREEN PEPPERS

These sweet and juicy green peppers from Galicia are fried hard and fast in olive oil to char the skins while keeping the insides soft. Popping hot Padrón peppers in your mouth is like playing roulette—most are mild, but every now and then you'll get one with a spicy kick! Padrón peppers really just need good olive oil and a sprinkling of sea salt to let their flavor shine. To me, they capture the essence of Spanish tapas—high-quality ingredients, simplicity in preparation, and bursts of flavor. A plate of blistered Padróns never lasts long with drinks being passed around. They liven up any tapas spread or table with their vibrant color and sweet-meets-spicy bite. —M.M.

30 shishito peppers or Padrón peppers

3 tablespoons extra-virgin olive oil

Coarse sea salt

1. Rinse the shishito peppers or Padrón peppers, then pat them dry using a clean kitchen towel or paper towels.

2. In a large, heavy skillet (preferably cast iron) over medium-high heat, add the extra-virgin olive oil. Allow the oil to heat up until it is shimmering but not smoking.

3. Carefully add the peppers to the hot oil, ensuring they are in a single layer. You may need to cook them in batches if your skillet isn't large enough to accommodate all the peppers at once.

4. Cook the peppers for 2 to 3 minutes on each side, turning occasionally with tongs, until their skin starts to blister and char in spots. Keep an eye on them to avoid burning.

5. Once the peppers are blistered and slightly softened, use tongs to transfer them to a serving plate.

6. While the peppers are still hot, sprinkle them generously with coarse sea salt.

SERVES 5

SPANISH-STYLE DEVILED EGGS

These Spanish-Style Deviled Eggs, a spin on the beloved appetizer, are inspired by classic Spanish tapas flavors. Smoky piquillo peppers, briny olives, capers, and paprika pack each bite with the iconic taste of Spain. Though not a traditional tapas dish, these deviled eggs fuse the spirit of tapas with a familiar favorite. For an inventive way to bring Spanish flavor to any occasion, these stuffed eggs offer all the vibrancy of España in one handheld bite.

12 eggs

1 tablespoon diced jarred piquillo peppers

1 tablespoon liquid from the piquillo pepper jar

¼ cup Spanish green olives, pitted and minced

2 tablespoons capers, minced

1 tablespoon parsley, finely chopped

⅓ cup mayonnaise

1 tablespoon Dijon mustard

Kosher salt and pepper, to taste

Smoked paprika, for sprinkling

1. Place the eggs in a single layer in a saucepan or pot. Cover with enough water that there's 1 to 2 inches of water above the eggs. Heat on high until water begins to boil, then cover, reduce the heat to low, and cook for 1 more minute. Remove from heat and leave covered in the pot for 14 minutes, then rinse under cold water continuously for 1 minute.

2. Crack eggshells and carefully peel under cool running water. Gently dry with paper towels. Slice the eggs in half lengthwise, removing yolks to a medium bowl and placing the whites on a serving platter.

3. To the egg yolks, add diced piquillo peppers, liquid from the pepper jar, minced green olives, minced capers, parsley, mayonnaise, and Dijon mustard. Mix everything together until smooth. Season with salt and pepper to taste.

4. Using a spoon or a pastry bag, fill each egg white half with the yolk mixture. The filling should be generous, mounding slightly above the surface of the egg white.

5. Lightly sprinkle smoked paprika over the filled deviled eggs for added flavor and a touch of color.

6. Serve immediately or refrigerate until ready to serve.

NOTE: These deviled eggs can be made a few hours in advance but are best consumed the same day for optimal flavor.

MAKES **24**

PAN CON TOMATO

COUNTRY BREAD WITH TOMATO

Pan Con Tomato epitomizes Catalonia's culinary spirit. With crusty bread, ripe tomatoes, fragrant garlic, and a touch of olive oil and salt, its flavors speak of rustic simplicity. Across Spain, from Seville to Madrid, this unassuming dish stands as a testament to the nation's love for authentic and impeccable flavors.

6 slices artisan country bread

Olive oil

2 cloves garlic

2 ripe heirloom tomatoes

Kosher salt, to taste

1. Turn on the broiler and place a rack 6 inches from the heat source. Drizzle both sides of each bread slice with olive oil and season with a pinch of salt.

2. Broil the bread, keeping a watchful eye to prevent burning, until one side is golden. Flip it and continue broiling until the other side is crisp.

3. After removing the bread from the broiler, gently rub the surface with a garlic clove. Use one clove for the first 3 slices, and the other clove for the remaining 3 slices.

4. Slice the ripe tomatoes in half, and if necessary, remove excess seeds and moisture. Press the cut side of a tomato onto a bread slice, massaging the pulp into all the crevices. Use one tomato for the first 3 slices, and the other tomato for the remaining 3 slices.

5. Complete the dish by drizzling a little more olive oil over each bread slice and adding a final sprinkle of salt.

MAKES **6**

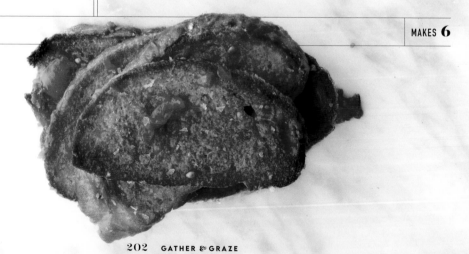

CROQUETAS DE POLLO

CHICKEN CROQUETTE

Beloved in bars across Spain, Croquetas de Pollo showcase two quintessential Spanish ingredients: chicken and béchamel. Béchamel sauce has been used in Spanish cooking since the fifteenth century. Combining it with chicken creates the ultimate comforting tapa. Rolled in breadcrumbs and fried, the creamy croquetas offer a taste of home in snackable form. Croquetas likely emerged in the nineteenth century as tapas bars shaped leftovers into fritters. While croquetas come in many flavors, chicken remains one of the most popular. Crisp on the outside and soft within, these Croquetas de Pollo exemplify how Spanish tapas blend tradition with culinary invention.

FILLING

3 tablespoons extra-virgin olive oil

1 medium white onion, grated

1 cup shredded chicken

BÉCHAMEL

4 cups whole milk

6 tablespoons (¾ stick) unsalted butter

1 cup all-purpose flour, sifted

Kosher salt to taste

Black pepper to taste

¼ teaspoon freshly grated nutmeg

BREADING

1 cup panko breadcrumbs

3 large eggs

FRYING

Peanut oil or other neutral oil for frying

1. **To prepare the filling:** Heat olive oil over medium heat in a pan. Sauté the grated onion for about 5 minutes, stirring frequently. Add the shredded chicken, season with salt and pepper, and mix well. Cook for 10 minutes on medium-low heat, stirring regularly. Set aside.

2. **To make the béchamel:** In a pot, warm the milk over medium heat for about 5 minutes without bringing it to a boil. Remove and set aside.

3. In another pot, melt the butter over low heat until it has a nutty color. Add the sifted flour to the butter, stirring continuously to form a roux. Continue stirring until the mixture thickens and turns golden in color. Slowly pour in half of the warmed milk while stirring constantly. Add salt, pepper, and freshly grated nutmeg to taste.

4. Continue stirring, adding the remaining milk gradually until the sauce thickens and is smooth. If any lumps form, use an immersion blender or whisk to smooth the sauce.

5. Let the béchamel sauce cool completely, then combine it with the chicken filling. Mix thoroughly.

6. **To shape the croquettes:** Line a large dish with parchment paper. Spread the croquette mixture evenly over the dish and cover it with plastic wrap. Refrigerate for at least 8 hours.

7. After chilling, divide the mixture into 18 to 20 equal portions and shape them into oval croquettes.

CONTINUED

8. Place the shaped croquettes on a baking tray lined with parchment paper and chill in the refrigerator for another 15 minutes.

9. To bread: Beat the eggs in a bowl. Place the breadcrumbs in a separate, deep plate. Dip each croquette into the beaten eggs, then coat them in breadcrumbs. Place the breaded croquettes back on the baking tray. Chill in the refrigerator for another hour.

10. To fry: Pour 2 to 3 inches peanut oil in a deep heavy-bottomed pan or Dutch oven. Clip a candy thermometer to pan. Preheat to 350°F over medium heat. Once the oil has preheated, gently add a few croquettes at a time to the pan or Dutch oven. Make sure not to overcrowd. Fry the croquettes until they are golden brown.

MAKES ABOUT **20**

PATATA BRAVAS

BRAVE POTATOES

During my travels across Spain and my quest to find the most authentic recipe for this beloved dish, I discovered that authenticity can be a fluid concept in cooking, especially with dishes as beloved and widespread as Patata Bravas. So the recipe below is my humble take on the dish. I love to serve my version with two sauces. —M.M.

POTATOES

4–5 medium-sized Yukon
  potatoes

Olive oil for frying

Kosher salt

BRAVA SAUCE

⅓ cup extra-virgin olive oil

3 cloves garlic, thinly sliced

2 pickled pepperoncini
  peppers, stems removed

1 small onion, diced

Kosher salt, to taste

Freshly ground pepper, to
  taste

1 teaspoon smoked paprika
  (pimentón)

½ teaspoon cayenne pepper
  (adjust for desired heat)

1 (28-ounce) can whole peeled
  tomatoes, roughly chopped

½ teaspoon brown sugar

2 tablespoons pepperoncini
  brine (from the pickled
  pepperoncini jar)

1. **To make the potatoes:** Peel the potatoes and cut them into small cubes or irregular shapes, about 1 to 2 inches thick.

2. Wash the potato pieces in cold water to remove excess starch. This helps in getting them crispier when frying. After washing, pat them dry with a kitchen towel.

3. In a deep frying pan or pot, heat the olive oil. Once hot, carefully add the potatoes. Fry them in batches if needed. Fry until they are golden and crisp. Once fried, transfer the potatoes to a plate lined with paper towels to remove excess oil. Sprinkle some salt over the hot potatoes.

4. **To make the brava sauce:** Heat the olive oil in a large skillet over medium heat. Once glistening, add the garlic and pepperoncini. Sauté until the garlic is aromatic, about 1 to 2 minutes.

5. Add the diced onions, season with salt and pepper, and cook until translucent, about 7 to 8 minutes. Sprinkle in the smoked paprika and cayenne pepper and mix to coat the onion and garlic. Add the tomatoes and brown sugar, stirring well. Reduce the heat to low and let the sauce simmer gently. Then add the pepperoncini brine.

6. After the sauce has simmered for about 25 to 30 minutes and the tomatoes have softened, remove from heat. Let the mixture cool.

CONTINUED

7. Blend the sauce until smooth using an immersion blender or countertop blender. Taste and adjust seasoning if necessary. Add a splash of water if the sauce is too thick.

8. Store in a sealed container in the fridge for up to a week. Warm gently before serving.

SERVES **6–8**

GARLIC AIOLI

MAKES ABOUT ¾ CUP

1 large egg yolk, at room temperature
1 tablespoon fresh lemon juice
1 teaspoon Dijon mustard
¼ teaspoon smoked paprika (pimentón)
Pinch of cayenne pepper (optional)
½ cup extra-virgin olive oil
2 large cloves garlic, minced
Sea salt, to taste
Splash of water (if needed, to adjust consistency)

1. In a medium bowl, whisk together the egg yolk, lemon juice, Dijon mustard, smoked paprika, and cayenne, if using. The mixture should be well combined. Add olive oil, drop by drop, into the yolk mixture while constantly whisking. This process requires patience. Once the mixture starts to emulsify and thicken, you can slowly drizzle in the remaining oil while continuing to whisk.

2. After you've incorporated all the oil and have a smooth, creamy texture, whisk in the minced garlic. Season with sea salt to taste. If the aioli is too thick for your liking, you can adjust the consistency by whisking in a splash of water.

3. Store the aioli in a sealed container in the refrigerator if not using immediately. It's best used within a day or two.

4. Serve this creamy garlic aioli alongside your Patata Bravas for a delightful combination of flavors and textures.

PAN DE CRISTAL

GLASS BREAD

Pan de Cristal, or glass bread, was developed in Barcelona and has an especially crusty outside with large holes in the inside, making for very little crumb. The process to get the beautiful hole-filled interior requires doing coil folds every 30 minutes for 3 hours and then another 1 hour and 30 minutes for the final rise. So you will want to make it on a day that you can be near the kitchen. The finished product will fill your house with the smell of crusty deliciousness and will be lovely sliced and perfect for dipping in the many dishes on this spread. —L.K.

1¾ cups warm water +
    2 tablespoons + more for
    pan and hands
1½ teaspoons yeast
2 teaspoons fine kosher salt
4 cups bread flour

1. In the bowl of a stand mixer with the hook attachment, mix water, yeast, and salt. Add flour 1 cup at a time, mixing on medium in between each addition. Dough will be sticky. Knead on medium for 8 minutes.

2. Set a small bowl with water near a 9 × 13-inch pan. Add 1 tablespoon water to pan and spread it with your hands so bottom of pan is slightly wet. This helps the dough stick less. Turn out dough into pan. Bowl-fold dough by stretching each corner up and folding it over the top of the dough. Stretch dough into a rectangle. Dough will be very sticky at this stage. If you find that it's sticking to your hands too much, wet your hands in the bowl of water. Cover pan with a damp cloth or plastic wrap. Allow to rest for 30 minutes.

3. After resting 30 minutes, do the first coil fold by wetting hands and grasping each side of center of dough. Lift from the center and allow dough to stretch, forming a fold. Lay back in pan folded. Stretch folded dough slightly to form a rectangle with the folded side as one of the short sides of rectangle. Grasp center of dough again and make another fold. Stretch dough into a rectangle and cover and allow to rest 30 more minutes. Repeat this step 3 more times, waiting 30 minutes between each time, for a total resting time of 3 hours.

4. After the last coil fold, allow dough to rest 30 more minutes. With a bench scraper, cut dough in half. On a generously floured surface, stretch first half to a rectangle roughly 15 × 5 inches. Generously flour the top of the dough. Place a piece of parchment on a cutting board or pizza peel and place first loaf on parchment. Repeat with second half of dough. Cover and allow to rest 1½ hours.

5. Place a heavy-bottomed sheet pan or baking stone in oven and preheat to 450°F. Carefully place first loaf on baking pan or stone by pulling out oven rack and sliding parchment onto baking sheet or stone. Bake until golden outside, about 15 to 20 minutes. Remove from oven and bake second loaf. Serve warm. Bread tastes best the first day and will lose most of its magic by day 2. Freeze leftover bread in an airtight container or use day-old bread for making homemade breadcrumbs.

MAKES **2** LOAVES

ROMESCO SAUCE

Legend claims Romesco sauce originated centuries ago in the countryside of Tarragona, where peasants crafted the nutty condiment to complement meat and calçots onions grilled over open fires. Today the blend of roasted peppers, tomatoes, garlic, and almonds stands as a pillar of Catalan cuisine. Beyond its homeland, the sweet, smoky, and vibrant sauce has become a staple in tapas bars across Spain where it elevates seafood, meat and vegetables alike. Capture the aroma and spirit of Spain in this richly hued sauce blending the region's iconic ingredients. A dollop of Romesco brings a burst of Mediterranean flavor to brighten any dish it accompanies. —M.M.

2 dried Nora peppers (or substitute dried California, New Mexico, or Pasilla chilies)

6 vine-ripened tomatoes

1 head garlic + 1 additional clove

Extra-virgin olive oil for frying

⅓ cup hazelnuts, preferably skinned

⅓ cup blanched almonds

4 half-inch-thick slices of baguette

1 cup loosely packed flat-leaf parsley leaves

3 tablespoons sherry vinegar

1 cup extra-virgin olive oil

Kosher salt, to taste

1. Place the dried peppers in a bowl and pour very hot (almost boiling) water over them. Let them stand at room temperature overnight.

2. Preheat the oven to 450°F. Line a rimmed baking tray with foil and place the tomatoes on it. Roast the tomatoes for 20 minutes, then add the whole head of garlic to the pan. Continue roasting until the tomatoes are blackened and blistered, and the garlic skin is brown, about 2 hours.

3. Drain the peppers, discarding the stems and seeds. Scrape out the flesh and reserve.

4. In a large skillet, heat enough oil to come ¼ inch up the sides over medium heat. Add the bread slices in a single layer, cooking until golden brown, about 30 seconds per side. Transfer the bread to a bowl.

5. Add the hazelnuts and almonds to the skillet, and cook until golden brown, shaking the pan often, about 1 minute. Combine the nuts with the bread. Remove the top ¼ inch of the head of roasted garlic. Squeeze the soft cloves into the bread and nut mixture.

6. In a blender, pulse the reserved Nora pepper flesh, roasted tomatoes, roasted garlic, raw garlic clove, fried bread, fried nuts, parsley, and vinegar until well mixed. With the blender running, slowly drizzle in 1 cup of olive oil until the mixture becomes smooth and thick, with some tiny parts remaining. Season with salt.

MAKES **3–4** CUPS

MOJO VERDE DE CILANTRO

CANARIAN GREEN SAUCE WITH CILANTRO

I first tasted this sauce with "papas arrugadas" (wrinkly potatoes) at a cozy, family-owned tapas bar that we stumbled upon in Seville. The flavors instantly blew me away and I had to thank the chef, who turned out to be the grandmother running the place. Before I left, she handed me a handwritten note with this very recipe. Every time I make it, I'm reminded of that special day and the generous grandma. —M.M.

1 green bell pepper, deseeded and cut in chunks

1 bunch fresh cilantro leaves, washed and coarsely torn

3 cloves garlic, minced

1 teaspoon ground cumin

1 tablespoon white wine vinegar

Sea salt to taste (a pinch or more)

½ cup extra-virgin olive oil

1. In your food processor, start by placing the bell pepper, cilantro, garlic, cumin, white wine vinegar, and a pinch of salt. Give the mixture a few pulses, blending until it takes on a paste-like texture.

2. Slowly stream in the olive oil while the processor is running. This will help emulsify the sauce and give it a smooth, velvety texture.

SERVING SUGGESTIONS

Grilled Meats and Seafood: Drizzle the sauce over grilled chicken, steak, or fish.

Dips: Serve it alongside tortilla chips, pita bread, or crudité.

Sandwiches and Wraps: Spread a layer inside sandwiches, wraps, or burritos.

Salads: Use the sauce as a unique dressing for salads, especially those with grilled veggies or proteins.

Potatoes: It pairs wonderfully with boiled or roasted potatoes. You can also mix it into mashed potatoes.

Eggs: Spice up your breakfast by adding it to scrambled eggs, omelets, or even drizzling over a sunny-side-up.

Pasta: Mix it with freshly cooked pasta for a light and aromatic alternative to traditional sauces.

Soup Garnish: Add a dollop on top of soups like gazpacho or black bean for an extra kick of flavor.

Marinade: Use the sauce as a marinade for meats or tofu. Let the protein marinate for a few hours or overnight to absorb the flavors.

MAKES **2** CUPS

POLVORÓNS

SPANISH SHORTBREAD

Polvo means "dust" in Spanish. Polvoróns have a generous dusting of confectioners' sugar on top and they also tend to crumble when eaten. Traditionally made for holidays in Spain, these simple treats are great year-round.

1¼ cups almonds

1 cup unsalted butter, softened

1½ cups confectioners' sugar + more for dusting

2 cups all-purpose flour

½ teaspoon salt

1 teaspoon cinnamon

1. Preheat oven to 350°F. Toast almonds 8 to 10 minutes. Allow to cool on pan. In the bowl of a food processor, grind cooled almonds until fine.

2. In the bowl of a stand mixer with the paddle attachment, add ground almonds, butter, and confectioners' sugar. Beat on medium speed for 2 to 3 minutes. In a small bowl, whisk together flour, salt, and cinnamon.

3. On a lightly floured surface, roll dough out to ½-inch thickness. Create cutouts with a 2-inch round cookie cutter. Bake for 10 to 12 minutes or until lightly golden.

4. Transfer polvoróns to cooling rack and dust generously with confectioners' sugar while still warm. Allow to cool completely and serve. Or store in an airtight container for up to 5 days or freeze for up to 3 months.

MAKES **36**

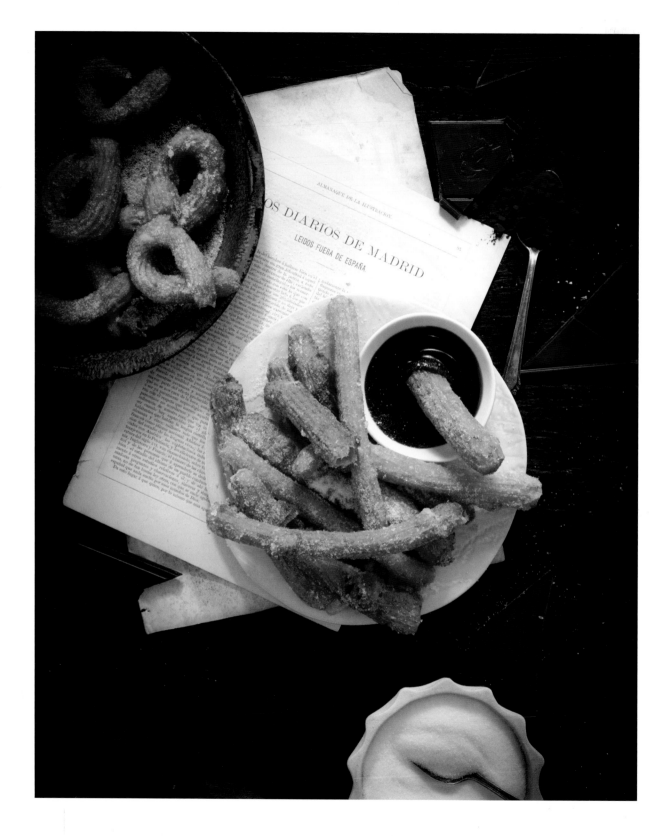

CHURROS

The name churros is said to have come from churra sheep that are native to the Iberian Penninsula. Legend says that shepherds fried dough that resembled the horns of the sheep. Spaniards brought these treats all over the world where they've been embraced by many cultures. Another legend says that Cortez brought churros to the Aztecs and they, in turn, taught him to make chocolate, and that since this exchange, chocolate has been the choice accompaniment for churros is Spain.

Peanut oil or other neutral oil for frying

2 cups flour

½ teaspoon fine kosher salt

½ teaspoon baking powder

1 cup whole milk

1¼ cups water

1 teaspoon sugar

2 tablespoons unsalted butter

2 teaspoons vanilla extract

COATING

⅔ cup sugar

Dark Chocolate Sauce (page 148)

1. Clip a candy thermometer to a deep heavy-bottomed pan or Dutch oven. Pour 2 to 3 inches peanut oil in pan. Preheat to 350°F over medium heat.

2. In the bowl of a stand mixer with the paddle attachment, combine flour, salt, and baking powder.

3. In a medium saucepan over medium-high heat, combine milk, water, sugar, butter, and vanilla. Cook until mixture reaches a boil. With stand mixer running on low, carefully pour hot milk mixture into mixer bowl. Continue to mix until a smooth dough forms and is cool enough to touch. Add dough to a large pastry bag with a large star tip.

4. Line a baking sheet with paper towels, and top with a cooling rack. Add sugar to a flat shallow bowl. Set near stove. If oil hasn't reached 350°F, increase stove to medium-high heat. When oil has preheated, pipe dough into oil. You can use a scissors to cut dough from piping bag. Fry until golden brown, about 2 to 3 minutes per side. Remove with a slotted spatula and place on prepared cooling rack to drain. After about 1 minute, place churro in bowl with sugar and lightly coat with sugar.

5. Serve churros warm with Dark Chocolate Sauce or your favorite topping.

6. If you have more dough than you need, pipe dough onto parchment and freeze. When dough has frozen, transfer to an airtight container and freeze for up to 2 weeks. Then you can make fresh churros by frying the frozen dough.

MAKES ABOUT **16**

PORTUGUESE PETISCOS

"Everything we eat in Portugal tells a story—of ancient dispersal, discovery, trade, war, occupation, resistance." —MARCIA LAIDLAW

My heart remains in Lisbon after spending two life-changing months immersed in its food and culture. I arrived eager to uncover the centuries-old culinary soul of this colorful seaside city. I lost myself winding through storybook streets, gazing at pastel façades under glowing sunsets. I broke bread with locals, listening to melancholic fado flow through the night. Each day brought new discoveries—obscure bakeries with fifteenth-century recipes passed down from nuns, arrays of spices from around the world that entered global trade through prolific Portuguese exploration. From Vasco de Gama to Magellan, Portuguese voyages propelled access and knowledge of captivating spices like black pepper, clove, nutmeg, and cinnamon. Through cooking classes, food tours and endless restaurants, I uncovered Portugal's genius for blending local fare, global flavors, and generations of tradition. Beyond the food, it was the Portuguese people who won my heart—their passion for life's pleasures, even in hard times. In those simple moments. sharing laughter over wine, cheering at soccer matches, and discovering recipe treasures from centuries past, I felt a true bond to this culture take root inside my heart. Two months felt both ephemeral and endless in this magical place. —M.M.

MAKE AHEAD

Make Tomato Jam in advance and store in an airtight container in the refrigerator.

Make Peri Peri Sauce in advance and store in an airtight container in the refrigerator.

Make Salame de Chocolate up to 3 days in advance. Store in an airtight container in the refrigerator. Set out about 2 hours before serving so chocolate becomes easier to slice.

EXTRAS

Cured Meats

Olives

Crackers

TIME SAVERS

Purchase peri-peri sauce.

Purchase crusty bread for the sandwiches.

Purchase tomato relish/jam.

Styling Ideas

For this board, I bought all the serving dishes from Portugal. I spent countless hours at antique shops and local markets and was able to find the most stunning pieces.

Combine local ceramics with rustic wood textures. Mix old with new.

RECPES

BOLINHOS DE BACALHAU

PORTUGUESE COD FRITTERS

While the original recipe often uses salted cod (bacalhau), this version with fresh cod offers a more delicate and fresher flavor while keeping the essence of the traditional Portuguese fritter.

1 pound fresh cod filets

1 pound russet potatoes, unpeeled

1 large onion, finely chopped

4 cloves garlic, minced

2 large eggs, beaten

1 bunch flat-leaf parsley, finely chopped

Kosher salt, to taste

Fresh ground pepper, to taste

Peanut oil or another neutral oil, for frying

NOTE: You can also shape the mixture into oval patties, about 2 to 3 inches long.

1. Place the fresh cod in a saucepan and cover with water. Bring to a boil, reduce heat, and simmer for about 10 to 12 minutes or until the fish is flaky and cooked through. Once cooked, drain and set aside to cool. After cooling, shred the fish using your fingers, making sure no bones are left behind.

2. Place the russet potatoes in another pot and cover them with water. Bring to a boil, then simmer until the potatoes are tender, roughly 20 minutes. Once cooked, drain the water. When cool enough to handle but still warm, peel the potatoes and then mash them in a large mixing bowl.

3. To the mashed potatoes, add the shredded cod, finely chopped onion, minced garlic, beaten eggs, and finely chopped parsley. Season the mixture with kosher salt and freshly ground pepper to taste. Stir everything together until the mixture is uniform.

4. To shape the fritters, take a spoon and scoop a generous amount of the mixture. Use a second spoon to shape and smooth the mixture into an oval or quenelle shape by transferring it back and forth between the spoons. This method creates a traditional, slightly elongated fritter. Once shaped, gently slide the fritter off the spoon and set it aside on a tray or plate. Repeat with the remaining mixture.

5. In a deep frying pan, heat the peanut oil to around 350°F. Once the oil is hot, fry the fritters in batches, ensuring not to overcrowd the pan. Fry each side for about 2 to 3 minutes or until they are golden brown and crispy.

6. After frying, place the fritters on a plate lined with paper towels to drain any excess oil.

MAKES ABOUT **24**

PEIXINHOS DA HORTA

FRIED GREEN BEANS

These crisp "little fish of the garden" offer a plant-based twist on classic Portuguese seafood dishes. Slices of tender green beans get dipped in a light tempura-style batter before frying up golden and crispy. The delicate exterior contrasts the tender bean interior in these irresistible fritters. They exemplify Portugal's talent for elevating humble vegetables into satisfying vegetarian bites.

1 pound green beans, trimmed, washed, and dried

1½ cups all-purpose flour

½ cup rice flour

1 teaspoon baking powder

½ teaspoon kosher salt

½ teaspoon ground black pepper

½ teaspoon paprika

2 cups cold club soda, sparkling water, or beer

Frying-grade oil for frying

1. To prepare the beans: Bring a large pot of salted water to a boil. Fill a separate large bowl with ice water and set it aside.

2. Add the green beans to the boiling water and blanch for about 2 minutes. Immediately transfer the blanched beans to the bowl of ice water to halt the cooking process. Once cooled, drain the beans and pat them dry using a kitchen towel. Set aside.

3. To prepare the batter: In a mixing bowl, whisk together the all-purpose flour, rice flour, baking powder, salt, ground black pepper, and paprika. Gradually add the club soda, stirring continuously to prevent clumps from forming. Adjust until the batter achieves a thick but pourable consistency. Let the mixture sit for 5 minutes.

4. To fry the beans: Heat frying-grade oil in a large pot until it reaches the appropriate frying temperature. Use a thermometer to accurately monitor the temperature. The oil should be about 3 inches deep.

5. Using tongs, dip each green bean into the batter, ensuring it's fully coated, and allow any excess batter to drip off. Carefully place the battered beans into the hot oil, frying them in small batches to avoid overcrowding.

6. Fry until the beans are golden and crispy, which should take about 3 to 4 minutes. Remove the beans from the oil and transfer them to a wire rack.

SERVES **4-6**

PORTUGUESE-INSPIRED "BIFANA" SANDWICH

SLOW COOKED BEEF SANDWICHES

In Lisbon's maze-like streets, an enticing aroma of sweet and salt drew me to a bodega alive with eager locals. Joining the line, I mistook their prized "bifana" for a beef sandwich, sharing the discovery with friends. It was, in fact, a pork classic. Since I don't eat pork, I've reinterpreted it here—not as a copy, but as homage. It might not echo Lisbon's exact notes, but it resonates with that memory. It's a nod to that unforgettable Lisboeta morning, and to Laura, who magically mastered the recipe for the iconic Papo Seco (page 226). —M.M.

3–4 pound chuck roast

¼ cup olive oil

Kosher salt and black pepper, to taste

1 large onion, thinly sliced

5 cloves garlic, minced

2 tablespoons tomato paste

1 teaspoon smoked paprika

1 teaspoon dried oregano

½ teaspoon nutmeg

¼ teaspoon cinnamon

½ teaspoon crushed red pepper flakes, to taste

1 cup red wine (preferably a Portuguese variety like Vinho Tinto)

2 bay leaves

1 cup beef broth

6 Papo Secos (page 226) or Ciabatta, for serving

Yellow mustard, to taste

Peri Peri Sauce (page 232), to taste

1. Generously season the chuck roast on all sides with salt and pepper. In a large skillet or pan, heat some oil over medium-high heat. Once hot, sear the chuck roast on all sides until browned, about 3 to 4 minutes per side. Transfer the roast to your slow cooker.

2. In the same skillet, sauté the sliced onion until translucent, then add the minced garlic, cooking until fragrant. Stir in the tomato paste, smoked paprika, dried oregano, nutmeg, cinnamon, and crushed red pepper flakes. Once combined, pour in the red wine, scraping any bits from the bottom of the skillet. Allow the wine mixture to simmer for about 2 minutes.

3. Transfer the onion-wine mixture to the slow cooker over the roast. Add the bay leaves and beef broth. Cover and cook on low for 7 to 8 hours, or until the beef is tender and can be easily shredded with a fork.

4. Once cooked, transfer the roast to a cutting board or plate. Use two forks to shred the meat, discarding any large fat pieces. Mix some of the cooking juices with the shredded meat for added flavor and moisture.

5. Slice the Papo Secos (Portuguese rolls) or Ciabatta in half. Pile the shredded beef onto one half of each roll. Add a few dollops of peri peri sauce and mustard.

MAKES **6**

PAPO SECOS

PORTUGUESE ROLLS

Papo Secos rolls are popular all over Portugal in homes and bakeries. They have a slightly crisp exterior with a soft inside, making them perfect for sandwiches. They are the base of the traditional bifana sandwich, and they also taste great with butter or cheese.

1⅔ cups warm water

1 teaspoon sugar

1 tablespoon active dry yeast

4 cups bread flour

2 teaspoons fine kosher salt

2 tablespoons unsalted butter, softened + more for bowl

1 egg white

2 cups water for steaming rolls

1. In a small bowl, mix water, sugar, and yeast. Allow to stand until a thick foam has formed at the top, about 10 minutes.

2. In the bowl of a stand mixer, with the dough hook attachment, stir together flour and salt. With the mixer on low, slowly pour in yeast mixture. Mix until a soft shaggy dough forms. If dough is too sticky, add more flour 1 tablespoon at a time until dough comes together. With mixer running, add butter in four portions. Allow butter to fully incorporate before adding the next portion.

3. Knead on medium speed for 8 minutes.

4. Lightly butter a large bowl and place dough in bowl. Cover bowl with plastic wrap or damp towel and allow dough to rise until it doubles in size. Bowl-fold dough by stretching from bottom to top. Allow to rise again for 30 minutes.

5. Divide dough into 18 equal portions (about 50 grams each). Form balls from each portion. Line a large baking sheet with parchment or a silicone baking mat. Place a dough ball on pan and flatten with palm of hand. Form crease in center with side of hand. Fold over and create points on ends by pinching dough on both sides of fold. Allow to rise on pan 30 more minutes.

6. Place one oven rack in center of oven. Place a second rack at the lowest level of oven. Place an empty 9 × 13-inch pan on the bottom rack. Preheat oven to 425°F. Beat egg white and brush on rolls. Set 1 cup of hot water near oven. Place first pan of rolls on the center rack of oven. Pull out bottom rack and carefully pour water in pan. Return rack and close oven as quickly as possible so steam is trapped in oven.

7. Bake until golden, about 18 to 22 minutes. Fresh bread tastes best on the same day it is baked. Store leftovers in an airtight container in the freezer for up to 1 month. To revive frozen rolls, preheat oven to 300°F. Place rolls on a baking sheet and warm for 7 to 10 minutes.

MAKES **18**

MARINATED SCALLOPS WITH AVOCADO CREAM & BREAD CRUMBLE

In homage to José Avillez, perhaps the second-most popular man in Portugal after Ronaldo, this recipe presents my ode to his masterpiece—scallops marinated in bright lemon and herb oil sit atop smooth avocado cream, topped with crunchy breadcrumbs. Textural contrasts meet coastal flavors in my rendition of Avillez's uniquely Portuguese approach to quality seafood handled simply, allowing fresh ingredients to sing. —M.M.

SCALLOPS

12 fresh scallops, cleaned

Zest and juice of 1 lemon

2 cloves garlic, minced

3 tablespoons extra-virgin olive oil

Kosher salt and freshly ground pepper to taste

AVOCADO CREAM

2 ripe avocados, pitted and peeled

Juice of 1 lime

1 small clove garlic, minced

2 tablespoons Greek yogurt or sour cream (optional for creaminess)

Kosher salt and pepper, to taste

Splash of water or olive oil for consistency

BREAD CRUMBLE

2 cups day-old rustic bread, broken into pieces

3 tablespoons extra-virgin olive oil

1 teaspoon smoked paprika (optional for flavor)

Kosher salt, to taste

1. To prepare the scallops: In a bowl, combine the lemon zest, lemon juice, minced garlic, olive oil, salt, and pepper. Mix well.

2. Add the scallops to the mixture, ensuring they're well coated. Let them marinate for about 15 to 20 minutes.

3. After marinating, sear the scallops in a hot pan for 1 to 2 minutes on each side or until they get a golden-brown crust. Avoid overcrowding the pan.

4. To prepare the avocado cream: In a food processor, combine the avocados, lime juice, garlic, and Greek yogurt or sour cream, if using. Pulse until smooth. If the mixture is too thick, you can thin it with a splash of water or olive oil. Season with salt and pepper. Set aside.

5. To prepare the bread crumble: Preheat the oven to 350°F.

6. In a food processor, pulse the bread until you get a coarse crumble. Transfer to a mixing bowl, add olive oil, smoked paprika (if using), and salt. Mix well. Spread the mixture on a baking sheet and bake for 10 to 12 minutes or until golden and crispy. Stir occasionally to ensure even cooking.

7. To assemble: On each plate, place a dollop of avocado cream. Place the seared scallops over the avocado cream. Sprinkle generously with the bread crumble. Garnish with fresh herbs or microgreens, if desired.

SERVES **12**

OVEN ROASTED NISA CHEESE WITH DOCE DE TOMATE

ROASTED NISA CHEESE

1 wheel Nisa cheese (around 7–9 ounces or 200–250 grams)

1 tablespoon olive oil

Pinch of dried oregano (optional)

Fresh thyme or rosemary sprigs (optional)

DOCE DE TOMATE

3 cups tomatoes

Peel of 1 orange

1 cup granulated sugar

3 cloves

1 cinnamon stick

1 star anise

1. To prepare the roasted Nisa cheese: Preheat the oven to 400°F. Place the Nisa cheese in an ovenproof dish. Drizzle with olive oil and sprinkle a pinch of dried oregano, if using. Add fresh thyme or rosemary sprigs around the cheese for added aroma.

2. Roast in the preheated oven for about 15 to 20 minutes, or until the cheese is soft and slightly golden on top. Remove from oven and let it cool slightly before serving.

3. To prepare the Doce de Tomate: Wash the tomatoes, cut them into quarters, and remove the seeds. After seeding, peel the tomatoes. Chop the peeled tomatoes into small pieces until you have about 3 cups.

4. Use a vegetable peeler or a sharp knife to peel the orange. Be careful to only take the orange part and not the bitter white pith. You can also use a zester if you want smaller pieces of peel.

5. Place the chopped tomatoes, sugar, cloves, cinnamon stick, star anise, and orange peel in a medium-sized, heavy-bottomed pot. Cook the mixture over medium heat, stirring occasionally, until the sugar has completely dissolved. Once the sugar has dissolved, reduce the heat to low and let the mixture simmer. Stir frequently to prevent it from sticking to the pot. Continue to cook the mixture on low heat for about 1 hour, or until it thickens to a jam-like consistency. The exact time will depend on the water content of your tomatoes.

6. Once the jam has thickened, remove the cloves, cinnamon stick, star anise, and orange peel. Let the jam cool slightly before transferring it to a clean jar. This makes around 3 cups.

7. To serve: Place the roasted Nisa cheese on a serving plate. Serve alongside the tomato jam. It pairs beautifully with crispy toasted bread or crackers.

NOTES: If you're unable to find Nisa cheese, there are a few alternatives that can give a similar texture and flavor profile when roasted:

Feta Cheese: Although it's Greek in origin, feta cheese has a creamy texture that becomes even creamier when baked. It won't have the exact same flavor as Nisa, but it will offer a tangy contrast to the sweet tomato jam.

Halloumi: This Cypriot cheese maintains its shape when heated and has a higher melting point, so it won't become overly gooey when roasted. It has a pleasant saltiness and a unique texture that's enjoyable when warmed.

Camembert or Brie: Both French cheeses have a soft, creamy interior with a mild flavor. When roasted, they become deliciously gooey.

Queso Fresco or Queso Blanco: These Mexican cheeses have a crumbly texture similar to feta but are milder in flavor. They can be used in the roasted cheese dish but will have a softer texture when warmed.

When selecting an alternative cheese, keep in mind the texture and melting point of the cheese. The goal is to achieve a creamy or soft texture when roasted, complementing the sweet and tangy tomato jam.

SERVES **6–8**

PERI PERI SAUCE

Iconic Peri Peri Sauce blends Portugal's passion for heat and brightness. Chili peppers join smoky paprika, herbs, and vinegar, transforming into an addictive condiment with African roots. Beloved especially in former colony Mozambique, this sauce likely originated with Portuguese explorers adopting the pili pili chili.

2 red bell peppers, coarsely chopped, seeds removed

½ cup extra-virgin olive oil + 2 tablespoons

3–4 dried peri peri chilies or 4–5 fresh red chili peppers, coarsely chopped, seeds removed

1 jalapeño pepper, coarsely chopped, seeds removed

3–5 cloves garlic, coarsely chopped

Handful fresh oregano leaves or 1 tablespoon dried oregano

4–5 large basil leaves

¼ cup chopped onions

1 tablespoon smoked paprika

1 lemon, juiced

1 teaspoon kosher salt, to taste

½ teaspoon freshly ground black pepper

¼ cup apple cider vinegar

1. Preheat your oven to 400°F.

2. Line a baking sheet with parchment paper. Spread the chopped red bell peppers evenly across the sheet and drizzle with 2 tablespoons of olive oil. Roast the peppers in the preheated oven until they're tender and slightly charred. Allow them to cool before proceeding.

3. In a blender or food processor, combine the roasted red bell peppers, chili peppers, jalapeño, garlic, oregano, basil, and onions. Pulse until a rough paste forms. With the blender or food processor running, slowly pour in the remaining olive oil until you achieve the desired consistency of your sauce. Add the smoked paprika, lemon juice, salt, and black pepper to the blender or food processor. Blend the mixture until everything is well combined. Add the apple cider vinegar last and give the sauce a final blend. You have the option to strain the sauce if you prefer a smoother texture. If not, you can keep the sauce as it is.

4. The Peri Peri Sauce can be stored in a refrigerator for up to 1 month.

MAKES ABOUT **2 ½** CUPS

PASTÉIS DE NATA

PORTUGUESE CUSTARD TARTS

I recently spent two amazing months in Lisbon, exploring its vibrant food scene, diving into its rich history, and enjoying the city's beautiful sights. As the haunting melodies of fado filled the air, I discovered Pastéis de Nata on almost every corner. This delightful custard tart is not just a dessert; it's a symbol of Lisbon's culinary heritage, with each vendor proudly claiming their recipe as the authentic nun's secret. —M.M.

SUGAR SYRUP

1½ cups sugar

⅔ cup water

Peel of 1 lemon without the pith

1 cinnamon stick

1 teaspoon vanilla bean paste

EGG CUSTARD

¼ cup flour

1 tablespoon cornstarch

1¼ cups whole milk, divided

6 large egg yolks

2 pounds Rough Puff Pastry (page xxi) or packaged puff pastry, thawed

Confectioners' sugar

1. **To make the custard:** In a large saucepan, combine sugar, water, lemon peel, a cinnamon stick, and vanilla bean paste. Heat the mixture to a boil, then reduce the heat and let it simmer for about 3 minutes. Strain and discard lemon peel and cinnamon stick. Allow syrup to cool for 10 minutes.

2. In the bowl of a stand mixer with the whisk attachment, combine flour and cornstarch. Add ¼ cup of the milk and beat until fully incorporated.

3. In a medium saucepan, cook the remaining 1 cup of milk until it boils. With the mixer on low, immediately pour hot milk into the flour mixture. Slowly pour syrup into the bowl and mix on low until fully combined and mixture is no longer hot.

4. When milk mixture has cooled, add egg yolks one at a time—waiting until each yolk is fully incorporated before adding the next. Pour custard through a fine mesh sieve into a bowl. Cover bowl with plastic wrap and set aside.

5. **To assemble the tarts:** Preheat oven 500°F.

6. On a lightly floured surface, form a log with puff pastry that is about 1 inch thick. Set a small cup of water near your work area. Slice 1 inch off log and add to the first egg tart tin. Wet fingers and press puff pastry into tin all the way to the top in an even layer. (Don't allow any holes in the puff pastry or custard will leak through and tart will stick to the tin.) Line all tart tins and set on a half-sheet baking pan.

CONTINUED

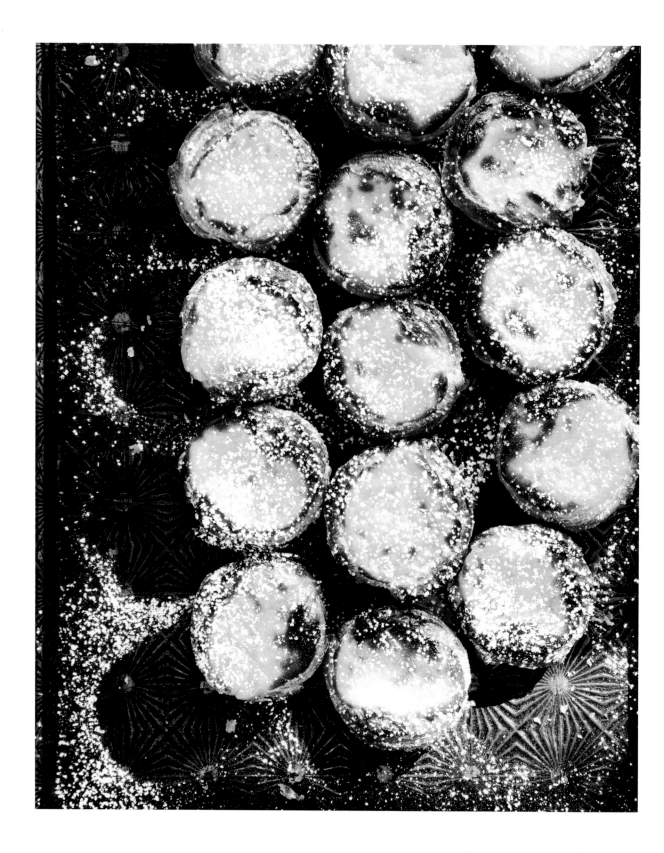

7. Fill each tart pan ⅞ of the way with egg custard. Be careful not to overfill. Bake the tarts for approximately 7 minutes, or until the egg custard has set and small black spots start to appear on the top of custard.

8. Allow the Pastéis de Nata to cool for about 10 minutes before removing them from their tins. Allow to cool until just warm. Dust with confectioners' sugar and serve. Pastéis de Nata are best on the day they are made. If you have leftovers, freeze in an airtight container. To revive frozen tarts, preheat oven to 275°F. Place frozen tarts on a baking sheet and warm them for 7 to 9 minutes.

SALAME DE CHOCOLATE

CHOCOLATE SALAMI

This is an easy, no-bake Portuguese treat that can be made in advance and is a sweet addition to a snacking board. You can tie twine around it, so it looks more like salami. Serve it on a cutting board with a knife to allow guests to make their own slices.

10–12 Maria or digestive biscuits

⅔ cup pistachios

½ cup unsalted butter, softened

1 teaspoon vanilla extract

1½ cups confectioners' sugar + more for dusting

½ cup Dutch-process cocoa powder

½ cup heavy cream

6 ounces dark chocolate, coarsely chopped

1. Break biscuits into chunks and place in a small bowl. Shell and coarsely chop pistachios. Set aside.

2. In the bowl of a stand mixer with the paddle attachment, beat butter, vanilla extract, and confectioners' sugar until well combined and fluffy, about 3 minutes. Add cocoa powder and beat until combined. Warm cream in a small saucepan over medium-high heat until steaming but not boiling. Remove from heat and add chocolate. Stir with a rubber spatula until chocolate is completely melted and smooth. If chocolate does not all melt, return to stove and warm over low heat, stirring constantly until all chocolate is melted. Do not leave pan on stove without stirring—chocolate burns easily.

3. With mixer running on low, pour chocolate mixture into mixer bowl. Beat until combined. Scrape sides and bottom of bowl, and beat again until all ingredients are fully incorporated. Add broken biscuits and pistachios. Mix on low until evenly distributed.

4. Place 2 feet of parchment on counter. Turn out chocolate mixture onto parchment. Coat hands with confectioners' sugar and form a log with chocolate. Dust log with confectioners' sugar on all sides. Roll log in parchment and tie ends with bakers' twine. Refrigerate for at least 1 hour. When ready to serve, open parchment and slice chocolate salami. Serve in slices or add the whole log to your table with a knife to allow guests to cut off their own pieces.

MAKES **1** LOG

MOROCCAN TABLE

Over centuries, Morocco's bustling crossroads fostered a cuisine shaped by diverse influences. Local crops like figs, dates, and olives blended with imported spices like cumin and saffron, creating signature flavor pairings that reflect the country's history as a culinary crossroads. Cooking techniques that prevail today, from handmade pastries to elaborate stews, reflect the heritage of Morocco's storied kingdoms. Following Islamic traditions, lamb and chicken prevail over pork. Clay tagines for slow-cooked stews evolved from ancient urns. Skewered and grilled meats retain nomadic imprints. Communal dishes like couscous and generous tea rituals encapsulate Moroccan hospitality. From market stalls to family tables, time-honored food traditions bridge past and present. The cuisine encapsulates the country's history at the intersection of African, Middle Eastern, and European influences. —M.M.

MAKE AHEAD

Make Jazar Bil Kamoun Wal Toum a day in advance and store in airtight container in the refrigerator.

Make Harissa in advance and store in airtight container in the refrigerator for up to 2 weeks.

Make dough and form Chebaki one day before. Fry and coat in syrup just before serving.

Make pastry and form Gazelle Horns the day before serving. Store in an airtight container in refrigerator and bake just before serving.

EXTRAS

Fresh pomegranate

Dried rose buds

Pistachios

Mint tea with fresh mint garnish

Radishes

Rustic bread or Pita (page 88) to dip in tagine

M'hanncha (snake cake)

TIME SAVERS

Harissa can be purchased.

Chebakia and Gazelle Horns can be purchased from a Moroccan bakery.

Styling Ideas

Add roses, jasmine, or orange blossoms to your table. Place them in a decorative vase or a traditional Moroccan pottery.

Use Moroccan-style plates, bowls, and platters. Mix and match different designs for added visual appeal. Use tagine dishes and decorative brass or silver serving ware and utensils.

Serve Moroccan mint tea in ornate tea glasses.

RECISPES

MAAKOUDA

POTATO FRITTERS WITH FETA AND CILANTRO

A staple Moroccan potato fritter, Maakouda's crispy exterior and fluffy interior reflects generations of local cooks resourcefully transforming simple ingredients into beloved street fare. Sold by vendors across cities like Marrakesh and Fez, the nostalgic aroma and sizzle of frying maakouda evokes memories of community in Moroccan culture. From market crowds to family gatherings, maakouda encapsulates cherished food traditions passed down through generations.

2 tablespoons butter

1 small onion, finely chopped

3 cloves garlic, minced

6 medium potatoes

Kosher salt, to taste

1 tablespoon ground cumin

½ teaspoon ground coriander

1 teaspoon harissa, homemade (page 249) or store-bought

¼ teaspoon black pepper

½ teaspoon turmeric

¼ cup crumbled feta

¼ cup finely chopped fresh cilantro

1 beaten egg (for binding)

1 cup semolina for dredging

Oil for frying (vegetable or sunflower oil)

1. Melt the butter over medium-low heat in a skillet. Add the finely chopped onion and sauté gently for 7 to 10 minutes or until translucent. Stir in the minced garlic and continue sautéing for an additional minute. Remove from heat and set aside.

2. Boil the potatoes in salted water until tender and easily pierced with a fork. Drain and let them cool. Once cooled, peel and grate them into a large mixing bowl.

3. Fold in the sautéed onion and garlic mixture. Then add salt, cumin, coriander, harissa, black pepper, and turmeric and mix using a wooden spoon or your hands.

4. Add crumbled feta and finely chopped cilantro. Stir in the beaten egg, ensuring the mixture binds well but without leaving excess egg at the bottom of the bowl.

5. Using a spoon or your hands, take about 2 tablespoons of the potato mixture and shape it into a ball. Flatten the ball into a patty that's approximately 1 inch thick. Repeat this process with the remaining mixture.

6. Spread the semolina evenly on a flat plate. Gently coat each patty in the semolina, ensuring it's lightly covered on all sides.

7. Heat oil in a frying pan or skillet over medium heat. Once the oil is hot, carefully add the dredged patties, ensuring not to overcrowd the pan. Fry until golden brown on each side. Transfer to a plate lined with paper towels to remove excess oil.

MAKES ABOUT 18

CHICKEN TAGINE WITH PRESERVED LEMONS, OLIVES & APRICOTS

This dish encapsulates the essence of Moroccan culinary storytelling. Traditionally cooked in the distinctively-shaped tagine pot, this dish draws from Morocco's age-old trade routes, merging the saltiness of preserved lemons and olives with the sweetness of apricots. As families gather to break bread and savor the harmonious flavors, this tagine carries tales of Berber nomads, ancient medinas, and bustling souks.

6–8 chicken pieces (like thighs or drumsticks, bone-in and skin-on)

½ teaspoon kosher salt

½ teaspoon freshly ground black pepper

½ teaspoon saffron threads

2 tablespoons warm water

2 tablespoons olive oil

2 large onions, finely chopped

2–3 cloves garlic, minced

1 tablespoon ground fresh ginger

1 teaspoon turmeric powder

1 teaspoon ground cumin

1 teaspoon ground coriander

1 teaspoon paprika

½ teaspoon cinnamon

1 cup chicken broth or water

2 preserved lemons, rinsed and thinly sliced, with pulp discarded (store-bought)

1 cup green olives, pitted

½ cup dried apricots

3 tablespoons cilantro, coarsely chopped (for garnishing)

1. Clean and pat dry the chicken pieces. Season generously with salt and black pepper.

2. Soak the saffron threads in 2 tablespoons of warm water for about 10 to 15 minutes to unlock their color and aroma.

3. In a tagine or a large heavy-bottomed pot, heat the olive oil over medium-high heat. Add the chicken pieces and brown on all sides. Once browned, remove and set aside.

4. Reduce the heat to medium. In the same pot, add the finely chopped onion, sautéing until translucent. Stir in the minced garlic and ground ginger and sauté for an additional minute.

5. Add the turmeric, cumin, coriander, paprika, cinnamon, and the soaked saffron (along with its soaking water). Cook for 2 to 3 minutes.

6. Return the browned chicken to the pot. Add the chicken broth. Cover the tagine or pot and let it simmer on low heat for about 30 minutes.

7. Add the preserved lemons, olives, and dried apricots and simmer on low heat for another 30 minutes until the chicken is tender. Garnish with fresh chopped cilantro. Serve with couscous.

SERVES **6**

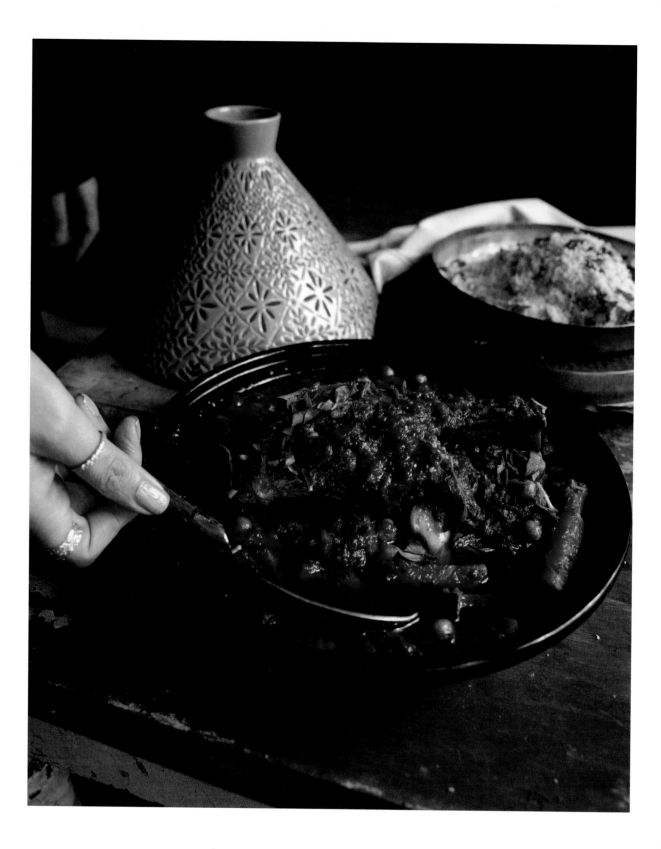

CAFÉ MOGADOR-INSPIRED LAMB SHANKS

Inspired by the iconic East Village eatery, Café Mogador, the slow-cooked lamb shanks with chickpeas and carrots exemplifies the fusion of authentic Moroccan flavors with modern culinary flair. Café Mogador, a beloved institution, has been instrumental in introducing and popularizing Moroccan dishes to New Yorkers. This dish, a nod to both the Moroccan pastoral practices and the culinary innovations of the vibrant East Village, is a delectable blend of history, community, and the spirit of sharing. With each bite, diners are transported from the bustling streets of New York to the aromatic souks and warm gatherings of Morocco.

1 red onion, quartered

4 cloves garlic, roughly chopped

2 teaspoons fresh ginger, roughly chopped

2 teaspoons ras el hanout spice blend

2 teaspoons ground cumin

1 tablespoon ground coriander

1 teaspoon paprika

1 teaspoon kosher salt

3 tablespoons olive oil

4 lamb shanks

1½ tablespoons harissa

1 (14-ounce) can chopped tomatoes

1 tablespoon tomato paste

2 carrots, peeled and chopped into large chunks

1 cinnamon stick

1 cup beef broth

1 (14-ounce) can chickpeas, rinsed and drained

Juice of 1 lemon

Fresh cilantro, for garnish (optional)

1. Blend the red onion, garlic, ginger, ras el hanout, cumin, coriander, paprika, and salt in a food processor until it forms a smooth paste.

2. On the Sauté or Brown setting of your slow cooker, heat olive oil. Brown the lamb shanks on all sides, about 2 to 3 minutes per side. Remove and set aside.

3. In the same pot, add the spice mixture. Sauté until aromatic, roughly 3 to 4 minutes. Add the harissa and continue cooking for another 2 minutes.

4. Place the browned lamb shanks back into the pot. Add the chopped tomatoes, tomato paste, carrots, and cinnamon stick. Pour in the broth, ensuring the shanks are mostly covered.

5. Turn off the Sauté or Brown mode, and switch to slow cook on low. Cook for 5 hours. After 5 hours, gently mix in the chickpeas, ensuring they are submerged in the liquid. Continue cooking for an additional 2 to 3 hours or until the lamb is tender.

6. Once done, incorporate the lemon juice and adjust the seasoning as necessary.

7. Dish out the lamb shanks accompanied by the sauce, chickpeas, and carrots. Garnish with fresh cilantro.

SERVES 4

COUSCOUS

Traditional Couscous stands as an emblem of Moroccan heritage, embodying centuries of culinary wisdom passed down through generations. A dish often reserved for special occasions, it speaks to the nation's communal ethos, where families gather around a steaming pot, sharing tales and moments of togetherness. Historically, its preparation became a rhythmic dance of hands expertly rolling semolina, symbolizing patience and artistry. Couscous isn't merely food; it's a ritual, weaving together the threads of ancestry, celebration, and Moroccan identity.

2½ cups couscous

2½ cups warm water

½ teaspoon kosher salt

2 tablespoons oil (preferably olive oil)

3 tablespoons butter, diced

Slivered almonds or pine nuts (optional for garnish)

Mint, cilantro, finely chopped (optional for garnish)

1. In a large oven-safe dish, spread the couscous evenly. Slowly pour the warm water over the couscous, ensuring it's evenly distributed. Add the salt and mix thoroughly, ensuring all the couscous grains are moistened. Allow the couscous to sit and absorb the water, letting it swell for about 10 minutes.

2. Drizzle the oil over the swelled couscous. Gently rub the couscous between your hands to separate any lumps and to ensure each grain is individual and not sticking together.

3. Preheat your oven to 400°F. Place the oven-safe dish containing the couscous into the preheated oven and bake for approximately 20 minutes. This allows the couscous to cook thoroughly and develop a fluffy texture.

4. Remove the couscous from the oven. While it's still hot, scatter the diced butter over the top. Using a fork, fluff the couscous, ensuring the butter is well-distributed and melted throughout.

5. Toast slivered almonds or pine nuts lightly in a pan and sprinkle on top. Finely chop and fold mint and cilantro into the cooked couscous. Serve the couscous warm with the tagine dishes in this section.

SERVES 5

HARISSA

A traditional Tunisian condiment, harissa's origins stretch back centuries, when chili peppers arrived from the new world. Hand-pounded together with herbs and spices, harissa paste reflects generations of meticulous North African culinary customs. Beloved for its intense heat and complex flavor, harissa beautifully encapsulates the legacy of artisanal food craft in North Africa.

½ pound fresh red chili peppers, seeded and roughly chopped

3 large red roasted bell peppers, roughly chopped

4 cloves garlic, minced

½ preserved lemon, deseeded and finely chopped

⅔ cup extra-virgin olive oil, divided

1 teaspoon ground coriander

1½ teaspoons ground cumin

1½ teaspoons kosher salt

2 tablespoons sugar

1½ teaspoons smoked paprika

1. In a food processor, combine the red chili peppers, roasted bell peppers, minced garlic, and preserved lemon. Process until it becomes a consistent paste.

2. In a medium skillet, heat half of the olive oil over medium heat. Once the oil is hot, add the paste from the food processor to the skillet.

3. Then add coriander, cumin, salt, sugar, and smoked paprika. Mix well.

4. Reduce heat to low and allow the harissa to simmer gently for 15 to 20 minutes, stirring occasionally. Once the sauce has thickened slightly, remove from heat.

5. Allow it to cool to room temperature and then transfer to a clean, airtight glass jar. Pour the remaining olive oil over the top to create a protective layer. This will help preserve the harissa.

MAKES ABOUT **2** CUPS

JAZAR BIL KAMOUN WAL TOUM

MOROCCAN CARROTS WITH CHILI AND CUMIN

Jazar Bil Kamoun Wal Toum is deeply rooted in Morocco's culinary traditions, representing the nation's affinity for infusing simple ingredients with profound flavors. A testament to the region's legacy of communal feasts and vibrant marketplaces, this dish reflects a timeless bond between farmers, spice traders, and home cooks. Often gracing family tables and festive gatherings, it encapsulates shared stories, local pride, and the age-old Moroccan spirit of hospitality.

2 cups shredded carrots

2 tablespoons olive oil

4 cloves garlic, finely minced

1½ teaspoons ground cumin

½ teaspoon harissa, homemade (page 249) or store bought

1 teaspoon sweet paprika

Juice of 1 lemon

1 teaspoon red wine vinegar

½ bunch fresh cilantro, minced

½ bunch fresh parsley, minced

Kosher salt, to taste

1. Begin by slicing each carrot lengthwise into four equal sections. Cut each section further lengthwise in half to create slender sticks.

2. In a large pot, bring salted water to a boil. Add the carrot sticks and blanch for about 7 to 8 minutes, ensuring they are tender yet retain some crunch. Drain the carrots and immediately transfer them to cold water to halt the cooking process. Set aside.

3. In a pan, heat the olive oil over medium heat. Add minced garlic, sautéing until fragrant. Stir in the cumin, harissa, and paprika, and sauté for another minute.

4. Add the blanched carrot sticks to the pan. Sauté for 3 to 4 minutes, ensuring they are well-coated with the spice mixture. Stir in the lemon juice, red wine vinegar, minced cilantro, and parsley. Season with salt as desired, then remove from heat.

5. Let the carrot mixture marinate for at least 30 minutes in the refrigerator, allowing the flavors to meld. Before serving, garnish with additional fresh cilantro or parsley.

SERVES **4 — 6**

HARCHA

Originating from the Middle Atlas region of Morocco, Harcha are buttery, delicious semolina flatbreads that resemble English muffins but have more of a cornbread texture and are much richer. Enjoy them plain or sliced with jam, butter, and honey.

3½ cups semolina flour + more for rolling

1 teaspoon fine kosher salt

1 tablespoon baking powder

1½ cups butter, softened

2 tablespoons olive oil

3 tablespoons honey

1¼ cups warm buttermilk

1. Whisk together flour, salt, and baking powder. Mix butter and olive oil into flour with hands until an even crumb forms. Whisk together honey and buttermilk. Slowly add to the flour mixture. Mix until a damp dough forms. Allow to rest for 10 to 15 minutes so the moisture can absorb into the flour.

2. Scoop out about 6 tablespoons dough. Form a ball and roll in extra semolina. Flatten ball to ½-inch thickness. Stack uncooked harcha between pieces of parchment or set on a parchment-lined baking sheet. Preheat a skillet over medium-low heat. Add 2 to 3 harchas to skillet and cook for 6 to 8 minutes or until the first side is golden brown. Flip and cook the second side an additional 6 to 8 minutes.

3. Serve warm with butter and honey. Harcha are best the same day. Freeze leftovers in an airtight container for up to 1 month. To revive frozen harcha, place in a frying pan over medium-low heat and warm for 3 to 4 minutes per side.

MAKES **18**

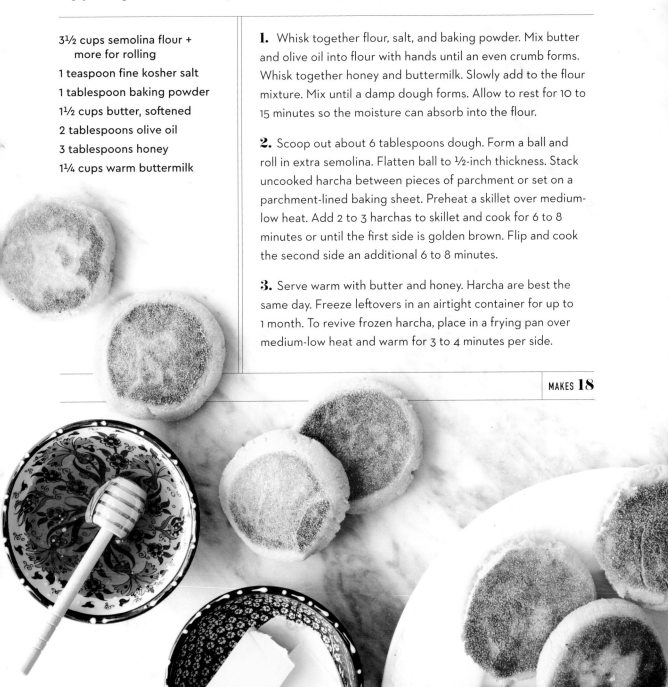

CHEBAKIA

A traditional favorite for Ramadan and other special occasions in Morocco—these flower-shaped cookies are fried and then dipped in a honey syrup and sprinkled with sesame seeds. The pastries are an important part of celebrations, and women traditionally gather to make them together. Shaping the dough takes some practice. If the flower shape is too challenging, simply cut strips and twist them. They will be crispy and chewy delicious regardless of shape.

CHEBAKIA

1 teaspoon yeast

1 teaspoon sugar

¼ cup warm milk

⅔ cup sesame seeds, toasted

2 cups all-purpose flour + more if needed

½ teaspoon baking powder

½ teaspoon fine kosher salt

½ teaspoon ground anise

1 teaspoon ground cinnamon

½ teaspoon saffron threads, crumbled

1 large egg

¼ cup unsalted butter, melted

2 tablespoons olive oil

1 tablespoon orange flower water

Peanut oil for frying

HONEY SYRUP

2 cups honey

1 tablespoon water

1 tablespoon orange blossom water

1. **To make chebakia:** Dissolve yeast and sugar in milk and set aside.

2. Reserve 2 tablespoons of toasted sesame seeds for garnish. Place the remainder in the bowl of a food processor and grind until paste-like. Add flour, baking powder, salt, ground anise, cinnamon, and saffron to ground sesame seeds and pulse to combine. Add flour mixture to the bowl of a stand mixer with the dough hook attachment. Add egg, melted butter, olive oil, orange flower water, and yeast mixture. Knead on medium until dough forms. If dough is too moist, add flour 1 tablespoon at a time until a firm dough is achieved. Continue to knead on medium for 5 more minutes.

3. Divide dough in two parts. Roll out one part to ⅛-inch thickness. With a pastry wheel, cut into 2½ × 3-inch rectangles. In center of one rectangle make 4 (2-inch) cuts parallel with the short side of rectangle to create 5 columns (see photo A). Slide two fingers through cuts, with column 1, 3, and 5 on top of fingers and column 2 and 4 below fingers (see photo B). Grasp column 5 and pull it through the space your fingers are holding open (see photo C). This will turn the dough inside out and form a flower shape. Pinch the dough on both sides (see photo D).

4. Clip a candy thermometer to a heavy-bottomed pot or Dutch oven, and preheat 2 to 3 inches oil to 350°F.

5. **While oil is preheating, make honey syrup:** In a small saucepan over medium heat, whisk together honey, water, and orange blossom water. Cook until mixture comes together. Reduce temperature to low to keep warm.

6. To fry chebakia: Line another baking sheet with parchment and set a cooling rack on top. Add 4 to 5 chebakia to the preheated oil and cook for about 2 to 3 minutes on each side, or until golden brown on both side. Remove with a metal skimmer or strainer. Allow oil to drain before placing them in honey syrup. Allow each to soak for 1 minute. Remove from honey syrup with tongs or slotted spatula. Allow syrup to drip back into your pan. Set chebakia on prepared baking sheet to drain. Sprinkle with sesame seeds and serve immediately. Chebakia tastes best on the day it's made. Store leftovers in an airtight container for up to 2 days.

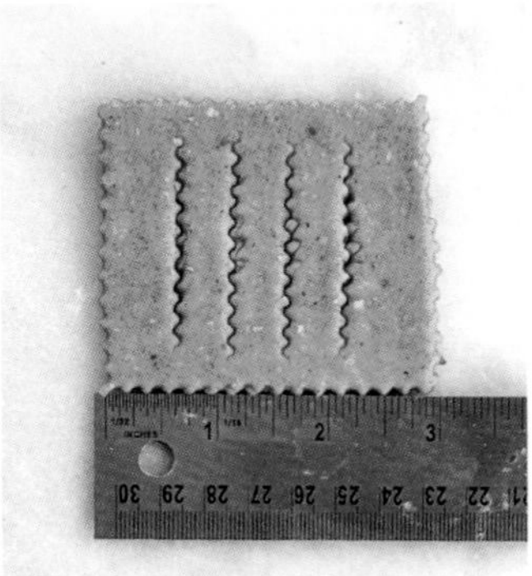

A

B

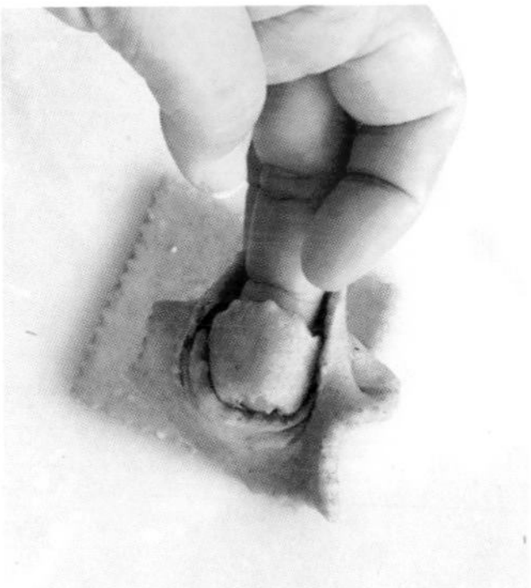
C

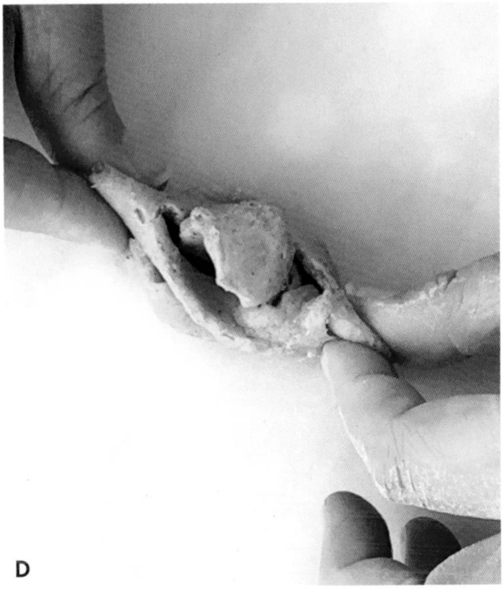
D

MAKES **40**

GAZELLE HORNS

Simple, delicious flavors make these pretty little pastries a hit with a crowd. Gazelle Horns are a traditional Moroccan treat and go great with coffee or tea.

PASTRY

2 cups all-purpose or pastry flour

1 teaspoon kosher salt

1 cup unsalted butter

¼–½ cup ice water

ALMOND PASTE

2 cups blanched whole almonds

¾ cup confectioners' sugar

½ teaspoon cinnamon

¼ cup unsalted butter, softened

1 tablespoon orange blossom water

1 teaspoon almond extract

Confectioners' sugar for dusting

NOTE: The almond paste may crumble while forming logs. The pastry will hold it all together so don't worry if the almond paste is in more than one piece when placing in the pastry.

1. **To make the pastry:** In a medium bowl, mix the flour and salt. Slice the butter into small pats and toss into the flour-salt mixture. Cut the butter and flour mixture with a pastry blender until you have a fine crumb. Do not overmix.

2. Sprinkle about half of the ice water over the crumb mixture. Combine with your hands, squeezing the crumbs together until a dough forms. If the dough doesn't come together, add more ice water 1 tablespoon at a time until you get the dough to form. Divide dough in half and form two discs. Wrap each in plastic wrap and refrigerate for 1 hour or up 24 hours.

3. **To make the almond paste:** Preheat oven to 325°F. Place almonds on a single layer on a baking sheet. Toast almonds for 5 minutes. Allow almonds to cool. In the bowl of a food processor, process cooled almonds until coarse. Add sugar and process until a paste forms. Add cinnamon, butter, orange blossom water, and almond extract. Process until fully combined. Scrape bottom and sides of food processor bowl, and then pulse to be sure ingredients are evenly combined.

4. **To assemble:** Preheat oven to 375°F. Line a baking sheet with parchment or a silicone baking mat. Roll out first pastry disc to ⅛-inch thickness. Cut 4-inch by 2½-inch rectagles. Scoop 2 to 3 teaspoons almond paste and form a log. Place on one pastry rectangle. Fold pastry over almond log and crimp edges. Curve to form a crescent shape. Using a pastry wheel cut off any extra pastry. Poke several holes in the pastry to release steam. Place on prepared baking sheet, leaving 1 inch between each Gazelle Horn.

5. Bake for 12 to 14 minutes. Gazelle Horns will still be quite light in color. The pastry is meant to stay soft, not golden and crisp. Dust with confectioners' sugar and allow to cool completely. Serve or store in an airtight container for up to 3 days.

MAKES **28**

ETHIOPIAN BOARD

Ethiopian cuisine, rich in history and communal values, is a compelling narrative of age-old social and religious ethos. Central to this narrative is Gursha, a tradition that goes beyond mere dining to a warm exchange of camaraderie. The sourdough flatbread, Injera, is not merely a staple, but a symbol of unity, inviting individuals to come together, share meals, and forge connections over a shared plate.

A fascinating aspect is the culinary parallel between Ethiopian and Indo-Pakistani cuisines, hinting at possible historical exchanges. Both culinary traditions exhibit a fondness for a spectrum of spices like cumin, coriander, cardamom, and fenugreek, infusing meals with unique, yet somewhat familiar flavors. The Ethiopian Berbere finds a distant cousin in Indo-Pakistani Garam Masala, each with its unique blend, embodying the culinary essence of their respective cultures.

The significance of lentils and legumes is another common thread, echoing a shared tradition of wholesome, comforting meals like the Ethiopian Misir Wat and the assortment of Dals in Indo-Pakistani cuisine. The communal experience of enjoying meals with flatbreads like Injera, Roti, or Naan underscores a shared dining ethos. Through these culinary intersections, one uncovers not only the subtleties of flavors but a dialogue of shared culinary traditions, enriching the narrative of these ancient, yet ever-evolving cuisines. —M.M.

RECIPES

EXTRAS

Berbere spice blend (store-bought)

Fresh chopped vegetables of your choice: tomatoes, onion, cucumbers, and peppers

Cilantro

MAKE AHEAD

Start injera process 6 days in advance of serving.

Niter Kibbeh can be made a week in advance.

TIME SAVERS

Purchase injera from a local Ethiopian restaurant.

Styling Ideas

Use traditional Ethiopian fabrics, baskets, and pottery.

SIX-DAY AUTHENTIC INJERA

Injera—a spongy, sour, fermented flatbread—is the foundation for many Ethiopian dishes, oftentimes even becoming the serving platter for a meal. Pieces of injera are torn off and used to scoop stews and salads, eliminating a need for utensils. Traditional injera is made with teff flour and takes days to achieve proper fermentation. If you want to make it with the most authentic flavor, plan six days ahead and use this recipe.

STARTER

2 cups ground teff flour

1¼ cups water

INJERA BATTER

3 cups ground teff flour

½ teaspoon fine kosher salt

1 cup starter

3 cups warm water

ABSIT

1 cup water + more to thin batter

½ cup batter

NOTE: Teff flour is made from an ancient, gluten-free grain that grows in the horn of Africa. It is available in both brown and ivory and you can use either color to make your injera.

1. Day 1: Make the starter: In a medium bowl, mix teff and water with hands until there are no lumps. Add starter mixture to a 1-liter glass mason jar. Cover tightly and allow to set at room temperature for 4 days.

2. Day 4: Make the batter: In a medium bowl, mix teff and salt. Carefully pour off water from the top of the starter and stir. Add starter and warm water to teff. Stir with a rubber spatula until completely incorporated. Clean any dough from sides of bowl. Cover and allow to rest for 2 days.

3. Day 6: Make the absit: Remove any water that formed on surface of the batter. Boil 1 cup of water over medium-high heat. Add ½ cup of batter and whisk constantly until a thick paste forms. Remove from heat. Allow to cool until absit is warm. Add absit to the rest of the batter. Whisk until there are no lumps. Add more water until batter is quite thin. Batter should be thick enough to coat the spatula but will run off quickly. Cover and allow to rest an additional 2 hours.

4. To cook the injera: Preheat a crepe pan or mitad over medium-high heat. Pour batter in a circle, starting at the edge and spiraling until you reach the center. Small bubbles will start to appear almost immediately. Allow most of the surface to form spots (or "eyes") and cover and cook 3 to 4 more minutes. Do not flip injera. When injera is finished cooking, the edges of the injera will have started to lift off the cooking surface. Use a flat plate or cutting board to remove injera from cooking surface. Place pieces of parchment between injera. Serve immediately by either using the injera as a platter for other dishes or roll injera and include as a side.

MAKES **5** 11-INCH INJERA

NITER KIBBEH

ETHIOPIAN SPICED CLARIFIED BUTTER

Niter Kibbeh is a spiced clarified butter integral to Ethiopian cuisine. Originating from centuries-old culinary traditions, it's crafted by slowly simmering butter with a medley of herbs and spices, resulting in a fragrant and flavorful base for many dishes.

1 pound unsalted butter

1 large yellow onion, chopped

3–4 cloves garlic, coarsely chopped

1½ tablespoons ginger, freshly chopped or grated

1½ teaspoons fenugreek seeds

1 teaspoon turmeric powder

3 black cardamom pods, lightly crushed

2–3 green cardamom pods, crushed

1 teaspoon whole allspice berries

1 cinnamon stick

2–3 cloves

1 teaspoon cumin seeds

1 teaspoon coriander seeds

¼ teaspoon nutmeg

1. In a heavy-bottomed saucepan, melt the butter slowly over medium-low heat, occasionally swirling it around. Once the butter is melted, add the onions, garlic, and ginger. Let them soften slightly in the butter but not brown.

2. Add in all the spices: fenugreek seeds, turmeric, black and green cardamom pods, allspice berries, cinnamon, cloves, cumin seeds, coriander seeds, and nutmeg.

3. Reduce the heat to the lowest setting and let the butter gently simmer for about 30 to 45 minutes. The butter will become clear, and milk solids will settle to the bottom of the saucepan. The spices and aromatics will infuse their flavors into the butter during this simmering. Ensure the butter doesn't boil too quickly to prevent the spices from burning.

4. After the simmering process, remove the saucepan from heat and let it cool slightly. Skim off any foam on top. Line a strainer with a dampened clean cheesecloth. Carefully ladle the butter through this strainer into a clean jar or container, leaving behind the milk solids and spices.

5. Allow the Niter Kibbeh to cool to room temperature. Once cooled, store in the refrigerator. It will solidify but easily melts upon heating.

TIPS: Ensure that the heat remains consistently low to prevent the butter from burning. The aim is to let the spices infuse their flavors into the butter without getting overcooked.

Niter Kibbeh has a long shelf life when stored in a cool place.

MAKES ABOUT 1½ CUPS

KEY SIR

BRAISED BEET WITH JALAPEÑOS

Key Sir, a dish of braised beets with jalapeños, is deeply rooted in Ethiopia's agricultural traditions. In a country where communal dining is the norm, dishes like this are more than just food; they're a reflection of shared experiences and centuries of agricultural practices. The fertile Ethiopian highlands, known for diverse crops, produce vibrant beets which are celebrated in this dish. The addition of jalapeños adds a layer of heat, echoing Ethiopia's penchant for spicy flavors, commonly seen with their berbere spice blends.

2 tablespoons canola oil

1 medium yellow onion, finely chopped

4 cloves garlic, finely chopped, divided

1 tablespoon grated fresh ginger

1 teaspoon berbere spice blend (store-bought)

Kosher salt, to taste

2 cups medium beets, shredded using a box grater or a food processor

2 jalapeño peppers, sliced

Juice of ½ lemon

1. In a large skillet or pan, heat the canola oil over medium heat. Once the oil is hot, add the chopped onions. Sauté until the onions are translucent and soft, about 5 to 7 minutes.

2. Add the chopped garlic and grated ginger to the skillet. Continue to sauté for another 2 minutes or until the garlic is fragrant.

3. Add berbere spice blend and salt and mix well. Then stir in the shredded beets. Allow the beets to cook, stirring occasionally, for about 10 to 12 minutes. They should begin to soften and meld with the other flavors in the pan.

4. Add the sliced jalapeño peppers to the skillet. Mix well to ensure the ingredients are evenly distributed.

5. Cover the skillet and reduce heat to low. Continue to cook for another 10 minutes. The beets should be tender at this point. Drizzle the lemon juice over the mixture and stir well. Continue to cook on a simmer for another 2 to 3 minutes until all the flavors are well combined.

6. Remove the skillet from the heat and transfer the Key Sir to a serving dish.

7. Key Sir can be enjoyed both warm and cold. Serve warm as a side dish with injera.

SERVES **4 – 6**

ATAKILT WAT

POTATOES AND CABBAGE IN GINGER TUMERIC SAUCE

Traditionally, carrots are also added to this dish. In my version, I chose to omit them. Feel free to add a cup of sliced carrots to your version. —M.M.

½ head green cabbage, cored and thinly sliced

2 tablespoons canola oil

2 medium yellow onions, finely sliced

1 tablespoon finely chopped fresh garlic

1 tablespoon finely chopped fresh ginger

½ teaspoon ground turmeric

1 teaspoon berbere spice blend (store-bought)

½ tablespoon ground cumin

½ tablespoon ground black pepper

½ teaspoon kosher salt

2 medium white potatoes, peeled and cut into bite-sized pieces

¾ cup water

Cilantro, for garnishing

1. Place the thinly sliced cabbage into a bowl with warm salted water. Gently swish the cabbage around to remove any dirt. After a few moments, drain the cabbage and set aside.

2. In a large skillet or pot, heat the oil over medium-low heat. Add the finely sliced onions, cooking them until they're translucent and soft, which should take about 10 minutes.

3. Add chopped garlic and ginger. Allow them to cook with the onions for 2 to 3 minutes, ensuring they become fragrant but don't burn.

4. Add the turmeric, berbere spice blend, ground cumin, black pepper, and salt, stirring well to evenly coat the onions.

5. Add the cabbage and potato pieces to the skillet. Mix well with the onion and spice mixture, ensuring an even coating.

6. Add the water to the skillet, then reduce the heat to low. Cover the skillet or pot with a lid and let everything simmer gently for about 20 to 25 minutes.

7. After the simmering time, check that the potatoes are tender and fully cooked. If not, you can continue cooking for an additional 5 to 10 minutes.

8. Transfer to serving dish and garnish with fresh cilantro. Sprinkle some Toasted Cumin Powder (page 54) for extra flavor.

SERVES **4 – 6**

ATER KIK ALICHA

YELLOW SPLIT PEA STEW

Ater Kik Alicha, an Ethiopian yellow split pea stew, mirrors the comforting essence of Pakistani Dal. A nod to shared culinary threads, it celebrates communal dining and age-old agricultural traditions.

1¼ cups yellow split peas

¼ cup niter kibbeh (you can substitute with canola or another neutral oil)

2 medium yellow onions, finely chopped

1 tablespoon finely chopped garlic

½ tablespoon freshly grated ginger

½ tablespoon turmeric powder

¼ tablespoon Ajwain (also known as Bishop's weed or carom seeds)

1 green pepper, deseeded and finely chopped

1. Start by rinsing the yellow split peas several times in cold water until the water runs clear. This removes any residual dirt or starch.

2. Place the washed split peas in a pot with enough water to cover them. Bring to a boil and then reduce to a simmer. Cook for 45 to 60 minutes or until the peas are soft but not completely mushy. Drain the water and set aside.

3. In a large pot or skillet, heat the niter kibbeh or oil over medium heat. Add the finely chopped onions, stirring occasionally until they become translucent and soft.

4. Add the chopped garlic and grated ginger. Sauté for another 2 to 3 minutes. Then add turmeric and Ajwain. Mix well, ensuring the onions are well-coated with the spices. Allow to cook for about 2 minutes, stirring occasionally.

5. Add the drained split peas to the pot. Gently stir, making sure the peas are well mixed with the spiced onion mixture. If you prefer a smoother consistency, you can mash some of the peas using the back of your spoon.

6. Finally, add the green pepper to the pot. Stir gently, cover, and let it simmer on low heat for about 10 to 15 minutes, allowing all the flavors to meld together. If the mixture is too thick, you can add a bit of water to achieve your desired consistency.

SERVES **4–6**

GOMEN WAT

COLLARD GREENS STEW

Gomen Wat, an Ethiopian collard greens stew, is seasoned with aromatic spices, bearing a resemblance to various leafy green preparations across cultures. Its deep, earthy flavors can remind one of the heartiness found in many Asian and African dishes, emphasizing the universality of using greens as a staple.

2 bunches fresh collard greens (you can substitute with kale)

¼ cup niter kibbeh (you can substitute with canola or another neutral oil)

2 medium yellow onions, finely chopped

3-4 cloves garlic, minced

1 tablespoon finely grated fresh ginger

2-3 green jalapeños, deseeded and sliced

½ teaspoon cardamom powder

1 teaspoon ground cumin

½ teaspoon turmeric powder

½ cup vegetable broth

½ teaspoon kosher salt

1. Thoroughly wash the collard greens to remove any grit. Remove the thick stems and roughly chop the leaves.

2. In a large pot of boiling water, blanch the chopped collard greens for 2 to 3 minutes. Drain and set aside. This step helps to soften the greens and remove any bitterness.

3. In a large pot or skillet, melt the niter kibbeh or oil of choice over medium heat. Add the onions and sauté until translucent, about 6 to 8 minutes.

4. Add the minced garlic, grated ginger, and sliced jalapeños to the pot and sauté for another 2 to 3 minutes. Then add the cardamom, cumin, and turmeric. Cook for an additional 1 to 2 minutes. Add the blanched collard greens to the pot, stirring well to coat the greens in the spiced onion mixture.

5. Finally, add vegetable broth. Reduce the heat to low, cover, and let the stew simmer for 20 to 25 minutes, stirring occasionally. If the mixture becomes too dry, you can add a bit more water.

6. Once the collard greens are tender, add the salt and take off the heat. Serve hot.

SERVES **4–6**

SHIRO WAT

CHICKPEA STEW

Shiro Wat is a hearty Ethiopian stew, central to many meals and made primarily from ground chickpeas or broad bean flour. A testament to the global love for legumes, its rich, spiced profile can evoke memories of other chickpea dishes, like Indian chana masala or Middle Eastern hummus, showcasing the chickpea's versatility across cuisines.

SHIRO POWDER

1 cup chickpea flour

2 tablespoons berbere spice blend (store-bought)

1 teaspoon cardamom powder

1½ teaspoons ground cumin

1 teaspoon garlic powder

SHIRO WAT

2 tablespoons niter kibbeh (Ethiopian spiced butter) or regular unsalted butter

1 large onion, finely chopped

2–3 cloves garlic, minced

1 tablespoon ginger, minced

2 tablespoons berbere spice blend (store-bought)

1 cup shiro powder

2½ cups low-sodium vegetable broth

½ teaspoon kosher salt

NOTE: If you live near an Ethiopian neighborhood, you can actually buy shiro powder off-the-shelf or order it online.

1. **To make the shiro powder:** In a dry skillet over medium heat, add the chickpea flour. Toast gently for about 5 to 7 minutes, stirring continuously to ensure it doesn't burn. The flour should turn fragrant and slightly darker in shade. Remove from heat and let it cool.

2. Combine the toasted chickpea flour, berbere spice mix, cardamom powder, ground cumin, and garlic powder in a bowl. Mix thoroughly to ensure even distribution of spices.

3. Store in an airtight container in a cool, dark place.

4. **To make the shiro wat:** In a pot or a large skillet, melt the niter kibbeh or unsalted butter over medium heat. Add the finely chopped onions and sauté until they become translucent and soft. This may take about 8 to 10 minutes.

5. Stir in the minced garlic and ginger to the onions and cook for another 2 to 3 minutes. Then add the berbere spice and sauté for another minute. Gradually add the shiro powder to the pot, 1 tablespoon at a time, continuously stirring to avoid lumps. Slowly pour in vegetable broth while stirring. The consistency you're aiming for is similar to a thick soup or stew. If it's too thick, you can always add a bit more broth.

6. Add salt and reduce the heat to low, cover the pot, and let the stew simmer for 15 to 20 minutes. Stir occasionally to avoid sticking at the bottom. The shiro will thicken as it cooks.

SERVES **4–6**

SPRIS

LAYERED FRUIT SMOOTHIE DRINK

A Spris is a blend of various fruit juices or purees layered artistically in a glass. While it can be made with any combination of fruits, some popular choices include avocado, mango, papaya, guava, orange, and banana. The charm of the Spris lies in its separate layers, each retaining its unique taste. This allows for a multi-sensory experience, where with each sip, you can either savor individual fruit flavors or mix them for a combined taste. I added pomegranate molasses in my version for added texture and flavor. —M.M.

2 ripe avocados, pitted and scooped

1 ripe mango, peeled, pitted, and chopped

1 ripe papaya, peeled, seeded, and chopped

Juice of 1 lime, freshly squeezed

6 ice cubes, divided

¼ cup pomegranate molasses or honey for drizzling (optional), divided

Fresh mint leaves, for garnish

1. Ensure the fruits have been chopped into manageable pieces for blending.

2. For the avocado layer, add the avocado to the blender, along with lime juice and 2 ice cubes. Blend until smooth. Pour the avocado blend as the first layer into your serving glass(es). Then lightly drizzle pomegranate molasses or honey for added sweetness (optional).

3. Clean the blender and add the mango and 2 ice cubes. Carefully pour this as the second layer. Then lightly drizzle pomegranate molasses or honey for added sweetness (optional).

4. Clean the blender one more time and blend the papaya with 2 ice cubes. Pour this as the third and top layer. Lightly drizzle pomegranate molasses or honey for added sweetness (optional).

5. Garnish with fresh mint leaves and serve immediately.

SERVES **2**

MEXICAN TABLE

"Tacos are like what the voices of a hundred angels singing Bob Dylan while sitting on rainbows and playing banjos would taste like if that sound were edible." —ISABEL QUINTERO

Mexican cuisine is a vibrant fusion of multiple heritages and influences with its heart in the ancient cultures of Mesoamerica. The Maya and Aztec based their diets on native crops—maize, beans, tomatoes, avocados, chilis, cacao, and squash. The Spaniards brought over new ingredients, such as cilantro, meats, dairy, onions, garlic, rice, and wheat. They also brought recipes that are now so much a part of Mexican cuisine that we often identify them as Mexican, such as chorizo, arroz con pollo, flan, and churros. The French brought cooking and baking techniques that evolved into complex sauces and sweet Mexican favorites like Orejas and Conchas. The complexity of the flavors and rich history of the ingredients make Mexican food one of the most popular around the world. Americans have long been enamored with Mexican food—especially tacos. Even if we haven't always gotten it right, our reverence and admiration for the cuisine is real. Since childhood, Mexican food has always been my most-loved, top-choice meal. This table is a roundup of some of our favorite flavors—wrapping the rich food of Spain in traditional Mayan and Aztec corn grains and covering the whole thing with avocado, cilantro, and lime deliciousness. This table will be loved by your guests any day of the week—not just on Tuesdays. —L.K.

MAKE AHEAD

Salsa Verde, Black Beans, and Chile con Queso can be made up to 3 days in advance and stored in an airtight container in the refrigerator.

Pickled Red Onions can be made up to 2 weeks in advance.

Marinate the chicken for Street-Style Grilled Chicken Tacos the night before.

Make Tres Leches Cake Cups the day before to give the cake time to soak in the milks.

Conchas can be made up to a month in advance. Freeze in an airtight container. Warm in a 275°F oven for 10 to 12 minutes.

EXTRAS

Tortilla chips

Queso fresco

Cilantro and lime wedges for garnish

Margaritas

Add roasted corn to Pico de Gallo for an extra salsa variety

TIME SAVERS

Purchase tortillas and warm before serving.

Purchase conchas from a Mexican Panaderia.

Use canned black beans to make refried black beans.

Styling Ideas

Create an assemble-yourself taco board. Wrap tortillas in towels to keep warm. Serve meats and fish on a platter. Serve vegetarian fillings separately. Surround tray with salsas and toppings.

RECIPES

FRESH CORN TORTILLAS

The ingredients couldn't get any simpler than homemade corn tortillas. The process takes some practice and sometimes a little trial-and-error. The consistency of the masa (dough) needs to be just right and your pan or griddle needs to be at the right temperature to cook properly. Wrapping tortillas in a towel immediately after cooking is an essential step to getting soft, pliable results. The steam trapped in the towel keeps the tortillas soft and hot until you're ready to eat them. Once you've gotten the hang of it, you'll never go back to packaged tortillas. A taco made with a homemade fresh tortilla is perfection, and simply can't be beat. —L.K.

EQUIPMENT
Tortilla press

2 cups (210 grams) Masa Harina

1¼ cups warm water + more if needed

½ teaspoon fine kosher salt (optional)

1. Combine all ingredients in a medium bowl and knead together with one hand—scooping masa from bottom of bowl and punching down with your fist. Work the dough this way for about 3 minutes. Check masa for the correct consistency. Make a small ball with the masa. If it sticks to your hands, it needs more masa harina, sprinkle in a little at a time, working the dough until it comes together. Keep adding a little at a time until you reach a workable consistency. If, when you make the masa ball, it cracks, then you need more water. Add a little water at a time, kneading the dough until you get the correct consistency.

2. Preheat a skillet or griddle over medium to medium-high heat. Set out a clean kitchen towel near stove. Cut two parchment pieces roughly the size of your tortilla press. Create a 1½-inch ball of masa. Place one piece of parchment on the bottom of open tortilla press. Place masa ball in center of parchment. Place second parchment on top of masa. Close lid and press. Open press and rotate parchment and dough 180 degrees and press again. Doing this second step will give you a more evenly flattened tortilla. Cook about 2 minutes on the first side. When you flip it, the tortilla should have some brown spots. If it appears undercooked, raise temperature a little. If the tortilla has black spots, reduce temperature and wait 3 to 4 minutes for pan to cool before trying again.

CONTINUED

3. When everything is working together correctly—thickness of tortilla, temperature—the tortilla will puff after flipping. If it doesn't puff, you can try lightly pressing around the edge of tortilla with an offset spatula. Don't worry if it doesn't puff—the tortilla will still be delicious. The tortilla is ready when both sides have light brown spots. Place tortilla in towel and wrap edge of towel over top of tortilla to keep warm. Continue pressing and cooking the rest of tortillas. You can usually cook multiple tortillas at the same time depending on how large your cook surface is.

4. Fresh corn tortillas taste best right after cooking. Try to estimate how many you need so you won't have many leftovers.

NOTES: If tortilla sticks to cooking surface, the masa is too wet. To resolve, work in a little more masa harina. Clean any masa stuck to skillet or griddle before cooking more tortillas.

Masa harina is easy to find in most grocery stores. Maseca is the most popular brand. It is also available in a variety of colors, made from different color corn. Add some variety to your spread by mixing up the colors.

MAKES ABOUT **20**

FRESH FLOUR TORTILLAS

Growing up eating packaged tortillas, I was floored the first time I had a fresh tortilla and I went about trying to find a place to get them. Most restaurants use the packaged kind, so the most reliable place to find these is your own kitchen. Once you get the hang of it, they are easy to make and so worth the effort. —L.K.

3 cups all-purpose flour + more for rolling

1 teaspoon baking powder

½ teaspoon kosher salt

⅓ cup butter, room temperature, or shortening

¾ to 1 cup hot water

1. Mix flour, baking powder, salt, and shortening or butter with a pastry blender until a crumb forms. Slowly add water until dough comes together. You may not need all of the water. Divide into 30 balls, flatten slightly. Cover with a damp towel and allow to rest 45 minutes.

2. Place a tortilla warmer or a pan with a lid near stove. Preheat a skillet or griddle over medium heat. Roll out first dough disk on a lightly floured work surface. Roll out very thin to about a 5½-inch circle. Use as little flour as possible when rolling out. Brush excess flour off tortilla with a pastry brush. Place tortilla on preheated pan and cook for 1 to 2 minutes. Flip when bottom has light brown spots on it. If it's cooking too slowly, increase the temperature slightly. Cook on second side for an additional minute or until light brown spots appear. Place in tortilla warmer or pan and cover. Trapped steam will keep tortillas pliable, soft, and hot. Continue cooking remainder of tortillas. You can usually cook multiple tortillas at the same time depending on how large your cook surface is.

3. Store leftover flour tortillas in an airtight container in refrigerator for up to 4 days. To revive cold tortillas, brush a skillet with vegetable oil and warm tortillas over medium heat for about 2 minutes each.

MAKES **30**

BAJA FISH TACOS

Epitomizing the seafood traditions of Mexico's Baja peninsula, Baja fish tacos balance lightly fried white fish with creamy Mexican crema and salsas, all tucked into a warm corn tortilla. This iconic beachside street food emerged locally in Ensenada before spreading across the Mexico-California border. The name honors Mexico's Baja California, where Pacific flavors first fused into the beloved fish taco.

FISH
2 pounds white fish filets (preferably cod, halibut, or mahi-mahi)

Kosher salt and pepper, to taste

Juice of 1 lime

BATTER
1½ cups all-purpose flour

½ cup rice flour

1 teaspoon baking powder

½ teaspoon kosher salt

½ teaspoon ground black pepper

½ teaspoon ground cumin

½ teaspoon paprika

2 cups cold club soda or beer

Frying-grade oil

CABBAGE SLAW
1 tablespoon apple cider vinegar

1 tablespoon honey

Juice of 1 lime

½ teaspoon kosher salt

1 cup finely shredded purple cabbage

¼ cup finely chopped fresh cilantro

½ small red onion, thinly sliced

1 jalapeño, seeded and minced

1. **To prepare the fish:** Slice the fish filets lengthwise, then cut diagonally into 3-inch strips. Season with salt, pepper, and lime juice. Marinate for 30 minutes in the fridge.

2. **To prepare the batter:** In a bowl, mix together all-purpose flour, rice flour, baking powder, salt, ground black pepper, ground cumin, and paprika. Gradually add the club soda, stirring continuously to prevent clumps from forming. Adjust until the batter achieves a thick but pourable consistency. Let the mixture sit for 5 minutes.

3. **To fry the fish:** Heat frying-grade oil in a large pot until it reaches the appropriate frying temperature. Use a thermometer to accurately monitor the temperature. The oil should be about 3 inches deep.

4. Dredge the marinated fish pieces in the batter, shaking off any excess, then carefully lower the fish into the hot oil. Fry the fish in small batches to prevent overcrowding. Once the fish is cooked and crispy, transfer it to a wire rack.

5. **To prepare the cabbage slaw:** In a medium bowl, combine the apple cider vinegar, honey, lime juice, and salt. Whisk until all ingredients are combined. Add the shredded cabbage, cilantro, red onion, and jalapeño and mix until everything is evenly coated.

CONTINUED

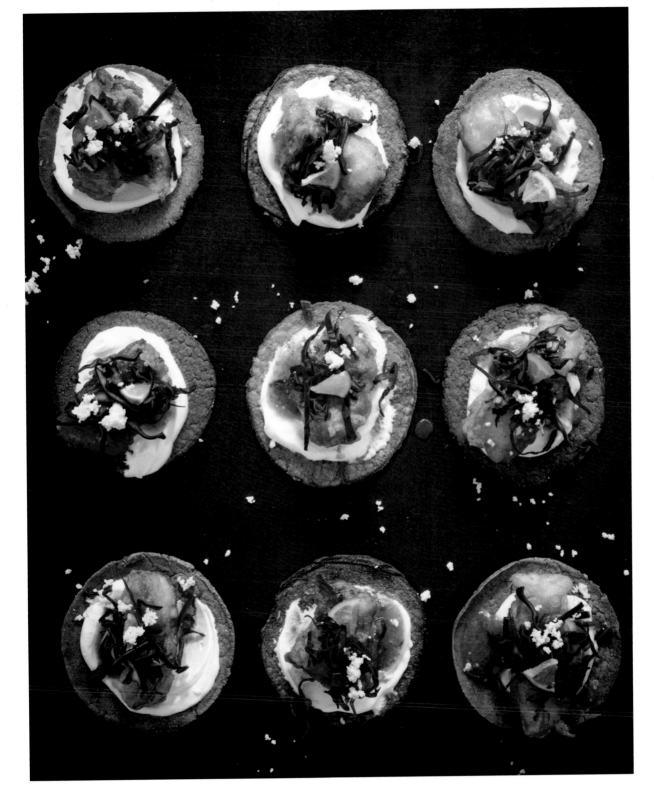

CREMA

½ cup sour cream

¼ cup yogurt

Juice and zest of 1 lime

1 tablespoon finely chopped
canned chipotle pepper
(optional)

GARNISH

1 lime, cut into wedges

1 avocado, sliced

Fresh cilantro

Tortillas

6. **To prepare the crema:** In a medium bowl, combine the sour cream, yogurt, lime juice, and finely chopped chipotle pepper. Mix until all the ingredients are well combined.

7. **To assemble the tacos:** Heat the tortillas in a dry pan over medium heat for about 30 seconds on each side.

8. Spread some of the crema onto a warm tortilla, add a piece or two of fried fish, top with slaw and avocado slices. Repeat with the remaining tortillas.

9. Serve the tacos with additional lime wedges on the side. Garnish the tacos with fresh cilantro for added flavor.

MAKES **8**

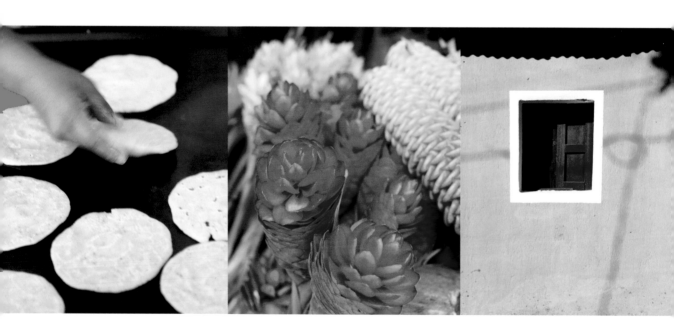

VEGETARIAN TACOS

Showcasing Mexico's affinity for fresh produce, these vegetarian tacos highlight colorful bell peppers and onions sautéed with classic Mexican seasonings of garlic, cumin, and oregano. Hearty black beans add protein. Wrapped in warm corn tortillas, the tacos balance flavor and nutrition. This meatless take encapsulates the resourcefulness of traditional Mexican cooking.

1 tablespoon olive oil

1 red onion, thinly sliced

1 red bell pepper, thinly sliced

1 green bell pepper, thinly sliced

1 jalapeño, seeded and minced

3 cloves garlic, minced

1 teaspoon cumin

1 teaspoon oregano

1 cup Refried Black Beans (page 286)

Fresh Corn Tortillas (page 273) or Fresh Flour Tortillas (page 275)

TOPPINGS

Lime, cut into wedges

1 avocado, sliced

Fresh cilantro chopped

Queso, crumbled

1. In a large skillet over medium-high heat, add the olive oil. When hot, add the onions and cook for 2 to 3 minutes until starting to soften. Add the bell peppers and cook for 3 to 4 more minutes until tender but still crisp. Add the jalapeño, garlic, cumin, and oregano. Cook for 1 minute until fragrant. Remove from heat.

2. Warm fresh tortillas or packaged tortillas on a dry grill or skillet for a few seconds on each side. Top with the black beans and then peppers. Add your choice of toppings and sauces.

MAKES **6**

GROUND BEEF TACOS

As much as us gringos love to add cheese, tomatoes, and lettuce to our tacos, none of these toppings are part of a typical Mexican taco. Being a huge fan of cheese, I never imagined that I could love a taco without it, but these are amazing with just the meat, white onion, a generous amount of cilantro, and a squeeze of lime. Of course a homemade fresh corn tortilla is the perfect base for this simple taco perfection. —L.K.

TACOS

1 pound ground beef

1 small onion, diced

2 cloves garlic, finely chopped

1 tablespoon chili powder

1 teaspoon ground cumin

¼ teaspoon paprika

¼ teaspoon oregano

½ teaspoon kosher salt

¼ teaspoon black pepper, freshly ground

2 tablespoons tomato paste

½ cup diced tomatoes

10 Fresh Corn Tortillas (page 273)

TOPPINGS

¾ cup chopped white onion

¾ cup chopped fresh cilantro

3 limes cut into wedges

1. Over medium heat, place the ground beef in a large skillet. Cook the beef until it is fully browned, breaking it up into crumbles as it cooks, for about 5 to 7 minutes.

2. Once the beef is browned, drain off the excess fat, leaving a small amount to cook the onions and garlic. Add the diced onion to the skillet with the beef, sautéing until it becomes translucent, about 3 to 5 minutes. Add the chopped garlic and cook for 1 additional minute.

3. Add the chili powder, ground cumin, paprika, oregano, kosher salt, and freshly ground black pepper to the beef mixture. Stir thoroughly, ensuring the spices are evenly distributed throughout the beef. Add tomato paste and diced tomatoes and stir again.

4. Cover the skillet and cook on simmer for about 10 to 15 minutes, enabling the flavors to fully integrate.

5. Divide meat between tortillas. Top with onion, cilantro, and serve with lime wedges.

MAKES **10** TACOS

STREET-STYLE GRILLED CHICKEN TACOS

A true homage to Mexico's bustling street food scene, these Street-Style Grilled Chicken Tacos encapsulate the essence of vibrant open-air markets. Succulent chicken, kissed by fire, melds with traditional spices, echoing the age-old traditions and spirited heartbeats of Mexican plazas.

3 cloves garlic, finely chopped

2 tablespoons fresh lime juice

1 tablespoon apple cider vinegar

¼ cup freshly squeezed orange juice

1 tablespoon olive oil

½ cup chopped cilantro

1 teaspoon ground cumin

1 teaspoon ancho chili powder (or substitute with chipotle chili or paprika)

1 teaspoon kosher salt

¼ teaspoon black pepper, freshly ground

1½ pounds chicken breast or thighs

Fresh Corn Tortillas (page 273) or Fresh Flour Tortillas (page 275)

1. **To marinate the chicken:** In a medium-sized bowl, create the marinade by combining the garlic, lime juice, apple cider vinegar, orange juice, olive oil, cilantro, ground cumin, ancho chili powder, salt, and black pepper. Stir until well mixed.

2. Add the chicken to the marinade. Ensure that the chicken is thoroughly coated. Let it marinate for at least 1 to 2 hours, but for best results, marinate overnight in the refrigerator.

3. **To cook the chicken:** Preheat a grill to medium-high heat. Once heated, remove the chicken from the marinade (discarding any leftover marinade), and place on the grill. Cook the chicken for about 6 to 7 minutes per side or until fully cooked.

4. Alternatively, the chicken can be cooked in the oven. Preheat the oven to 425°F, place the marinated chicken on a sheet pan and bake for about 30 minutes or until it's fully cooked and the edges are crisp.

5. After cooking, allow the chicken to rest for a few minutes. Then, slice lengthwise or dice it into medium-sized cubes.

6. To assemble the tacos, warm the corn tortillas on a dry grill or skillet for a few seconds on each side. Stack two warmed tortillas together, then top with the chopped chicken.

7. Add your choice of toppings and sauces.

SERVES **6**

BLACK BEANS

These beans get their excellent flavor from fresh epazote—a large, leafy Central American herb with a pungent flavor with notes of mint and oregano. My family from Central America swear by this herb and don't consider black beans to be quite right without it. If you have trouble finding it in your grocery store, try Latin American markets or try growing it in your garden. Don't bother with dried epazote as it has almost no flavor. Even if you can't find epazote in your area, these beans will still be delicious. I like to cook a large pot and portion it out for future meals. —L.K.

2 pounds black beans

16 cups water + more as needed

1 large white onion

2 jalapeños

6 cloves garlic, peeled

1 tablespoon chili powder

1 tablespoon dried oregano

2 teaspoons ground cumin

1 bunch fresh epazote

1 tablespoon kosher salt + more to taste

1. In a 7-quart pot, add black beans and water and cook over medium-high heat. Coarsely chop onion. Cut slits in both jalapeños. Add onion, jalapeños, garlic, chili powder, oregano, and cumin to pot and stir. Cut off stems of epazote and discard. Coarsely chop epazote leaves and mix in with beans. Continue cooking until mixture reaches a boil. Reduce heat to medium or medium-low so liquid is at a simmer. Beans should be covered by water throughout the cooking process. If needed, add hot water to cover beans. Continue to cook uncovered until beans are tender but not mushy, about 1½ to 2 hours. Add salt and stir, then cook an additional 2 to 3 minutes. Taste beans to check if salt is to your taste and add more if needed.

2. Remove jalapeños and garlic cloves and discard. Serve hot or divide and store. This large batch is perfect for freezing. Divide beans into freezer-safe airtight containers in portions that will work for future meals. Include cooking liquid with beans. Leave ½ inch head space in containers and freeze or refrigerate until ready to use.

MAKES ABOUT **13** CUPS

REFRIED BLACK BEANS

Growing up, refried beans in the states were usually made with pinto beans, but after my travels in Central America I almost exclusively use black beans now. Using the flavor-packed homemade black beans is the ideal way to make the perfect refried beans. They go great on tacos, inside burritos, and are the base of our Huevos Rancheros (page 340)—or garnish with queso and serve them up as a side dish with Mexican food. —L.K.

EQUIPMENT
Immersion blender

½ medium white onion
¼ cup olive or vegetable oil
2½ cups black beans with
    liquid

1. Finely chop onion and set aside. In a large skillet, heat oil over medium heat for 1 minute. Add onions and cook until golden brown, about 8 minutes. Turn off heat for 2 minutes before adding beans. If oil is too hot, it will splatter when adding beans. Mix beans with oil and onions and turn stove back to medium heat. Blend beans while cooking with an immersion blender. Keep blending until you get a smooth consistency. If you don't have an immersion blender, use a potato masher. Mash until beans are as smooth as you can get them. They won't be as smooth as they are with a blender, but they will still be delicious.

2. After blended, continue to cook beans until they have reached your desired thickness. Use a rubber spatula to scrape the bottom of skillet as you cook to prevent beans from sticking. This step varies in time based on how much liquid was on beans. Serve immediately. Store leftovers in an airtight container for up to 2 days. To revive refrigerated refried beans, add to a small saucepan with 1 to 2 tablespoons water, plus more if needed. Cook over medium heat, stirring continuously, until hot and serve.

MAKES ABOUT **2** CUPS

CHILE CON QUESO

It is debatable if Chile con Queso is actually Mexican in origin. The flavors are undoubtedly rich in Mexican ingredients, but this party favorite is more likely the result of the melding of Mexican flavors with the local foods in Texas. What is not debatable is the overall joy that this creamy cheesiness brings to the table.

2 poblano chilis

2 Anaheim chilis

2 tablespoons butter

1 medium white onion, chopped

1 jalapeño, cored, seeded, and finely chopped

2 cloves garlic, minced

2 tablespoons flour

2½ cups whole milk

8 ounces American cheese

16 ounces Monterey jack cheese

1 cup diced tomatoes

1. Char chilis on gas stove or under broiler until skins have blackened. Add to paper bag and fold over top of bag so chilis can steam. Allow to rest in paper bag for about 10 minutes. Rub off blackened skins from chilis and discard. Core and dice chilis and set aside.

2. In a large pot or Dutch oven, melt butter and cook onions in butter over medium heat for 4 minutes. Add jalapeño and garlic. Cook 1 more minute. Whisk in flour. Slowly add milk, continuously whisking. Whisk until flour is completely incorporated. Add cheeses, 1 cup at a time, whisking until smooth. Stir in diced tomatoes and chilis.

3. Serve warm or store in an airtight container.

MAKES ABOUT **7** CUPS

PICO DE GALLO

Pico de gallo is one of the most essential additions to almost any Mexican dish, and it's so fast and easy to pull together. Fresh, ripe tomatoes make this especially delectable.

3 medium tomatoes, diced

½ white onion, chopped

½ cup coarsely chopped cilantro + more for garnish

Juice of 1 lime

½ teaspoon kosher salt or more to taste

1 jalapeño, cored, seeded, and finely chopped (optional)

1. Prepare about 1 hour before serving. In a medium bowl, combine all ingredients. Stir until well combined. Taste to see if it has enough salt and add more if needed. Cover with plastic wrap and refrigerate. The resting time allows flavors to meld.

2. To serve, uncover, stir, and garnish with whole cilantro leaves.

MAKES ABOUT **3** CUPS

SALSA VERDE

Tomatillos are indigenous to Mexico and Central America. Their use in sauces dates back to the Aztecs. This cooked green salsa has a more tart flavor profile than the more common red salsa. It makes a great topping for tacos or for dipping chips. I especially love it with chicken dishes. —L.K.

2 pounds tomatillos, husked
1 small white onion, chopped
2 cloves garlic, peeled
2 jalapeños, cored and sliced
1 teaspoon cumin
1 bunch cilantro
2 teaspoons salt
2 tablespoons vegetable oil

1. Fill a large pot half full with water. Add tomatillos, onion, garlic, and jalapeños. Over medium-high heat, bring to a boil. Reduce temperature to medium and simmer for 25 to 30 minutes until onions and jalapeños are tender and tomatillos have darkened in color. The tomatillos will float; flip them a couple of times while cooking. Remove from heat and allow to rest for 10 minutes. Using a slotted spoon, scoop vegetables into a blender pitcher. Add ½ cup of cooking liquid and cumin to blender pitcher. Cover and blend for 15 seconds. Add cilantro to pitcher, stems down. The blender will pull cilantro down by the stems for even blending. Blend until salsa is completely smooth.

2. Empty pot and wipe dry. Heat oil over medium heat. Add salsa to pan and bring to a simmer. Cook for 10 to 15 minutes. Allow to cool completely and serve. Store extra salsa in an airtight container in refrigerator for up to 5 days.

MAKES ABOUT **3** CUPS

GUACAMOLE

2 large ripe avocados, peeled, pitted, and mashed

¼ cup finely diced white onion

1 clove garlic, minced

1 serrano pepper, seeded and minced

½ teaspoon Toasted Cumin Powder (page 54)

2 tablespoons fresh lime juice

1 teaspoon kosher salt

2 tablespoons fresh cilantro, chopped

1. In a bowl, gently combine the mashed avocados, onion, garlic, serrano pepper, cumin, lime juice, and kosher salt. If you have a mortar and pestle, you can use that instead of a bowl for a more traditional approach.

2. Fold in the chopped cilantro, reserving a little for garnish.

3. Garnish the top of the guacamole with the reserved cilantro and a sprinkle of additional toasted cumin, if desired.

NOTE: Guacamole is best enjoyed fresh due to avocados' tendency to brown after exposure to air. However, a layer of lime juice or plastic wrap directly on the surface of the guacamole can help prevent this if you need to store it briefly before serving.

MAKES ABOUT **2** CUPS

PICKLED RED ONIONS

These tangy, salty, purpley-pink onions are so easy to make, and they keep for a long time. They're great to have on hand to top tacos, sandwiches, salads, avocado toast, or huevos rancheros. They add so much flavor and a beautiful pop of color to your dish or table spread, too.

1 large red onion

1 cup white vinegar

1 cup water

3 tablespoons pure maple syrup

2 teaspoons kosher salt

1. Thinly slice red onion and pack tightly into a 32-ounce glass jar. Set jar with onions in sink. In a medium saucepan, cook vinegar, water, maple syrup, and salt until mixture comes to a boil. Immediately pour boiling vinegar mixture over onions. If any onions are above the liquid, press down with a spoon. Allow the onions to set until cool and then close the lid of the jar and refrigerate for up to 1 month.

2. To use: Scoop onions with a fork and allow liquid to run off before adding to your entrée.

MAKES ABOUT **2** CUPS

MANGO SALSA

Mango salsa, with its harmonious blend of sweet and tangy, complements the rich flavors of tacos splendidly. While variations exist across Latin America, this bright concoction elevates any dish, embodying the vibrant spirit of festive Mexican gatherings.

1 ripe mango, diced into cubes

1 small red onion, finely diced

½ jalapeño, seeded and finely diced

2 tablespoons cilantro, finely chopped

4–6 cherry tomatoes, quartered

2 tablespoons freshly squeezed lime juice

Kosher salt and pepper, to taste

1. Combine all the prepared ingredients (mango through tomatoes) in a medium-sized bowl. Add in the freshly squeezed lime juice. Season the mixture with kosher salt and pepper according to taste.

2. Stir all ingredients together thoroughly, making sure everything is well-mixed.

3. Allow the salsa to rest for 10 to 15 minutes before serving. This allows the flavors to meld together.

MAKES ABOUT **2** CUPS

TRES LECHE CAKE CUPS

Multiple Latin American countries claim to be the original source of tres leche cake. Though there is no definitive answer to where the first tres leches cake was made, it is certainly a popular fixture in most of Latin America and is Mexico's national pastry. The three-milk soaked cake elicits nostalgia for those who grew up in Latin America—it is a favorite in our household among my Guatemalan family. For this version the cake is soaked in individual serving dishes. Be sure to cut your cake smaller than the dish so there's room for plenty of milk. Topped with whipped cream and a sprinkle of cinnamon sugar, these are a beautiful addition to your table.

EQUIPMENT
12 dessert cups

Round cookie cutter

CAKE
6 large eggs

1¼ cups sugar, divided

4 tablespoons unsalted butter, softened

1 tablespoon vanilla extract

2 cups all-purpose flour

2 teaspoons baking powder

¾ teaspoon kosher salt

½ cup buttermilk

TRES LECHES
1 (14-ounce) can sweetened condensed milk

1 (12-ounce) can evaporated milk

⅓ cup heavy cream

1 teaspoon pure vanilla extract

TOPPING
2 cups heavy cream

½ cup confectioners' sugar

1 teaspoon vanilla extract

3 tablespoons sugar

2 teaspoons cinnamon

Caramel (page 149) (optional)

1. To make cake: Preheat oven to 350°F. Coat a 9 × 13-inch pan with nonstick spray and set aside.

2. Separate eggs; set aside egg yolks. Add egg whites to the bowl of a stand mixer. Using the whisk attachment, beat egg whites on medium until foamy. Increase the speed to high, and slowly add ¼ cup sugar, 1 teaspoon at a time. Beat until stiff peaks form. Scoop out the egg whites into a bowl and set aside.

3. Switch to the paddle attachment. Add butter, 1 cup of sugar, and vanilla to the bowl of the stand mixer. Beat on medium for 3 to 4 minutes. Add egg yolks and beat an additional 3 to 4 minutes. Scrape the bowl including the bottom to ensure even mixing. In a medium bowl, whisk together flour, baking powder, and salt. Slowly add flour mixture to egg yolk mixture. Add buttermilk and beat on low until combined.

4. Remove bowl from stand mixer. Using a rubber spatula, carefully fold egg whites into cake batter. Try not to completely deflate the egg whites. Stir with spatula until fully combined and no white streaks appear in the batter. Pour into prepared pan and bake for 25 to 30 minutes or until a cake tester comes out clean.

5. To make tres leches and assemble: Allow cake to cool for 5 minutes and then turn out the cake onto a board or platter. Allow cake to cool completely. In a medium bowl with spout, whisk together all of the tres leches ingredients. Cut rounds

CONTINUED

½ to ¾ inch smaller than your dessert cups to allow room for milk. Add cake rounds to dessert cups. Poke top of cake with a fork several times. Pour the three-milk mixture over each cake cup. Allow to soak into cake and then pour more milk mixture on cake. Refrigerate cups for 1 hour or up to 24 hours.

6. **To make topping:** When ready to serve, add heavy cream, confectioners' sugar, and vanilla to the bowl of a stand mixer with the whisk attachment. Beat on medium-high until soft peaks form, about 2 to 3 minutes. Add whipped cream to top of each cake cup. Mix sugar and cinnamon and sprinkle on top of whipped cream. Drizzle with caramel, if using. Serve immediately.

MAKES **12**

CONCHAS

Conchas are a beautiful and delicious *pan de dulce* (sweet bread) originating in Mexico. The brioche-like dough is most likely the result of French influence on baking methods and recipes in Mexico. The crisp cookie-like top is scored with a knife or cut with a concha cutter to look like a shell. The bread is such a favorite that it has spread beyond Mexico and is one of the most popular choices at *panaderies* (bakeries) all over Latin America. We love to bake them at home and have them with coffee for breakfast or an afternoon snack.

ROUX
⅔ cup whole milk
¼ cup all-purpose flour

DOUGH
2 cups bread flour
2 teaspoons fine kosher salt
⅓ cup cold whole milk
1 tablespoon yeast
1 cup sugar
1 tablespoon vanilla extract
4 large eggs, room temperature
4 cups all-purpose flour
¾ cup unsalted butter, softened + more for the bowl

1. To make the roux: Add milk and flour to a small saucepan and cook over medium heat, whisking continuously until paste forms.

2. To make the dough: Butter a medium or large bowl and set aside. In a small bowl, combine bread flour and salt and set aside. Add roux to stand mixer and beat with ⅓ cup milk using the paddle attachment. Add yeast, sugar, and vanilla and beat on medium until well combined. Add 1 egg at a time and beat on medium for 1 minute between each addition. Add bread flour–salt mixture and beat until well combined. Switch to dough hook and add all-purpose flour. Mix on medium for 10 minutes. Add butter 1 tablespoon at a time and mix on low until fully incorporated. Increase the speed to medium-high and mix for 4 additional minutes. Add dough to prepared bowl and bowl-fold dough. Cover and allow to rise in a warm place until it has doubled in size, about 1 to 2 hours.

3. To make the topping: Add butter, confectioners' sugar, flour, and extracts to bowl of stand mixer, and mix with paddle attachment until well combined. Dough should form a workable consistency, in which it is easy to roll into balls.

4. Divide mixture in three portions. Cover 2 portions and set aside. Return 1 portion to mixer bowl. Crush strawberries with fork, if using. Strain and retain juice. Add juice and food coloring to mixer bowl and mix until combined. Add 1 tablespoon flour, plus more if needed to get topping to a

CONTINUED

TOPPING

1¼ cups unsalted butter, softened

1¼ cups confectioners' sugar

3 cups all-purpose flour

1 teaspoon almond extract

2 teaspoons vanilla extract

2 medium strawberries (optional)

2 drops pink gel food coloring

2 medium strawberries (optional)

1–2 tablespoons flour

3 tablespoons Dutch-process cocoa

1–4 teaspoons whole milk

workable consistency. Remove from bowl, cover, and set aside. Wash and dry bowl and add another portion to the bowl. Add cocoa and 1 teaspoon of milk and mix on medium until well combined. Add more milk if needed to reach a workable consistency.

5. Divide dough into 36 portions (about 50 grams each). Roll each portion into a ball. Place on three baking sheets. Flatten slightly. Cover dough balls loosely and allow to rest 30 minutes.

6. Preheat oven to 350°F.

7. Divide each topping into 12 equal potions. Roll each into a ball. Place each ball between two pieces of parchment and flatten with a tortilla press or a rolling pin. Press a design on the flattened topping with a concha cutter or create your own design with a sharp knife. Use a round cookie cutter to trim topping so it fits a roll. It should overlap the sides.

8. Bake about 17 to 20 minutes or until conchas are puffed and lightly golden brown on edges.

9. Like most homemade bread, Conchas taste best on the day they are baked. Freeze any Conchas that you won't eat in an airtight container. To warm frozen Conchas, place on a pan in a preheated 275°F oven for 10 to 12 miunutes.

NOTE: To make a marbleized top, take a small portion of each color, roll into a ball taking care to not over mix the colors, and press ball with tortilla press.

MAKES **36**

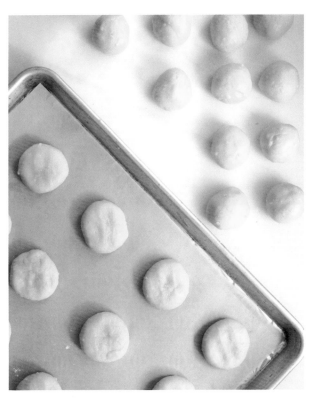

TROPICAL TABLE

"Cooking is all about people. Food is maybe the only universal thing that really has the power to bring everyone together. No matter what culture, everywhere around the world, people get together to eat."

—GUY FIERI

We prepared this spread for a birthday party while visiting my extended family in Guatemala. We were inspired by the fresh local produce, the bright bougainvillea toppling over stone walls, and the rich colors of the Mayan textiles. The ingredients included are not specifically Central American. One could create this for a summer pool party or a Hawaiian-themed party. Once assembled, this spread hits all the bright beautiful colors of the tropics and is perfect for summer. Our guests enjoyed everything down to the last drop of Dark Chocolate Nutella Fondue. More than one child wore the remnants of thoroughly enjoyed, chocolate-dipped fruit on his face. —L.K.

MAKE AHEAD

Sweet and Sour Chili Sauce can be made ahead up to 2 days and stored in an airtight container in the refrigerator. Shake sauce before serving.

Assemble kebabs a few hours in advance and store them in the refrigerator.

Bake Piña Colada Cookies a day ahead. Frost and add garnishes to cookies just before serving.

Make Mango Crumb Tart the day before. Cover and refrigerate. Before serving, refresh the tart in a 300°F oven for 10 minutes.

EXTRAS

Pineapple, papaya, kiwi, strawberries, and mangoes cut into bite-size pieces.

Toasted coconut

Banana leaves

Cold cut meat and cheese roll ups

Tropical flowers

TIME SAVERS

Purchase fruits already cut and ready to add to your spread.

Sweet-and-sour chili sauce can be purchased jarred.

Styling Ideas

Banana leaves make a perfect platter for this board. You can also curl a section of a banana leaf into a cup to hold the Coconut Crusted Shrimp.

Cut a pineapple in half, scoop out the fruit and fill with cut fruit for a beautiful fruit bowl.

An emptied out coconut works great for serving sauces and sides. Use a round cookie cutter to stabilize coconut halves.

RECIPES

COCONUT CRUSTED SHRIMP

Originating from tropical regions, Coconut Crusted Shrimp marries the rich flavors of the ocean with the sweet allure of coconut. This dish, a testament to island communities' ingenuity, showcases how locally sourced ingredients can harmonize in taste and texture. Paired beautifully with our Mango Salsa (page 292), it's island cuisine at its finest.

2 pounds raw shrimp, peeled and deveined with tails removed

¼ cup fresh lime juice

½ teaspoon cayenne pepper

½ teaspoon ground cumin

1 teaspoon kosher salt

3 eggs

1½ cups panko breadcrumbs

2 cups unsweetened shredded coconut

½ cup oil for frying

Mango Salsa (page 292), for serving

1. In a medium bowl, add shrimp, lime juice, cayenne pepper, ground cumin, and salt. Toss and set aside.

2. Whisk eggs in a bowl until frothy and set aside.

3. Toss the panko and shredded coconut in a shallow bowl and set aside.

4. Using tongs, dip each shrimp in egg mixture and then coat with the breadcrumb and coconut mixture. Set aside on a large plate. Repeat with remaining shrimps.

5. Heat oil in a skillet on medium heat. Add shrimps in a single layer. Make sure not to overcrowd.

6. The oil should sizzle when you add the shrimp. Work in batches and cook until the shrimp is golden brown all around. Cook on each side for 2 minutes.

7. Serve immediately with Mango Salsa.

SERVES ABOUT **12**

TROPICAL CHICKEN KEBABS

These chicken kebabs marinate in a gingery pineapple glaze before hitting the grill. Grilling infuses the chicken with char while basting it in more of that sweet and spicy sauce. Skewered with juicy pineapple, mango, and bell peppers, each tropical-scented bite bursts with a balance of savory and fruity flavors.

1 pound chicken breast, cut into 1-inch pieces

MARINADE AND SAUCE

1¼ cups pineapple juice

¼ cup light brown sugar

2 teaspoons sriracha

2 tablespoons low-sodium soy sauce

2 tablespoons sesame oil

2 tablespoons rice vinegar

1 teaspoon grated fresh ginger

2 teaspoons cornstarch

Kosher salt, to taste

Freshly ground black pepper, to taste

SKEWERS

1½ cups cubed pineapple

1½ cups cubed mango

2 large red, green, or yellow bell peppers cut into thick 1-inch pieces

1 large red onion, cut into larger wedges

2 tablespoons vegetable oil for brushing

1. **To prepare the sauce:** In a small saucepan, whisk together pineapple juice, brown sugar, sriracha, soy sauce, sesame oil, rice vinegar, ginger, and cornstarch until well combined. Place the mixture over medium-high heat, bringing it to a boil. Reduce the heat to medium and simmer until the sauce thickens to a glaze-like consistency, about 5 minutes. Once done, divide the sauce into two equal portions: one for marinating and one for brushing while grilling.

2. In a mixing bowl, toss the chicken pieces with half of the prepared sauce, ensuring all pieces are well-coated. Cover the bowl and refrigerate, allowing it to marinate for at least 1 hour.

3. **To assemble:** If you're using wooden skewers, it's advisable to soak them in water for about 30 minutes. This prevents them from charring or burning during the grilling process. Preheat your grill or grilling pan to medium-high heat.

4. Thread a piece of chicken onto a skewer, followed by a piece of pineapple, mango, sweet bell pepper, and a chunk of red onion. Repeat this sequence until the skewer is filled, ensuring you leave about an inch free at each end for easy handling. Prior to grilling, lightly brush each kebab with vegetable oil.

5. Place the skewers on your preheated grill. Grill them for about 4 to 6 minutes on each side, ensuring the chicken is thoroughly cooked. While grilling, regularly brush the kebabs with the reserved half of the sauce. After grilling, transfer the kebabs to a serving plate and let them rest for a few minutes before serving.

SERVES **4–6**

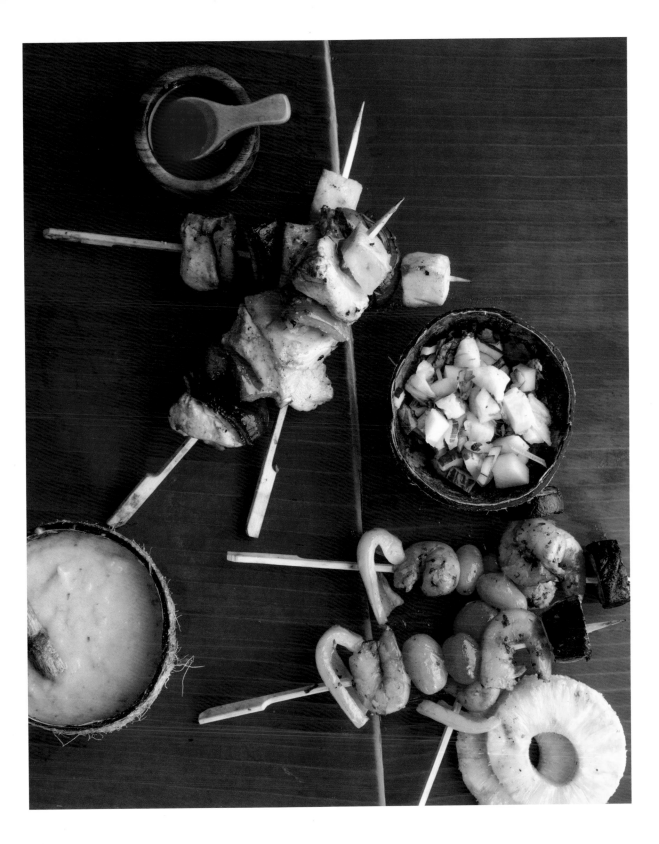

TROPICAL SHRIMP KEBABS

These shrimp kebabs marinate in a bright citrus-herb blend before hitting the grill. The coconut milk and cilantro marinade infuses the shrimp with tropical flavor. Skewered with juicy pineapple, onion, and peppers, the shrimp get caramelized and charred while retaining moisture. Grilling brings out the marinade's spice and complexity.

1 pound uncooked shrimp, peeled and deveined

MARINADE
½ cup coconut milk

⅓ cup minced fresh cilantro

¼ cup lime juice

¼ cup fresh orange juice

2 teaspoons soy sauce

2 cloves garlic, minced

2 teaspoons olive oil

½ teaspoon Toasted Cumin Powder (page 54)

¼ teaspoon kosher salt

¼ teaspoon coarsely ground pepper

SKEWERS
1 large red bell pepper, cut into 1-inch squares

1 red onion, cut into wedges and separated into 2 or 3 layers each

A handful of cherry tomatoes

Grilled pineapple cubes (you can grill them ahead of time or use fresh)

Fresh cilantro leaves for garnish

Wooden or metal skewers (if using wooden, soak in water for at least 30 minutes prior to prevent burning)

1. **To prepare the marinade:** In a large mixing bowl, whisk together the coconut milk, cilantro, lime juice, orange juice, soy sauce, garlic, olive oil, cumin, salt, and pepper until well combined.

2. Add the shrimp to the marinade, ensuring each shrimp is well-coated. Cover and refrigerate for 30 minutes to 2 hours. Do not marinate for longer than 2 hours, as the citrus juices can start to "cook" the shrimp.

3. **Prepare the skewers:** If using wooden skewers, soak them in water. This will prevent them from burning on the grill.

4. Start by skewering a piece of red bell pepper, followed by onion, a shrimp, cherry tomato, and then a pineapple cube. Repeat this sequence until the skewer is filled, leaving about an inch at both ends for handling.

5. Preheat grill to medium-high heat. Place the skewers on the grill and cook for 2 to 3 minutes on each side, or until the shrimp are opaque and have a nice char on them.

6. Remove from the grill and let them rest for a few minutes. Garnish with fresh cilantro leaves and serve with wedges of lemon on the side.

SERVES **4-6**

SPICY MANGO DIPPING SAUCE

1 ripe mango, peeled, pitted, and roughly chopped

½ cup full-fat coconut milk

1 small red chili, like a Fresno or serrano, seeds removed

2 tablespoons fresh lime juice

1 tablespoon agave syrup or honey

1 clove garlic, minced

¼ cup fresh cilantro, finely chopped

Kosher salt, to taste

1. In a blender or food processor, add the mango chunks, coconut milk, red chili, lime juice, honey or agave, and minced garlic. Add salt to taste. Blend until smooth and creamy.

2. Pour the sauce into a bowl and fold in the chopped cilantro.

3. Chill and serve with coconut-crusted shrimp.

MAKES 1½ CUPS

DARK CHOCOLATE NUTELLA FONDUE

I love this fondue because it doesn't have to be kept warm, making it an easy addition to a spread. Serve it with fruit, pound cake cubes, or graham crackers. —L.K.

10 ounces dark chocolate, finely chopped

1 cup heavy cream

¾ cup Nutella

¼ cup unsalted butter

1 vanilla bean

1. In a double boiler, heat water to just a simmer in the bottom pan. Place dark chocolate in the top pan, taking care not to spill any water into the chocolate.

2. In the microwave or stovetop, heat heavy cream until it is steaming but not boiling. Pour over chocolate and stir chocolate with a rubber spatula until chocolate is melted and cream is fully incorporated. Add Nutella, butter, and the seeds of one vanilla bean. Stir until smooth.

3. Serve immediately in a heatproof bowl. Fondue will remain fluid even at room temperature, making it ideal for a spread with no need for a heated fondue pot.

MAKES ABOUT **3** CUPS

MINI BANANA BUNDT CAKES

We grow bananas in Guatemala and there are alway an abundance, so I love to use them in cakes and quick breads. These little cakes are based on one of my mother's favorite recipes. They have a sweet caramelized sugar top with a soft cake base. —L.K.

TOPPING

¼ cup unsalted butter

¾ cup brown sugar

1 teaspoon vanilla extract

CAKE

½ cup unsalted butter, softened

1 cup sugar

2 eggs, room temperature

3 medium ripe bananas, mashed

1 tablespoon vanilla extract

1½ cups flour

½ teaspoon baking soda

1½ teaspoons baking powder

½ teaspoon kosher salt

½ cup buttermilk

1. Preheat oven to 350°F.

2. To make the topping: Melt butter in a medium heatproof bowl. Stir in brown sugar and vanilla until combined. Set aside.

3. In a medium bowl, beat together butter and sugar until light and fluffy, about 3 minutes. Add eggs and beat until combined. Add bananas and vanilla and beat until combined.

4. In a medium bowl, whisk together flour, baking soda, baking powder, and salt. Add flour mixture to butter mixture and mix. Pour in buttermilk and mix just until combined.

5. Spray a 6-well mini bundt pan with nonstick spray. Add 1 heaping tablespoon of topping to each well, using about half of the mixture. Top with cake batter until each well is about ¾ full. Bake for 25 to 30 minutes or until a cake tester comes out clean. Turn out mini cakes onto a sheet pan immediately. Leaving the cakes in the pan too long will make them stick. Repeat with second half of batter. Serve immediately or store in an airtight container for up to 3 days.

MAKES 12

MANGO CRUMB TART

I love to make this tart in Guatemala where the local mangos are especially delicious, but it's also amazing at home. When I come across ripe, fragrant mangos in the grocery store I bring them home to make a little tropical sweetness in the my Midwest kitchen. —L.K.

CRUST
¾ cup unsalted butter
½ teaspoon fine kosher salt
2 teaspoons vanilla extract
½ cup confectioners' sugar
1½ cups all-purpose flour

FILLING
1⅔ cups (300 g) diced mango
¼ cup + 2 tablespoons sugar
1 tablespoon cornstarch

CRUMB
½ cup unsalted butter
¼ teaspoon fine kosher salt
½ teaspoon cinnamon
¼ cup unsweetened coconut
½ cup brown sugar
¼ cup sugar
1 cup + 2 tablespoons all-purpose flour

1. Preheat oven to 350°F. Lightly butter the bottom of an 11-inch tart pan and set aside.

2. To make the crust: In a medium heatproof bowl, melt butter. Stir in salt, vanilla, and confectioners' sugar. Add flour and combine until dough forms. Press dough into prepared pan going up the sides of pan. If dough is too loose to work with, refrigerate 10 to 15 minutes before pressing into pan.

3. To make the filling: Combine all filling ingredients in the bowl of a food processor or a blender. Process until smooth. Pour into crust.

4. To make the crumb: In a medium heatproof bowl, melt butter. Stir in salt, cinnamon, coconut, and sugars. Add flour and combine with hands until crumb forms. Evenly sprinkle crumb over mango. Bake for about 40 minutes, or until crumb and crust are golden brown.

5. Allow tart to cool for 15 minutes before removing from pan. Serve warm or store in an airtight container in refrigerator for up to 5 days.

SERVES **16**

PIÑA COLADA COOKIES

I have made soft cookies with buttercream frosting as a favorite for holidays and celebrations. I changed up my recipe to bring in the tropics with the classic flavor combination of pineapple and coconut. These make a beautiful and delicious addition to your tropical table. —L.K.

COOKIES

¾ cup unsalted butter, softened

4 ounces cream cheese

1½ cups sugar

2 eggs, room temperature

1 teaspoon vanilla extract

2 teaspoons rum extract

3¼ cups flour

½ teaspoon fine kosher salt

2 teaspoons baking powder

¼ cup shredded unsweetened coconut

PINEAPPLE BUTTERCREAM

½ cup unsalted butter

4 ounces cream cheese

3–4 cup confectioners' sugar

1 teaspoon vanilla extract

¼ cup fresh pineapple, finely chopped and drained

¼ cup pineapple juice

GARNISH

¾ cup fresh pineapple, coarsely chopped and drained

¾ cup shredded unsweetened toasted coconut

1. **To make the cookies:** In a medium mixing bowl, beat butter, cream cheese, and sugar with a mixer until light and fluffy, about 3 minutes. Add eggs, vanilla, and rum extract and beat on high until combined.

2. In a small mixing bowl, combine flour, salt, baking powder, and coconut. Add to the butter mixture and beat just until combined. Divide the dough into two portions. Cover in plastic wrap and refrigerate for 30 minutes, up to overnight.

3. When ready to bake, preheat oven to 350°F. On a floured surface, roll out one portion until it is about ⅜ inch thick. This will be thicker than most rolled-out cookies. Cut out rounds with a 2½-inch cookie cutter. Repeat with second portion.

4. Transfer cutouts to a cookie sheet. Leave about 1½ inches between cookies. Bake for 12 to 15 minutes. Allow cookies to cool on the pan for 5 minutes before transferring them to a cooling rack.

5. **To make the buttercream:** Beat butter, cream cheese, and 1 cup of confectioners' sugar on high until light and fluffy, about 3 minutes. Add vanilla, pineapple, and pineapple juice. Beat until well combined. Add the remaining confectioners' sugar ½ cup at a time, beating between additions. Add until a spreadable consistency is reached.

6. After cookies have cooled completely, frost with your pineapple buttercream and garnish with fresh pineapple and toasted coconut. Store in a sealed container in refrigerator for up to 2 days.

MAKES **36**

PAN-SOUTH AMERICAN TABLE

Many worlds meet in the cuisines of South America. The foods native to the land: corn, peppers, cacao, tomatoes, quinoa, tropical fruits, potatoes, yucca, and alpaca meat are still a part of South American meals. For thousands of years the Incas cultivated land and raised animals, creating elaborate systems of irrigation and adapting high altitude land for crops. Spanish, Portuguese, and Italians brought new livestock, plants, and cooking methods that fused into the indigenous food. Later, African culture would impact food and cooking methods through the forced migration of millions of Africans. Today the cuisines of the many cultures have merged into a vibrant and flavorful array of dishes. With proteins from both land and sea, meals range from churrasco to ceviche. Delicious spiced empanadas and fresh, bright sauces grace tables, and sweets with European roots are shared throughout the continent. With its heart in indigenous foods and traditions, the South American table is as beautifully diverse as its people.

MAKE AHEAD

Marinate the Churasco the day before serving.

Prepare and shape Colombian Carimañolas a day in advance and store in an an airtight container in the refrigerator.

Prepare the filling for the Argentine Beef Empanadas a day in advance and store in an airtight container in the refrigerator.

Brigadeiros can be made several days in advance and stored in an airtight container in the refrigerator.

Make dulce de leche for Alfajores 2 to 3 days in advance and store in refrigerator. Toast coconut and store in an airtight container. Bake cookies and freeze for up to a week in advance. Assemble Alfajores just before serving.

EXTRAS

Grilled scallions

Lime wedges

Tortilla chips to go with Peruvian Ceviche

TIME SAVERS

Purchase jarred chimichurri sauce to go with Churasco.

Purchased jarred dulce de leche to use in Alfajores.

Styling Ideas

Use rustic serveware.

Incorporate South American textiles and pottery.

Use coconut halves as serving bowls. Stabilize coconut bowls by placing round cookie cutters below the coconut halves.

RECIPES

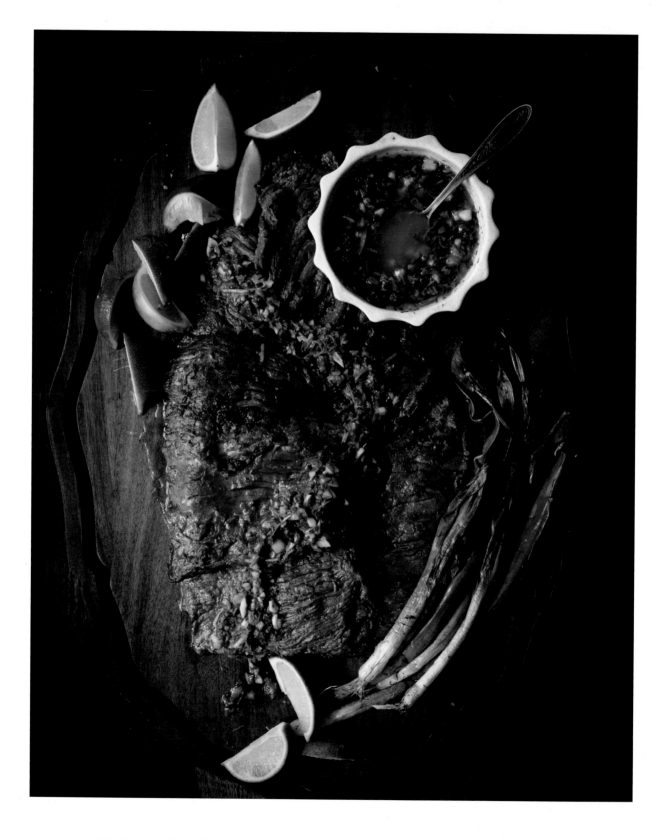

CHURRASCO WITH CHIMICHURRI SAUCE

ARGENTINIAN SKIRT STEAK

Argentina is famous for its flatland plains where cattle roam and graze on green pastures, producing some of the most delicious beef in the world. Churrasco originated in Brazil but is now a popular dish across much of Latin America. Pair this delicious skirt steak with traditional Argentinian Chimichurri Sauce for an amazing meal. The meat also goes great sliced with Fresh Corn Tortillas (page 273).

2 pounds grass-fed skirt steak

MARINADE
⅓ cup olive oil

Juice of 1 lime

Juice of 1 lemon

2 tablespoons Worcestershire sauce

2 tablespoons apple cider vinegar

6 cloves garlic, minced

1 teaspoon chili powder

Kosher salt and pepper to taste

CHIMICHURRI SAUCE
1 cup chopped fresh cilantro leaves

1 cup chopped fresh parsley leaves

3 cloves garlic

1 shallot, finely chopped

½ cup olive oil

2 tablespoons apple cider vinegar

Juice of 1 lime

½ teaspoon kosher salt

1. **To marinate steak:** In a medium bowl, whisk together all marinade ingredients. Add salt and pepper to both sides of steak. In a large airtight container, coat steak with marinade. Cover and refrigerate overnight.

2. **To make the chimichurri sauce:** Add cilantro, parsley, garlic, and shallot to a mortar and pestle. Smash ingredients with pestle until well combined. In a small bowl, combine parsley mixture with olive oil, vinegar, lime juice, and salt. Cover and allow to rest in refrigerator for at least a half hour to overnight.

3. **To grill steak:** Preheat grill to medium heat. If using charcoal, allow to burn 15 to 20 minutes before grilling. If using fire, use dry wood and allow to burn 30 to 40 minutes before grilling; flames should be low with hot embers. Place steak with marinade directly on grill, and cook about 3 minutes per side. Depending on heat of grill, it may take a little longer. To serve, slice skirt steak against the grain. Top with a strip of Chimichurri Sauce.

SERVES **8**

PERUVIAN CEVICHE

Ceviche, a marvel of culinary simplicity and sophistication, finds its roots in ancient coastal civilizations. As it journeyed through time, the Spaniards introduced citrus, which transformed the dish into what we recognize today. Central to Peruvian gastronomy, this dish showcases the purity of its ingredients: fresh fish "cooked" in zesty lime juice, harmonized with aromatic herbs and spices. This Peruvian Ceviche recipe captures the very essence of the ocean, uplifted by the vibrancy of South American flavors.

1 pound firm sole filet, cut into ½-inch cubes (substitution: halibut or sea bass)

1 cup freshly squeezed lime juice (about 8–10 limes)

½ red onion, thinly sliced

1 green chili (such as serrano or jalapeño), seeds removed and finely sliced

1 clove garlic, minced

1 teaspoon kosher salt

½ teaspoon freshly ground black pepper

¼ cup extra-virgin olive oil

¼ cup fresh cilantro leaves, finely chopped

1–2 teaspoons hot sauce (such as Tabasco)(optional)

1. In a glass or ceramic bowl, combine the cubed sole filet with the freshly squeezed lime juice. Ensure the fish is completely submerged. Cover and refrigerate for 15 to 20 minutes. The fish will turn opaque as it "cooks" in the lime juice.

2. Thinly slice the red onion and soak it in a bowl of cold water for about 10 minutes. This helps to remove some of the onion's sharpness. Drain and set aside.

3. After the fish has marinated, add the drained red onion slices, green chili, minced garlic, kosher salt, and black pepper to the bowl. Gently mix.

4. Stir in the olive oil and finely chopped cilantro. For those who like it spicier, add hot sauce to taste at this point. Serve immediately in small bowls, garnished with extra cilantro.

TIPS: Always use the freshest fish you can find. Make sure it's from a reputable source and ideally sashimi-grade.

Freshly squeezed lime juice is crucial for authentic flavor.

Adjust the amount of chili and hot sauce according to your heat preference.

SERVES **4**

ARGENTINE BEEF EMPANADAS

Savory pastries filled with history, Argentine empanadas encapsulate the country's cattle ranching roots. Finely chopped beef and onion get a kick of paprika and cumin for a flavorful filling tucked into tender, flaky pastry. Portable and satisfying, empanadas make the perfect hearty snack or appetizer with chimichurri for dipping.

DOUGH

2¾ cups all-purpose flour

½ teaspoon kosher salt

½ cup unsalted butter, chilled and cut into small pieces

1 large egg, beaten

1 tablespoon white wine vinegar

⅓ cup ice-cold water, more if needed

FILLING

2 tablespoons olive oil

1 large red onion, finely chopped

3 cloves garlic, minced

1 small red bell pepper, seeds removed and finely chopped

½ pound ground beef

1 tablespoon ground coriander

1 teaspoon ground cumin

1½ teaspoons sweet paprika

1 teaspoon paprika

Kosher salt and pepper to taste

2 hard-boiled eggs, crumbled

ASSEMBLY

1 large egg, beaten (for egg wash)

1. **To prepare the dough:** In a large bowl, combine the flour and salt. Cut the chilled butter into cubes and add to the flour. Mix with your hands until it resembles breadcrumbs.

2. Make a well in the center, add the beaten egg, vinegar, and start with ⅓ cup of ice-cold water. Mix until a dough forms, adding more water if needed. Shape the dough into a disc, wrap in plastic, and chill for at least 1 hour.

3. **To prepare the filling:** In a skillet over medium heat, add olive oil. Sauté the onion, garlic, and red bell pepper until softened. Add ground beef and cook until browned. Break apart any large chunks. Stir in the coriander, cumin, both paprikas, salt, and black pepper. Remove from heat, drain excess liquid, and let it cool. Once cooled, mix in the hard-boiled eggs.

4. **To assemble and bake:** Preheat the oven to 375°F and line a baking sheet with parchment paper. Roll out the chilled dough to about ⅛-inch thickness. Use a 4-inch cookie cutter to cut rounds. Place a spoonful of filling onto each round, fold into a half-moon, and seal by crimping with a fork.

5. Brush each empanada with the beaten egg. Place empanadas on the prepared baking sheet and bake for 20 to 25 minutes or until golden brown.

6. Serve with Chimichurri Sauce (page 321) or Spicy Venezuelan Guasacaca (page 328).

MAKES **12**

COLOMBIAN CARIMAÑOLAS

Carimañolas are a beloved Colombian snack, marking the marriage of creamy yuca dough and flavorful beef filling. This traditional street food, often seen in coastal regions, has a unique torpedo shape, with a crisp exterior and tender inside.

YUCA DOUGH

2 pounds fresh or frozen yuca, peeled and cut into chunks

1 teaspoon salt

Frying-grade oil for frying

BEEF FILLING

2 tablespoons vegetable oil

1 clove garlic, minced

¼ cup finely chopped red bell pepper

½ cup finely chopped yellow onion

1 scallion, finely chopped

½ pound ground beef

Kosher salt and pepper to taste

1 teaspoon ground cumin

1 tablespoon tomato paste

1. **To prepare the yuca dough:** Place yuca chunks in a pot, cover with water, and add 1 teaspoon of salt. Boil until yuca is soft and easily pierced with a fork, about 30 to 40 minutes. Drain and let cool. Once cooled, mash the boiled yuca until smooth, removing any fibrous veins. You should have a pliable dough.

2. **To prepare the beef filling:** Heat 2 tablespoons of vegetable oil in a skillet over medium heat. Add garlic, red bell pepper, yellow onion, and scallion. Sauté until soft, about 5 minutes. Add ground beef, breaking it apart with a spoon. Cook until no longer pink.

3. Stir in salt, pepper, ground cumin, and tomato paste. Cook for an additional 5 minutes. Remove from heat and let cool.

4. **To assemble and cook:** Take a golf ball–sized amount of yuca dough and flatten it into a disc. Place a spoonful of beef filling in the center. Fold the dough over the filling and shape it into a torpedo-like form, sealing the edges.

5. Heat oil in a large pot until it reaches the appropriate frying temperature. Use a thermometer to accurately monitor the temperature. The oil should be about 3 inches deep. Carefully lower the filled carimañolas into the hot oil and fry until golden brown, turning as needed, about 5 to 7 minutes.

6. Remove from oil and drain on paper towels. Serve immediately. Serve hot, optionally with a side of aji (Colombian hot sauce) or salsa for dipping.

MAKES **12**

URUGUAYAN SALSA CRIOLLA

Uruguayan Salsa Criolla, a staple in the country's cuisine, offers a harmonious blend of fresh tomatoes, onions, and bell peppers. Enhanced by the zest of red wine vinegar and rounded out by olive oil, this salsa gets its distinct depth from cilantro and a hint of cumin. Traditionally accompanying grilled meats or bread, its vibrant colors and flavors mirror the lively spirit of Uruguayan gatherings.

2 medium tomatoes, finely chopped

1 medium onion, finely chopped

1 green bell pepper, finely chopped

2 tablespoons extra-virgin olive oil

1 tablespoon red wine vinegar

2 tablespoons coarsely chopped cilantro

½ teaspoon kosher salt

¼ teaspoon freshly ground black pepper

¼ teaspoon ground cumin

1. In a medium bowl, combine the chopped tomatoes, onion, and green bell pepper.

2. Add the extra-virgin olive oil, red wine vinegar, cilantro, salt, pepper, and cumin to the vegetable mixture. Stir everything together until well mixed.

3. Let the salsa sit for at least 30 minutes to allow the flavors to meld together. For best results, cover and refrigerate for a couple of hours before serving.

4. Serve chilled or at room temperature with any dish for added texture and flavor.

MAKES ABOUT **2** CUPS

SPICY VENEZUELAN GUASACACA

Guasacaca, Venezuela's vibrant answer to guacamole, melds the creaminess of avocados with a symphony of herbs and spices. Often dubbed the "Venezuelan green sauce," its zesty blend of red onion, jalapeño, and garlic combined with cilantro and parsley makes it distinct. Enhanced with a hint of vinegar and olive oil, this sauce pairs brilliantly with grilled meats, arepas, or as a dip.

3 ripe avocados, peeled and pitted

1 medium red onion, roughly chopped

1 jalapeño, seeded and roughly chopped

2 cloves garlic, peeled

½ cup fresh cilantro leaves, tightly packed

¼ cup fresh parsley leaves, tightly packed

¼ cup red wine vinegar

1 tablespoon kosher salt (or to taste)

¼ teaspoon freshly ground black pepper

½ teaspoon ground cumin

1 teaspoon hot sauce (such as sriracha or a habanero sauce)

¾ cup extra-virgin olive oil

1. In a blender or food processor, add the avocados, red onion, jalapeño, garlic, cilantro, parsley, red wine vinegar, kosher salt, freshly ground black pepper, ground cumin, and hot sauce.

2. Pulse until the ingredients are well combined but still slightly chunky. With the blender running, slowly drizzle in the extra-virgin olive oil until well incorporated and the sauce becomes creamy.

3. Place the sauce in a sealed container and refrigerate for at least 1 hour to allow flavors to meld together before serving.

MAKES ABOUT **2½** CUPS

COCADAS

LATIN AMERICAN COCONUT MACAROONS

Cocadas are a coconut confection that can be found across much of Central and South America and are sold in both bakeries and by street vendors. They come in many varieties and colors and multiple countries claim them as their own. The recipe cocadas are based on was likely brought over by European explorers and takes it root from the Italian macaroon. This version combines the delicious crunch of macadamia nuts with the sweet chewy coconut.

3 cups shredded unsweetened coconut

3 cups shredded sweetened coconut

1 cup coarsely chopped macadamia nuts

2 egg whites

1 (14-ounce) can sweetened condensed milk

1 teaspoon vanilla extract

½ teaspoon almond extract

8 ounces dark chocolate, coarsely chopped

1 teaspoon coconut oil (optional)

1. Preheat oven to 325°F. Line a baking sheet with parchment or a silicone baking mat.

2. In a large bowl, mix coconuts and macadamia nuts. In a medium bowl, lightly beat egg whites. Add sweetened condensed milk, vanilla, and almond extract to egg whites and whisk until combined. Pour sweetened condensed milk mixture over coconut and stir until fully incorporated.

3. Use a 1-ounce (2 tablespoons) cookie scoop to scoop dough onto prepared baking sheet. Space cocadas about 1 inch apart. Bake for about 20 to 25 minutes or until tops are golden brown. Transfer to a cooling rack.

4. After cocadas have cooled, melt chocolate. In a double boiler, heat water to just a simmer in bottom pan. Water should not touch top pan. Place chocolate in top pan, taking care not to spill any water into the chocolate. Stir chocolate with a rubber spatula until melted. If chocolate is too thick, add 1 teaspoon coconut oil. Stir until coconut oil is melted and completely incorporated.

5. Line a baking sheet with parchment. Dip bottoms of cocadas in chocolate and set on baking sheet. Allow to rest for 30 minutes or until chocolate has set completely. Serve immediately or store in an airtight container in refrigerator for up to 5 days.

MAKES **36**

BRIGADEIROS

BRAZILIAN TRUFFLES

Brigadeiros are a traditional Brazilian confection popular across the country especially during special occasions. The candy was developed in Rio de Janeiro for a presidential candidate in the 1940s—made and sold to support Brigadier Eduardo Gomes. The truffles are traditionally covered in chocolate sprinkles but can be customized with a variety toppings to bring delightful flare to your table.

2 tablespoons unsalted butter

14 ounces sweetened condensed milk

⅓ cup unsweetened cocoa

¼ teaspoon fine kosher salt

1 cup chocolate sprinkles

ALTERNATE TOPPINGS

Unsweetened coconut

Chocolate cookie crumbs

Colored sprinkles

Malt powder

Unsweetened cocoa

Confectioners' sugar

1. Butter a medium bowl and set aside.

2. Over medium heat in a braiser or deep frying pan, melt butter. Add sweetened condensed milk. Stir with heatproof rubber spatula to combine. Add cocoa and salt and stir continuously until cocoa is completely incorporated. Continue cooking until mixture has thickened, about 10 minutes. It is ready when you can scrape rubber spatula across the bottom of pan and it takes 2 to 3 seconds to fill in. Pour into prepared bowl. Cover with plastic wrap and refrigerate for 1 to 2 hours.

3. Pour chocolate sprinkles in a small bowl. Line a 9 × 13-inch airtight container with parchment or fill with truffle liners. Remove chocolate mixture from refrigerator. Scoop a 1-tablespoon portion and roll into a ball. Roll ball in chocolate sprinkles (or alternate toppings) and set in prepared container. Store brigadeiros covered in refrigerator until ready to serve. Serve on a plate or in truffle liners.

MAKES **24**

ALFAJORES

ARGENTINIAN DULCE DE LECHE SANDWICH COOKIE

These little sandwich cookies are an excellent example of culinary travels and influences. The early origins come from the Arabic word الفاخر, al-fakhir, meaning luxurious. Arabs brought their stuffed treats to Spain and later the Spaniards brought them to South America. Bakers of Argentina and Uruguay started replacing the nuts and dried fruits in the Spanish version with jams and dulce de leche creating the modern alfajore—a light, airy, slightly crisp cookie with a sweet filling and toasted coconut finish.

EASY DULCE DE LECHE
2 (14-ounce) cans sweetened
    condensed milk

TOASTED COCONUT
½ cup shredded sweetened
    coconut

COOKIES
1 cup unsalted butter

¾ cup sugar

1 tablespoon vanilla extract

3 egg yolks, room
    temperature

1½ cups flour

1⅔ cups cornstarch

2 teaspoons baking powder

½ teaspoon salt

Confectioners' sugar for
    dusting

1. To make the dulce de leche: Remove label from sweetened condensed milk cans. Place unopened cans in a deep pot. Fill pot with water until it is 2 to 3 inches higher than the can. Place pot on stove over medium-high heat. Bring water to a boil. After it boils, reduce temperature so water remains at a simmer. Continue to cook for 2¾ more hours. Make sure can stays completely submerged in water. Add more water if it gets too low. After 2¾ hours, remove can from water with tongs and set in sink or on a hot pad. Allow can to cool completely before opening. When you open the can, it should be a rich golden brown.

2. To toast the coconut: Preheat oven to 350°F. Place coconut on a baking sheet in a single layer. Bake for 8 to 10 minutes, stirring every 3 minutes. When coconut turns golden brown, remove from oven and allow to cool on baking sheet.

3. To make the cookies: Beat butter, sugar, and vanilla for 2 to 3 minutes until fluffy. Add egg yolks and beat until combined. In a medium bowl, whisk together flour, cornstarch, baking powder, and salt. Add to the butter mixture and beat until well combined. Divide the dough into two portions. Wrap each portion in plastic and refrigerate for 1 hour, up to overnight.

4. When ready to bake, preheat oven to 350°F. On a floured surface, roll out one portion until it is about ¼-inch thick. Cut out rounds with a 2-inch cookie cutter. Transfer cutouts to a cookie sheet. Leave about 1½ inches between cookies. Bake for 10 to 12 minutes. Allow cookies to cool on the pan for 5 minutes before transferring them to a cooling rack.

5. After cookies have cooled completely, spread dulce de leche on a cookie and top with a second cookie. Roll sides in toasted coconut and dust top with confectioners' sugar. Store in an airtight container for up to 5 days. Over time, the cookies will absorb the moisture from the dulce de leche. For crisp cookies, assemble the cookies just before serving. Store any extra dulce de leche in an airtight container in refrigerator for up to 2 weeks.

MAKES **30**

NEW YORK CITY BRUNCH

"New York is not a city. It's a world." — IMAN

New York City is a crossroad for the people of the entire earth. It is the meeting place of all humans, all cultures, all languages. The cobblestone and blacktop streets—rife with food vendors; the smell of nuts cooked in sugar; the dingy subways; tall glass skyscrapers; the rush of feet; faces with determined expressions; the rich smelling restaurants where tables and chairs pour out onto sidewalks and people dine al fresco with friends and a dog sleeping at their feet; the trees blossoming in spring in the Village; and the late-night-after-the-bar feel of the wind while trying to hail a cab are all part of my memories of life in New York. This was Mumtaz and my common ground, where we met from the distance of half a world. When we started talking about the many table ideas we could do for New York, possibilities abounded. We share many culinary adventures in the city, but brunch seemed quintessential, and we knew this had to be the choice. Saturday might be the best evening for a dinner party or staying out late for drinks, but it is Sunday that captivates food-craving hearts for the leisurely-minded hoping for a plate of shakshuka or stack of lemon ricotta pancakes, and of course a mimosa or two. The dishes on this spread are like the people of New York—they come from a variety of places and cultures. Take time to savor the many flavors and huge helpings of comfort on this spread of brunch favorites. —L.K.

MAKE AHEAD

Make the Refried Black Beans (page 286) 1 to 2 days ahead. Make the Pico de Gallo (page 288) several hours ahead.

Make the smoothie mixtures a day in advance and store in the freezer until you are ready to use.

Bake bagels up to 2 weeks in advance. Freeze in an airtight container as soon as they have cooled. Warm frozen bagels in a 275°F oven for 7 to 10 minutes just before serving.

TIME SAVERS

Purchase fresh mini bagels and black and white cookies from your local bakery.

EXTRAS

A variety of cream cheese flavors

Lox/smoked salmon

Capers

Labne

Za'atar

Pita (page 88)

Granola

Mimosas

Bloody Marys

Coffee

Styling Ideas

Use an assortment of eclectic dishes, linens, and service ware.

Use fresh flowers from your local farmers' market.

Add color with seasonal fruits and vegtables from the local farmers' market.

RECIPES

SHAKSHUKA WITH FETA

Shakshuka always reminds me of leisurely Brooklyn brunches with friends. The dish is made complete with the addition of tangy and creamy feta cheese and runny egg yolks that create a luxurious sauce, perfect for dipping crusty bread. Preparing Shakshuka feels like taking a culinary journey to the Middle East, the birthplace of this comforting and always crowd-pleasing dish. —M.M.

3 tablespoons olive oil

1 medium-sized onion, finely chopped

2 large red bell peppers, seeded and diced

4 cloves garlic, finely chopped

1 teaspoon ground cumin

¼ teaspoon kosher salt

¼ teaspoon black pepper

2 teaspoons Harissa (page 249)

2 tablespoons tomato paste

5 large ripe tomatoes or 1 (28-ounce) can crushed tomatoes

5 ounces feta cheese

4 large eggs

Chopped cilantro, for garnish

1 avocado, sliced (optional)

1. Preheat the oven to 375°F.

2. In a cast-iron pan or a shallow Dutch oven, heat the olive oil over medium heat.

3. Add the diced onion to the pan and stir for 2 minutes.

4. Add the diced red peppers, finely chopped garlic, ground cumin, kosher salt, black pepper, harissa, and tomato paste. Cook for 8 to 10 minutes until the peppers have softened.

5. Add the tomatoes and cook on simmer for another 10 minutes. Crumble feta cheese over the tomato mixture.

6. Make four dips in the sauce and carefully crack the eggs into the holes.

7. Transfer the pan to the oven and bake for 8 to 10 minutes, depending on how runny you want your yolks.

8. Garnish with chopped cilantro and sliced avocado.

SERVES 4

HUEVOS RANCHEROS

Huevos rancheros translates to farm eggs. It is a popular breakfast in northern Mexico and in Texas. It was often served as a second hearty breakfast for farm and ranch workers. I first tried this dish homemade in my friend Michelle's home near Union Square. Though it doesn't have its origins in New York, this dish fits perfectly in a New York brunch spread where the people hail from all over the world and cultures and cuisines meld colorfully and deliciously. Years later, I now raise my own hens, and with eggs in abundance, this is a favorite dish for any meal at our house. —L.K.

¼ cup vegetable oil + more, if needed

16 Fresh Corn Tortillas (page 273)

2 cups Refried Black Beans, warmed (page 286)

3 tablespoons butter

8 large eggs

Kosher salt and pepper, to taste

2 cups Pico de Gallo (page 288)

8 ounces queso fresco

2 avocados

Fresh cilantro

1 jalepeño, sliced

Pickled Red Onions (page 290) (optional)

1. Set out eight medium plates or one large platter. Gather all ingredients before you begin so you can assemble each serving and be able to serve Huevos Rancheros hot.

2. Preheat oil in a small frying pan over medium-high heat. Set 7 pieces of paper towels, each folded in half near stove. Using tongs, pan-fry each tortilla for 1 to 2 minutes or until slightly crisped on each side. Allow tortilla to drain into pan and then set on paper towel. Cook remaining tortillas, placing 2 tortillas per paper towel and covering with another layer of paper towel to drain any excess oil. If pan dries out, add more oil.

3. Stack 2 tortillas per plate. Spread the top tortilla with refried black beans. Wipe the frying pan to use for frying eggs. Over medium heat, melt 2 teaspoons of the butter. Crack 1 egg into pan. Add salt and pepper to taste. Fry until whites are set and edges are slightly browned. Add egg to top of beans on one of the tortilla stacks. Add 1 more teaspoon of butter and cook the second egg. Continue cooking until all of the Huevos Rancheros are topped with eggs.

4. Top each with Pico de Gallo, queso fresco, avocado slices, fresh cilantro, jalepeño slices, and Pickled Red Onions, if using. Serve immediately.

SERVES **8**

POTATO LATKES

Latkes, deeply rooted in tradition, have found their modern niche in the New York brunch scene. These crispy potato pancakes, golden outside and tender within, are now a Big Apple brunch staple, best savored with a dollop of spiced labneh.

4–5 pounds russet potatoes, washed and scrubbed

1 medium yellow onion

1 teaspoon kosher salt, divided

¼ teaspoon black pepper

¼ cup plain dried breadcrumbs

1 teaspoon baking powder

2 large eggs, lightly beaten

1 teaspoon minced fresh parsley

Vegetable oil, for frying

1. Shred the russet potatoes and yellow onion using a box grater or the large shredding disc of a food processor. Preheat the oven to 200°F. Place a rimmed baking sheet in the oven to keep cooked latkes warm.

2. In a large mixing bowl, combine shredded potatoes and onion. Add ½ teaspoon of salt and mix gently. Using a dish towel or triple-layered cheesecloth, wring out the moisture from the potato and onion mixture. Let the extracted liquid sit for 4 to 6 minutes to allow the potato starch to settle at the bottom. Decant the liquid, retaining the potato starch.

3. In a separate bowl, combine breadcrumbs, baking powder, the remaining ½ teaspoon of salt, pepper, and lightly beaten eggs. Add the potato and onion mixture, the reserved potato starch, and minced parsley. Mix until well combined. The mixture should not be thick and not runny.

4. Heat vegetable oil, about ¼ inch deep, in a 12-inch skillet over medium-high heat until shimmering. Once the oil is heated, scoop approximately ¼ cup of the potato mixture, forming it into a ball. Gently place the ball in the hot oil and use a spatula to press it down, shaping it into a latke that's about ⅓ inch thick. Ensure you fry the latkes in batches, taking care not to overcrowd the skillet.

5. Fry each latke until golden brown on one side, about 3 minutes, then flip and cook the other side for an additional 3 minutes. Remove the latkes from the oil and let them drain on a wire rack set over a rimmed baking sheet. If needed, you can also first place them on paper towels to absorb excess oil.

6. Transfer the drained latkes to the baking sheet in the oven to keep them warm. Season the cooked latkes with additional salt and pepper. Serve with spiced labneh.

MAKES **16–20**

MINI BAGELS

When I lived in the New York City area, I took fabulous bagels for granted. Not everyone has access to this caliber of chewy, fresh deliciousness. After coming back to the Midwest, I once bit into a bagel from a breakfast spread and was shocked by how horrible it was. It's unusual for me to leave a bagel uneaten, but this one was—in fact—inedible. The best solution: start baking my own. Freshness is one of the most important factors in the creation of an amazing bagel. So plan to eat them right away, and freeze extras. —L.K.

2 cups warm water

1 tablespoon active dry yeast

1½ tablespoons granulated sugar

2 teaspoons salt

4¾–5¼ cups (570–630 grams) bread flour

TOPPING OPTIONS

Everything Bagel Seasoning

Poppy seeds

Sesame seeds

Turbinado sugar

1. In the bowl of a stand mixer, with the dough hook attachment, add water, yeast, sugar, and salt. Mix on low for 30 seconds. Allow to stand until a thick foam has formed at the top, about 10 minutes.

2. Add 4½ cups of flour to water mixture. Mix on low until a soft shaggy dough forms. Add more flour ¼ cup at a time until mixture comes together into a smooth dough.

3. Knead on medium speed for 6 minutes. Line two large baking sheets with parchment or silicone baking mats and set aside. Place 2 to 3 feet of parchment on counter near stove.

4. Spray a large bowl with nonstick spray and place dough in bowl. Bowl-fold dough by stretching some dough from bottom to top, flip over dough ball. Cover bowl with plastic wrap or damp towel, and allow dough to rise until it doubles in size, about 1 to 2 hours, depending on how warm your kitchen is.

5. Punch down dough and turn out onto a lightly floured surface. Divide dough into 28 equal portions (about 50 grams each). Form balls from each portion. Pierce a hole in center of dough ball with one finger. Stretch hole a little while stretching and flattening dough into a bagel shape. Place on parchment. Allow to rest 30 more minutes.

6. Preheat oven to 425°F. Fill a large pot halfway with water and heat over medium high heat until water boils. Carefully place 5 to 6 bagels in boiling water. Cook for 1 minute on each side. Remove from boiling water with a slotted spoon or spatula. Allow water to drain before placing them on the prepared baking sheet. Space bagels about 1 inch apart. Bagels expand during boiling process and will not expand much more in oven. Sprinkle with desired toppings.

7. Bake until golden, about 18 to 22 minutes. Transfer to a cooling rack and allow to cool completely. Or break one open immediately and slather with cream cheese to eat warm.

8. Fresh bagels taste best on the same day they are baked. Store leftovers in an airtight container in the freezer for up to 1 month. To revive frozen bagels, preheat oven to 275°F. Place bagels on a baking sheet and warm for 7 to 10 minutes.

MAKES **28**

AVOCADO TOAST WITH MEDITERRANEAN FETA AND ROASTED RED PEPPER DIP

A culinary emblem of the New York brunch culture, Avocado Toast has graced almost every menu, uniting simplicity with gourmet flair. While the creamy avocado base remains a constant, the toppings offer a canvas for creativity. The juxtaposition of crispy shallots and toasted sesame introduces a textural dance, while the Mediterranean Feta and Roasted Red Pepper Dip melds savory with a hint of tang. Not to be overshadowed, the Avocado Toast with Fig Preserves (page 348) effortlessly bridges the sweet and savory gap. These variations pay homage to the versatility of this beloved dish, ensuring there's an Avocado Toast for every palate in the city that never sleeps.

2 slices of your preferred bread (sourdough, multigrain, rye, etc.)

1 ripe avocado

¼ cup Mediterranean Feta and Roasted Red Pepper Dip (page 90) (homemade or store bought)

Salt and pepper, to taste

¼ cup crispy shallots

Fresh herbs (like parsley or basil) for garnish

1 tablespoon olive oil

Pinch of red pepper flakes or smoked paprika (optional)

1. Preheat your toaster or oven to a medium-high setting. Place the slices of bread in the toaster or on a baking sheet if using an oven. Toast until the bread is golden brown and crispy.

2. Cut the avocado in half and remove the seed. Carefully scoop out each half of the avocado from its skin, ensuring it remains intact. Slice each half into even, thin slices.

3. Spread a generous amount of the Mediterranean Feta and Roasted Red Pepper Dip onto each toasted bread slice. Carefully fan out and place the sliced avocado on top of the dip.

4. Season with salt and pepper, if desired.

5. Top with crispy shallots and fresh herbs. Drizzle with olive oil and sprinkle with red pepper flakes.

MAKES **2**

AVOCADO TOAST WITH FIG PRESERVES

2 slices of your preferred bread (sourdough, multigrain, rye, etc.)

1 ripe avocado

¼ cup fig preserves (store-bought)

Lemon zest for garnish

Pomegranate seeds for garnish

Salt and pepper, to taste

1. Preheat your toaster or oven to a medium-high setting. Place the slices of bread in the toaster or on a baking sheet if using an oven. Toast until the bread is golden brown and crispy.

2. Cut the avocado in half and remove the seed. Carefully scoop out each half of the avocado from its skin, ensuring it remains intact. Slice each half into even, thin slices.

3. Spread a generous amount of fig preserves onto each toasted bread slice. Carefully fan out and place the sliced avocado on top of the preserve.

4. Garnish with lemon zest and pomegranate seeds. Season with salt and pepper.

MAKES **2**

AVOCADO TOAST WITH CRISPY SHALLOTS AND TOASTED SESAME

2 ripe avocados

1–2 tablespoons lime juice, adjust to taste

Kosher salt, to taste

1–2 shallots, thinly sliced

2–3 tablespoons toasted sesame oil

1 handful pine nuts

2 slices multigrain bread

1 tablespoon toasted sesame seeds

1 handful cherry tomatoes, halved or quartered

Fresh herbs (such as basil, parsley, or cilantro), chopped

1. To prepare the avocado: Halve and pit the avocados. Scoop out the flesh into a medium bowl. Add lime juice and a pinch of kosher salt. Using a fork or a potato masher, mash the avocados until they're creamy and smooth. Taste and adjust the seasoning. You can also add to a food processor or blender for an extra velvety texture. Set aside.

2. To prepare the crispy shallots: In a small skillet over medium heat, add toasted sesame oil. Once the oil is hot, add the thinly sliced shallots. Fry them until they're golden brown and crispy, stirring frequently to ensure even cooking.

3. Remove the crispy shallots with a slotted spoon and place them on a paper towel to drain any excess oil. Sprinkle with a pinch of kosher salt.

4. In the same skillet over medium heat, toast the pine nuts, stirring frequently, until they're golden brown. This should take 2 to 3 minutes. Remove from heat and set aside.

5. Toast the multigrain bread slices until they're golden brown and crispy.

6. To assemble the avocado toast: Spread a generous amount of the whipped avocado mixture onto each slice of toasted bread.

7. Sprinkle the toasted sesame seeds over the avocado. Top with cherry tomatoes, crispy shallots, toasted pine nuts, and fresh herbs. Feel free to add other toppings to your toast such as crumbled feta. Finish with an extra sprinkle of kosher salt, if desired, and a drizzle of good-quality olive oil or a squeeze of lime.

MAKES **2**

BLACK & WHITE COOKIES

Barack Obama called these "unity cookies." A long-standing popular fixture of New York City, starting in a Manhattan bakery owned by Bavarian immigrants and becoming popular in NYC Jewish bakeries, black and white cookies are especially delicious homemade. The cookie is cake-like and topped half with a vanilla glaze and half with a Dutch-processed cocoa glaze. They are an all-time favorite at our house. —L.K.

COOKIES

¾ cup unsalted butter, room temperature

1 cup granulated sugar

2 eggs, room temperature

1 tablespoon vanilla extract

2¾ cups all-purpose flour + more for rolling

1 teaspoon kosher salt

1 tablespoon baking powder

¾ cup buttermilk

GLAZE

¼ cup whole milk + 1–2 tablespoons, divided

2 tablespoons corn syrup

1 teaspoon vanilla extract

3–4 cups confectioners' sugar

¼ cup cocoa, Dutch-process or black cocoa powder

1. **To make the cookies:** In a medium mixing bowl, beat butter, sugar, eggs, and vanilla with a mixer for 2 to 3 minutes.

2. In a small mixing bowl, combine flour, salt, and baking powder. Add to the butter mixture and mix until combined. Add buttermilk and mix just until combined. Cover dough and refrigerate for 1 hour (or up to 24 hours). The dough is sticky and difficult to handle at room temperature, so this step is essential.

3. When ready to bake, preheat oven to 350°F. Scoop refrigerated dough with a 1-ounce cookie scoop (about 2 tablespoons) and roll into a ball. If dough is too sticky, lightly coat hands in flour. Place dough ball on a cookie sheet and flatten slightly. Space dough discs about 2 inches apart.

4. Bake for about 12 to 15 minutes. Allow the cookies to cool for about 5 minutes before transferring them to a cooling rack. Allow to cool completely before icing.

5. **To make the icing:** In a medium mixing bowl, beat ¼ cup milk, corn syrup, and vanilla using the whisk attachment. Add 3 cups of confectioners' sugar and beat until smooth. Add more confectioners' sugar ¼ cup at a time until desired consistency is reached. Icing should be thin enough to drip off beater but thick enough not to run off cookie. Pour a little more than half the icing into a disposable piping bag or a small bowl. Add cocoa to the remaining icing. Icing will become too thick; thin it back out by adding 1 tablespoon milk. Beat until smooth. Add more milk 1 teaspoon at a time until desired consistency is reached. Pour chocolate icing into a disposable piping bag or a small bowl.

6. Place 2 feet of parchment on counter. If using disposable piping bags, cut tip off each bag to create a small opening. Ice one half of each cookie with vanilla icing either by piping or using an offset spatula. Create a straight line down middle of each cookie. Ice second half with chocolate icing, creating a straight line down middle. Allow icing to set for about 1 hour. Store in an airtight container for up to 5 days.

MAKES **40**

LEMON RICOTTA PANCAKES WITH BLUEBERRY COMPOTE

One of my favorite things about eating brunch in New York was the variations on pancakes, waffles, and French Toast. I loved to try the creative recipe combinations on sweet classic breakfasts. This combination of lemon and blueberry is a favorite twist on breakfast. —L.K.

PANCAKES

1 cup whole milk ricotta cheese

¼ cup unsalted butter, softened + more for the griddle

3 tablespoons sugar

4 eggs, room temperature

2 tablespoons fresh lemon juice

2 teaspoons lemon zest

1 teaspoon vanilla extract

2 cups all-purpose or pastry flour

1 teaspoon fine kosher salt

1 tablespoon baking powder

BLUEBERRY COMPOTE

2 cups blueberries

½ cup pure maple syrup

½ teaspoon lemon zest

1 teaspoon vanilla extract

1. To make the pancakes: Add ricotta, butter, and sugar to the bowl of a stand mixer. Mix on medium speed until light and fluffy, about 4 minutes. Add eggs and mix for 2 more minutes until combined. Scrape sides and bottom of bowl to ensure even mixing. Add lemon juice, zest, and vanilla, and mix just until combined. Remove bowl from stand mixer.

2. In a medium bowl, whisk together flour, salt, and baking powder. With a rubber spatula, mix flour into ricotta mixture. Mix just until all the flour is incorporated. It's okay to have some lumps.

3. Preheat griddle over medium heat. Butter griddle and pour about ¼ cup batter rounds. Space pancakes about 1 inch apart. When batter starts to bubble on top, flip pancake. Cook second side about 2 to 3 minutes longer or until both sides are a light golden brown. Serve pancakes immediately.

4. To make the blueberry compote: Add blueberries and maple syrup to a medium saucepan and cook over medium-high heat. Stir occasionally with a wooden spoon. Berries will break down and mixture will begin to bubble. Cook for a total of 10 to 12 minutes. Stir in lemon zest and vanilla extract and cook 1 more minute. Serve warm. Store leftover compote in a jar or airtight container in refrigerator for up to 5 days.

TIP: When adding flour to pancake batter, always mix by hand, careful not to overmix.

MAKES **24**

CREAM CHEESE WHIPPED CREAM

MAKES ABOUT 2 CUPS

8 ounces cream cheese
1 teaspoon vanilla extract
3 tablespoons confectioners' sugar
1 cup heavy cream

1. In a medium mixing bowl, beat cream cheese on high with whisk attachment until fluffy, about 3 minutes. Add vanilla, confectioners' sugar, and heavy cream and beat on high again for 3 to 4 more minutes. Serve immediately or refrigerate covered for up to 2 hours.

DRAGON FRUIT SMOOTHIE BOWL

Smoothie bowls, beyond being nutritional powerhouses, are a delightful play of colors and textures, allowing the culinary artist in all of us to shine. In the bustling New York brunch scene, they've become a picturesque staple, embodying the idea that we truly eat with our eyes first. With creations like the vibrant Dragon Fruit Smoothie Bowl, the rich Date and Tahini Smoothie Bowl (page 356), and the refreshing Tropical Sunshine Smoothie Bowl (page 356), every bowl becomes a canvas, waiting to be adorned with an array of toppings and swirls. Embrace the artistry and let your imagination run wild with every spoonful.

1½ cups frozen dragon fruit chunks

⅓ cup frozen mixed berries (you can use a combination of blueberries, raspberries, and strawberries)

2 frozen bananas

2½ tablespoons plant-based protein powder (such as pea or hemp protein)

⅓ cup creamy coconut milk (ensure to stir well if separated in the can)

SUGGESTED TOPPINGS

Toasted coconut shreds

Seasonal fresh fruits

1 tablespoon chia seeds

1. In a high-quality blender, add the frozen dragon fruit chunks, mixed berries, bananas, protein powder, and coconut milk (starting with about ¼ cup).

2. Process until you attain a velvety smooth texture. Blend it slowly and incorporate the coconut milk gradually to maintain the thickness.

3. Once blended, transfer the smoothie blend into bowls.

4. Add toppings of choice and serve immediately.

SERVES **2–3**

DATE AND TAHINI SMOOTHIE BOWL

3 frozen ripe bananas

2 tablespoons tahini

3 pitted Medjool dates

2 fresh figs

½ teaspoon pink Himalayan sea salt

¼ cup cashew milk

SUGGESTED TOPPINGS

Homemade granola

Fresh figs

Hemp seeds

Date syrup

1. In a high-quality blender, add the bananas, tahini, dates, figs, Himalayan sea salt, and cashew milk.

2. Process until you attain a velvety smooth texture. Blend it slowly and incorporate the coconut milk gradually to maintain the thickness.

3. Once blended, transfer the smoothie blend into bowls.

4. Top with granola, fresh figs, and hemp seeds. Drizzle with date syrup.

SERVES **2–3**

TROPICAL SUNSHINE SMOOTHIE BOWL

1 cup frozen mango chunks

1 cup frozen pineapple chunks

1 frozen banana

1 teaspoon raw honey

¼ cup Greek yogurt

1 tablespoon lime juice

SUGGESTED TOPPINGS

Fresh fruit such as kiwi and raspberries

Fresh mint

Toasted coconut

Chia seeds

1. In a high-quality blender, add the mango and pineapple chunks, banana, honey, yogurt, and lime juice.

2. Process until you attain a velvety smooth texture.

3. Once blended, transfer the smoothie blend into bowls.

4. Top with fresh fruit, garnish with mint, and sprinkle toasted coconut and chia seeds.

SERVES **2–3**

ICED MINI LEMON POPPYSEED MUFFINS

There's nothing especially New York about these classic muffins, but for me they will always signal my days of rushing from the subway through Rockefeller Center, running late of course, but still making time to grab a muffin on my way into work. The glazed tops are my favorite. Fresh-baked, these will be a hit on any breakfast or brunch spread.

MUFFINS

¾ cup sugar

Zest of 1 lemon

½ cup butter, softened

2 eggs, room temperature

1 teaspoon vanilla extract

2 cups flour

1 teaspoon baking powder

1 teaspoon baking soda

½ teaspoon kosher salt

2 tablespoons poppy seeds

2 tablespoons lemon juice

⅔ cup buttermilk

ICING

3 tablespoons lemon juice

1½ cups confectioners' sugar

1. Preheat oven to 350°F. Spray a 24-well mini muffin pan with nonstick spray and set aside.

2. In the bowl of a food processor, add sugar and lemon zest. Process for 1 minute. In a medium mixing bowl, beat butter and lemon sugar until light and fluffy, about 3 minutes. Scrape the sides and the bottom of the bowl in the middle of mixing time to ensure even mixing. Add eggs and vanilla and beat until combined.

3. In a small mixing bowl, combine flour, baking powder, baking soda, salt, and poppy seeds. Add to the butter mixture and beat for 1 minute. Add lemon juice and buttermilk and beat just until combined. Scrape the sides and bottom of the bowl with a rubber spatula and stir by hand to ensure even mixing. Scoop batter into prepared pan.

4. Bake for 12 to 15 minutes or until tops of muffins are lightly golden and a cake tester inserted comes out clean. Allow muffins to cool completely.

5. Make glaze by mixing lemon juice and confectioners' sugar in a medium bowl. Lay out 2 feet of parchment on countertop. Dip tops of muffins in glaze and set on parchment. Allow glaze to dry completely. Store in an airtight container for up to 2 days.

MAKES ABOUT **36**

HEARTLAND COOKOUT

"Urban friends ask me how I can stand living here, 'so far from everything?' When I hear this question over the phone, I'm usually looking out the window at a forest, a running creek, and a vegetable garden, thinking: Define everything." —BARBARA KINGSOLVER, *ANIMAL, VEGETABLE, MIRACLE: A YEAR OF FOOD LIFE*

When you're born in the Midwest and have even a little curiosity about the world, you become restless to escape it. I found my way to Ireland and then to Boston and eventually to my work in New York City. So it is with some wonder that I find myself back where I started in the land of casseroles and bake sales. After so much concrete and tight squeezes, I appreciate the wide open air in a way I never did in my teens. I take joy in my overflowing flower garden, raising chickens, and picking peaches in orchards and turning them into pies. Many people think of this as fly-over country, but it is also the heartland—the center of the country and the source of much of our sustenance. The food of the heartland is quintessential American and is the very essence of farm-to-table. I still miss the people of New York, but the rush hour and endless bus lines I can live without. Here, there is magic in the way October light filters through the yellow canopy of one-hundred-year-old maples, peace in the bounce of the curled white fluff tail of my husky in front of me on the trail through the woods, past the river where ramps grow in the spring and wood ducks lay clutches of eggs. What could be more heartland than a summer walk to the garden at dusk, dog in tow, to fetch a handful of herbs while the pizza bakes, hearing the neighbors over the wild tangle of bushes playing basketball, heirloom tomatoes in the garden just turning red, sunflowers turning their huge faces East waiting for morning, and the smell of of Genovese basil on fingertips? —L.K.

MAKE AHEAD

Make garlic butter for vegetable skewers up to 2 days in advance. Store in an airtight container in the refrigerator.

Make homemade marshmallows (page 367) up to 3 days in advance. Store at room temperature in an airtight container.

Make Onion Jam (page 365) up to a week in advance. Store in an airtight container in the refrigerator.

Bake pound cake for Strawberry Shortcake Jars (page 371) up to 1 month before and freeze in an airtight container. Remove from freezer the night before serving and assemble jars just before serving.

EXTRAS

Heirloom tomatoes

Fresh mozzarella

Pesto (page 102)

Grilled sweet corn

Watermelon

TIME SAVERS

Purchase pound cake for the Strawberry Shortcake Jars (page 371).

Use packaged marshmallows for S'mores Skillet Brownies (page 367).

Purchase jarred pesto.

Purchase slider buns.

Styling Ideas

Add fresh garden flowers to the table such as peonies, hydrangeas, garden roses, and poppies.

Serve food in rustic metal platters and vintage sheet pans.

RECISE S

BURGER SLIDERS

Nothing says "summer cookout" like the smell of burgers on the grill. We like to cook over a wood fire, but a gas or charcoal grill will also work perfectly for this American classic. For tender, juicy burgers, use ground beef that has not been stuffed tightly into a package and do not overhandle the beef when forming patties. Serve on a homemade, freshly-baked Brioche Slider Roll (page 364) for heartland perfection.

1½ pounds freshly ground chuck (80/20 meat/fat ratio)

8 cheddar cheese slices

Kosher salt

Freshly ground pepper

Olive oil for the grill

8 Brioche Slider Rolls (page 364)

2–3 tablespoons salted butter

Onion Jam (page 365)

Bibb lettuce

2 roma tomatoes, sliced

INTERNAL TEMPERATURES FOR BEEF:
Medium-rare: 130°–135°F
Medium: 140°–145°F
Medium-well: 150°–155°F
Well-done: 160°F

1. Cut 9 (4-inch) square pieces of parchment. Divide ground chuck into 8 (3-ounce) portions. Form into balls. Press with a burger press or the bottom of a flat pan or plate until burgers are about ½ inch wider than your bun. Burgers will shrink while cooking. With your thumb, press a shallow dimple in the center of each burger. Stack between pieces of parchment. Cut out cheese slices with a round cookie cutter so they are the right size for rolls.

2. Preheat grill to medium-high heat. If using charcoal, allow to burn 10 to 15 minutes before grilling. If using fire, use dry wood and allow to burn 20 to 30 minutes before grilling. Add salt and pepper to taste just before grilling. Cook for 3 to 4 minutes on each side. Timing will depend on the heat of grill and how done you want your burgers. Use time as a guide, but measure the temperature on the inside of burgers with a quick read thermometer for the most accurate results. About 1 minute before burgers finish cooking, add cheese.

3. While burgers cook, prepare rolls: Slice rolls and preheat a cast-iron skillet over medium high. You can add the skillet directly to your grill or grill buns on a stovetop. Add 2 teaspoons butter to skillet and spread around. Add 4 roll halves, cut side down, to pan. Cook for about 30 seconds to 1 minute or until golden and crisp on cut sides. Don't leave rolls unattended, as they can burn quickly. Add more butter and toast the rest of the burger rolls.

4. Assemble burgers with toppings plus any of your favorite condiments. Serve immediately.

MAKES **8**

BRIOCHE SLIDER ROLLS

¼ cup warm water

¼ cup warm whole milk

1 tablespoon active dry yeast

2 tablespoons sugar

5 large eggs, room temperature, divided

1 tablespoon kosher salt

4½ –5 cups all-purpose flour

1 cup unsalted butter, room temperature

Poppy seeds (optional)

1. In the bowl of a stand mixer, combine water, milk, yeast, and sugar and allow to rest until foamy, about 4 to 5 minutes. Add 4 of the eggs and the salt and beat with the paddle attachment until well incorporated. Switch to dough hook and add 4 cups of the flour. Add more flour ¼ cup at a time until dough holds together and slaps the side of bowl. Knead at medium speed for about 3 minutes. With mixer running, add butter 1 teaspoon at a time, waiting for each addition to incorporate before adding the next. Increase the speed to medium and knead for 6 minutes.

2. Spray a large bowl with nonstick spray and place dough in bowl. Cover with plastic wrap or a damp towel. Allow to rise in warm place until doubled in size, about 1 to 2 hours. Line two heavy-bottomed baking sheets with parchment or silicone baking mats and set aside.

3. Punch down dough and turn out onto a lightly floured work surface. Using a bench scraper and a kitchen scale, cut off 50-gram pieces. Roll each piece into a tight ball by rolling it across work surface with one hand for about 45 seconds. Place each ball on prepared pan and flatten slightly. Leave 1½ inches between dough balls. Cover with plastic wrap and allow to rise for 45 minutes.

4. Preheat oven to 350°F. Beat remaining egg in a small bowl. Brush tops and side of dough balls with egg wash. Sprinkle with poppy seeds, if using. Score top with a bread lame. Bake 25 to 30 minutes or until golden brown. Allow to cool on pan for 10 minutes. Slice and serve warm or at room temperature. Rolls taste best the same day they are baked. If you don't use them all, freeze leftovers in an airtight container in the freezer for up to a month. To revive frozen rolls, preheat oven to 300°F. Place frozen rolls on a baking sheet and place in oven for 8 to 10 minutes.

MAKES ABOUT **24**

ONION JAM

I grew up in a house on a hill overlooking massive rich-black-soiled fields. Every year, onions were the choice crops that the farmers planted. By midsummer, the outdoors smelled faintly of onions, and at the time, I tired of the smell quickly and was not at all fond of onions. Now I can't get enough onions with my savory meals. This jam brings out the sweetness of the onions and is an excellent complement to a savory burger or sandwich. —L.K.

3 medium Vidalia onions
¼ cup olive oil
2 teaspoons salt
½ cup balsamic vinegar
1 sprig fresh rosemary
¾ cup sugar
1 teaspoon fresh thyme leaves
Fresh cracked black pepper, to taste

1. Peel and chop onions. In a deep frying pan or braiser, preheat olive oil over medium-high heat for about 3 minutes. Add onions and sprinkle with salt. Cook until golden brown, about 12 to 15 minutes. Add balsamic vinegar and rosemary and cook for an additional 10 minutes.

2. Add sugar and stir to combine. Cook until sugar melts and mixture thickens, about 15 minutes. Remove from heat and stir in thyme leaves and add pepper. Remove and discard rosemary sprig. Taste to assess if jam needs more salt. If so, add a little at a time until you reach desired taste.

3. Use immediately or transfer jam to a glass jar and store in refrigerator for up to 10 days.

MAKES ABOUT 1½ CUPS

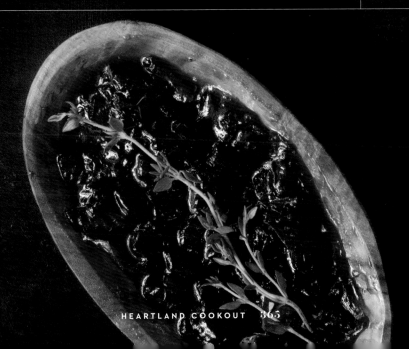

GARDEN VEGETABLE SKEWERS

Fresh local vegetables are in abundance during the summer months—pick them up at a farmers' market, roadside stand, or from your own garden. Swap in any of your favorite veggies to customize.

GARLIC BUTTER

⅓ cup salted butter

4 cloves garlic

3 tablespoons finely chopped fresh cilantro

3 tablespoons finely chopped fresh parsley

1 teaspoon fresh thyme leaves

VEGETABLES

1 medium zucchini

1 medium yellow squash

1 orange bell pepper

1 red bell pepper

1 large red onion

2 tablespoons olive oil

Salt and pepper, to taste

1. To make the garlic butter: In a small heatproof bowl, melt butter in microwave. Mince garlic and add to butter. Stir in chopped cilantro, parsley, and thyme. Set aside.

2. Soak 6 wooden skewers in water for 30 minutes. Wash vegetables. Slice squash and zucchini into half-inch slices and cut in half. Core bell peppers and cut into roughly 1½-inch squares. Peel onion and cut into roughly 1½-inch squares. Poke skewers through the center of vegetables, alternating between colors, reserving about an inch on each end. Brush skewered vegetables with olive oil. Add salt and pepper to taste. Preheat grill to medium high or if using charcoal or fire, allow to burn for 10 to 15 minutes. Place skewers directly on grill. Cook for about 8 minutes, flip, and cook another 8 minutes. Time may vary depending on how hot your grill is and how soft you like your vegetables. Place on platter and brush with garlic butter. Serve hot. Store leftovers in an airtight container in refrigerator for up to 2 days. Leftovers can be reheated as a side dish or used in an egg scramble or omelet.

MAKES **6** SKEWERS

S'MORES SKILLET BROWNIES

Growing up in the Midwest, summers meant camping, swimming in Lake Michigan, riding bikes with friends, fireflies at dusk, and campfire s'mores. I pulled these delicious, classic summertime flavors together so I could serve up some nostalgic camping sweetness at a party, even without the campfire. If you want to make this recipe easier, replace the homemade marshmallows with large, packaged marshmallows. —L.K.

HOMEMADE MARSHMALLOWS

1 cup water, divided

3 envelopes unflavored gelatin

2 cups sugar

½ cup corn syrup

½ teaspoon salt

1 tablespoon vanilla bean paste

1⅓ cups confectioners' sugar + more for the pan

NOTE: Use extra Homemade Marshmallows to top off hot chocolate or as a sweet snack all by themselves.

1. Make marshmallows 4 hours or longer in advance: Generously spray a 8 × 8-inch pan with nonstick spray. Coat the pan with confectioners' sugar and set aside.

2. In the bowl of a stand mixer, combine ⅓ cup water and gelatin. Use whisk attachment and mix for 10 seconds and allow to bloom.

3. Clip a candy thermometer to a large pot and set hot pads within reach of the stove. Cook ⅔ cup water, sugar, corn syrup, salt, and vanilla bean paste over medium-high heat. Stir constantly until mixture reaches 240°F. Use hot pads to remove pot from stove and pour into mixer bowl over gelatin. Start mixer on lowest setting and gradually increase the speed to high. Mix for 7 to 8 minutes, stopping occasionally to scrape down the bowl. Mixture will be fluffy and very sticky.

4. Pour marshmallow mixture into prepared pan. If mixture is too sticky to smooth out, coat hands with confectioner's sugar and press into pan. Allow to cool and then cover pan with plastic wrap. Allow marshmallows to set for at least 4 hours.

5. Place confectioners' sugar in a bowl. Generously dust a cutting board with some of the sugar. Turn out marshmallows on cutting board. Sprinkle more confectioners' sugar on the slab of marshmallows. Cut 8 rows by 8 rows to make 1-inch square marshmallows. Add more confectioners' sugar if the knife gets too sticky. Coat each cut marshmallow in confectioners' sugar to keep them from sticking to each other. Store in an airtight container for up to 2 weeks.

CONTINUED

CRUST

10 tablespoons unsalted butter

1½ cups graham cracker crumbs

BROWNIE

1 cup brown sugar

1 cup sugar

4 eggs, room temperature

1 tablespoon vanilla bean paste

1 cup unsalted butter, melted

1 cup unsweetened cocoa

1 cup all-purpose flour

½ teaspoon salt

3 (1½-ounce) milk chocolate bars, broken into pieces

6. **To make the crust:** Melt butter in a medium heatproof bowl. Stir in graham cracker crumbs until well combined. Evenly divide crust into 4 mini skillets. Lightly flatten crust with fingers.

7. **To make the brownie:** Preheat oven to 325°F. In the bowl of a stand mixer, beat sugars, eggs and vanilla bean paste on medium speed until light and fluffy, about 4 minutes. Scrape the sides and bottom of bowl to ensure even mixing. In a medium bowl, mix melted butter and cocoa until well combined. Add to egg mixture and beat just until combined.

8. In a medium bowl, whisk together flour and salt. Sift mixture into butter mixture. With a rubber spatula, stir by hand just until combined. Divide batter between the 4 skillets.

9. Bake for 20 minutes. Carefully add 3 to 4 marshmallows in center of each skillet, pressing down lightly to so they go partially into the brownies. Poke pieces of chocolate bar in surface of brownie. Bake for 4 to 8 more minutes or until edge of brownies are set and centers still jiggle a little. Marshmallows will be soft and gooey. To give them more of a campfire flavor, you can toast them with a kitchen torch or by placing skillets directly under the broiler for about 1 minute. Keep an eye on skillets under the broiler and remove as soon as they start to brown.

MAKES **4** SKILLETS

STRAWBERRY SHORTCAKE JARS

I have so many fabulous memories of summers when my family brought home whole flats of fresh local strawberries to be turned into jams, pies, shortcakes, and of course to eat all by their juicy selves. This version of shortcake—served in small mason jars—makes it easy to prepare in advance, and they will look adorable on your spread. —L.K.

EQUIPMENT
12 (8-ounce) mason jars

STRAWBERRIES
6 cups fresh strawberries + more for garnishing

⅓ cup sugar

POUND CAKE
1 cup unsalted butter, softened

1½ cups sugar

2 teaspoons vanilla extract

1 teaspoon almond extract

4 large eggs

2¼ cups all-purpose flour

½ teaspoon salt

½ cup heavy cream

¼ cup maple syrup

Cream Cheese Whipped Cream (page 353)

1. **To prepare strawberries:** Wash and hull berries. Place in a 9 × 13-inch pan or casserole dish. Sprinkle sugar over berries. Mash berries with a potato masher until sugar is dissolved and berries are mostly liquid with small chunks. Cover pan and refrigerate for 30 minutes up to 4 hours.

2. **To make pound cake:** Preheat oven to 325°F. Generously spray a 9 × 9-inch pan with nonstick spray. In the bowl of a stand mixer beat butter, sugar, vanilla extract, and almond extract on medium speed until light and fluffy, about 4 minutes. Add eggs one at a time, beating between each addition. Scrape the sides and bottom of bowl to ensure even mixing.

3. In a medium bowl, whisk together flour and salt. Add flour mixture to butter mixture in two parts, adding heavy cream after the first part. Add maple syrup and mix on low just until combined. Scrape the sides and bottom of bowl to ensure even mixing. Pour into prepared pan and bake for 40 minutes or until a cake tester comes out clean. Allow cake to cool in pan for 10 minutes and then turn out onto a platter or cutting board. Allow to cool completely. Cut into ½-inch cubes.

4. **To assemble cups:** Add a layer of cake at the bottom of a mason jar. Scoop 2 to 3 tablespoons strawberry mixture on top of cake. Add a layer of Cream Cheese Whipped Cream. Add another layer of cake followed by more strawberries and whipped cream. Garnish with a small whole strawberry. Serve immediately or cover and refrigerate for up to 3 hours.

MAKES **12** JARS

SONOMA WINE & CHEESE BOARD

"The air is wine. The grapes on a score of rolling hills are red with autumn flame. Across Sonoma Mountain, wisps of sea fog are stealing. The afternoon sun smolders in the drowsy sky. I have everything to make me glad I am alive. I am filled with dreams and mysteries." —JACK LONDON

Crossing the Golden Gate Bridge and traveling into wine country is an exhilarating journey of beautiful landscapes, vineyards with propped-up vines heavy with grapes, and endless wines to sample. What could be better with California wine than a picnic of cured meats, cheeses, fruit, and a crusty loaf of freshly baked bread? We built this charcuterie board to be a collection of our favorite things to sample with wine. It is a celebration of gathering and grazing with a little something for everyone—this board is for snacking and conversation. In the spirit of global sharing of food, from the Greek tradition of Meze to Spanish Tapas and Portuguese Petiscos, this board is all about sharing and savoring and connecting with friends and family. Fill your board with fresh food from the abundant California harvest of fruits, nuts, and cheeses and uncork a few bottles of wine. —L.K.

RECIPES

California-Style Crab Cakes ✖ 375

Dutch Oven Bread ✖ 376

Rosemary Flatbread Crackers ✖ 379

Garlic Butter ✖ 380

Sun-Dried Tomato Butter ✖ 380

CHEESE SUGGESTIONS

Sonoma Jack: A semi-hard cheese with options like garlic, jalapeño, or pepper flavors.

Vella Dry Jack: A firm, aged cheese with a nutty and sweet flavor profile.

Bellwether Farms Carmody: A semi-soft, cows' milk cheese with a buttery and rich taste.

Laura Chenel Chèvre: A fresh goat cheese (chèvre) that adds a tangy and creamy element.

Point Reyes Original Blue: A creamy and tangy blue cheese that adds a bold and savory note to the selection.

EXTRAS

Heirloom tomato slices with salt, pepper, and thyme

Mixed nuts

Fresh fruit

Fig salami with pistachio

Dried california apricots

Mini toasts

Fig jam

California ripe olives

Styling Ideas

Decide on the right size board for your gathering and fill it with colorful snacks. Add layering with slate, bowls, and parchment paper.

CALIFORNIA-STYLE CRAB CAKES

These California-Style Crab Cakes pay homage to Napa's proximity to the Pacific, showcasing the freshest seafood. A reflection of the valley's melding of tradition with innovation, this dish embodies the spirit of West Coast gastronomy.

1 egg

¼ cup mayonnaise

Juice of ½ lemon

1 tablespoon Worcestershire sauce

½ tablespoon fresh thyme leaves

1 tablespoon Dijon mustard

½ teaspoon ground cumin

½ teaspoon paprika

1 pound lump crab meat

5 saltine crackers, finely crushed

¼ cup panko breadcrumbs

1. Preheat the oven to 450°F.

2. In a large bowl, whisk together egg, mayonnaise, lemon juice, Worcestershire sauce, thyme, Dijon mustard, cumin, and paprika until well-blended. Gently fold the crab meat into the prepared mixture. Add the crushed saltine crackers and panko breadcrumbs. Mix lightly, ensuring the crumbs are distributed evenly. Cover and refrigerate the mixture for 30 minutes.

3. Portion the crab mixture using a small ring mold, pressing gently to compact and shape. Transfer the formed crab cakes to a tray lined with plastic wrap and chill.

4. When ready to bake, place crab cakes on a greased baking tray. Brush top and sides with olive oil. Bake for 8 to 10 minutes or until golden and heated through.

MAKES **6–8**

DUTCH OVEN BREAD

This is my absolute favorite, go-to recipe for easy, crusty bread perfection. My family devours it and it's always a favorite at parties. The moment it hits the cutting board to the time it is gone is usually not even long enough for it to fully cool. Freshness is key, so plan your baking to have it come out of your oven and still warm for a meal or party. —L.K.

2 cups warm water

2½ teaspoons active dry yeast

2 teaspoons salt

4¼ to 4¾ cups bread flour + more for forming

1. In the bowl of a stand mixer with the dough hook attachment, add water, yeast, and salt. Mix on low for 30 seconds. Add flour one cup at a time, mixing between each addition. Continue to add flour until dough starts to come together and slap the sides of the bowl. The dough will not form a firm ball and should still be sticky.

2. Knead with the mixer on medium for 5 to 6 minutes. Spray a large bowl with nonstick spray. Place the dough inside. Cover the bowl with a damp towel. Allow to rise about 1½ hours. Do a bowl-fold by stretching the edges of the dough to the center of the dough ball. Cover and allow to rise an additional 1 to 2 hours, or until roughly doubled in size.

3. On a generously floured surface with floured hands, punch down and form a ball. Cover the dough ball with the damp towel and allow to rest for 30 minutes.

4. Place a 5-quart or larger Dutch oven in the oven and preheat the oven to 450°F. Place dough ball on a piece of parchment. With a bread lame or very sharp knife make cuts into the top of dough ball in whatever pattern you like. Remove the hot Dutch oven when it reaches 450°. Lower the parchment and dough ball carefully into the Dutch oven. Cover with lid and bake covered for about 25 minutes. At 25 minutes, remove the lid and continue baking another 15 minutes or until the top is golden brown. All ovens are different so timing may vary. Serve warm.

MAKES 1 LOAF

ROSEMARY FLATBREAD CRACKERS

These easy-to-make little flatbread crackers are an excellent snack to go with dips, cheeses, and meats. The rosemary and whole wheat flour make an excellent flavor accompaniment on a vibrant wine and cheese board.

2 cups whole-wheat flour

⅔ cup all-purpose flour

2 tablespoons finely chopped fresh rosemary

1 teaspoon salt

¾ cup water

¼ cup olive oil

Coarse salt for sprinkling

2 tablespoons sesame seeds

Rosemary leaves, for garnish

1. Preheat oven to 375°F.

2. In the bowl of a stand mixer, add flours, rosemary, and salt. Mix on low until salt and rosemary are evenly distributed. With mixer on low, pour in water, and add olive oil. Continue mixing until dough forms.

3. Divide dough into 4 equal portions. Cut two pieces of parchment to the size of your baking sheet. Place one dough portion in the center of one piece of parchment. Top with second piece and roll out at thin as you can. Remove top parchment and place bottom parchment directly on baking sheet. Top with sesame seeds and coarse salt, to taste. Poke surface with fork. Bake for 15 to 20 minutes or until flatbread is crisped.

4. Repeat with remaining dough. Allow flatbreads to cool and then break them up into smaller pieces. Garnish with rosemary leaves and serve. Store in an airtight container for up to 1 week.

MAKES **4** LARGE FLATBREAD CRACKERS

GARLIC BUTTER

½ cup unsalted butter, room
temperature

2 cloves garlic, minced

2 teaspoons finely chopped
fresh parsley

1 tablespoon grated Parmesan
cheese

¼ teaspoon Dijon mustard

Zest of ½ lemon

½ teaspoon kosher salt

Freshly ground black pepper,
to taste

1. In a mixing bowl, combine the room-temperature unsalted butter, minced garlic, chopped parsley, grated Parmesan cheese, Dijon mustard, lemon zest, kosher salt, and freshly ground black pepper.

2. Mix until all the ingredients are well incorporated. Transfer the mixture to an airtight container or form it into a log shape using parchment paper. Refrigerate until ready to use or allow it to soften at room temperature for immediate use.

MAKES ½ CUP

SUN-DRIED TOMATO BUTTER

½ cup unsalted butter, room
temperature

¼ cup sun-dried tomatoes,
chopped

2 scallions sliced

1 tablespoon fresh thyme
leaves

½ teaspoon kosher salt

Freshly ground black pepper,
to taste

1. In a mixing bowl, combine the room-temperature unsalted butter, sun-dried tomatoes, scallions, thyme, kosher salt, and freshly ground black pepper.

2. Mix until all the ingredients are well incorporated. Transfer the mixture to an airtight container or form it into a log shape using parchment paper. Refrigerate until ready to use or allow it to soften at room temperature for immediate use.

MAKES ½ CUP

METRIC CONVERSIONS

If you're accustomed to using metric measurements, use these handy charts to convert the imperial measurements used in this book.

Weight (Dry Ingredients)

1 oz		30 g
4 oz	¼ lb	120 g
8 oz	½ lb	240 g
12 oz	¾ lb	360 g
16 oz	1 lb	480 g
32 oz	2 lb	960 g

Oven Temperatures

Fahrenheit	Celsius	Gas Mark
225°	110°	¼
250°	120°	½
275°	140°	1
300°	150°	2
325°	160°	3
350°	180°	4
375°	190°	5
400°	200°	6
425°	220°	7
450°	230°	8

Volume (Liquid Ingredients)

½ tsp.		2 ml
1 tsp.		5 ml
1 Tbsp.	½ fl oz	15 ml
2 Tbsp.	1 fl oz	30 ml
¼ cup	2 fl oz	60 ml
⅓ cup	3 fl oz	80 ml
½ cup	4 fl oz	120 ml
⅔ cup	5 fl oz	160 ml
¾ cup	6 fl oz	180 ml
1 cup	8 fl oz	240 ml
1 pt	16 fl oz	480 ml
1 qt	32 fl oz	960 ml

Length

¼ in	6 mm
½ in	13 mm
¾ in	19 mm
1 in	25 mm
6 in	15 cm
12 in	30 cm

INDEX

———◆———

ACKNOWLEDGMENTS

To my mother, Nergis, who introduced me to the joys of cooking and gathering around a table before I even knew how important that would be. Thank you for those first lessons in hummus, pesto, and béchamel sauce, which gave me a head start in the kitchen when my friends were just starting to boil water. Your inexhaustible culinary inventiveness continues to dazzle me, each dish a testament to your imaginative genius.

Mehreen, you've been our rock during the hectic times on set. From photography to videography, from sous chef to prop master, your contributions have been immeasurable. My heartfelt gratitude goes out to you; in you, I have found the quintessence of chosen family.

Tehmina, your constant support and cheers have always given me strength. I'm grateful for the meals we've shared and your generous feedback. Your nutritional knowledge has been a gift, and I cherish the hope that we'll collaborate on a health-focused cookbook someday.

Ashu, thank you for always being there, from setting up to cleaning up, for curating the best culinary adventures from Lisbon to Marrakesh, and for being my go-to buddy for farmers' market adventures.

Vivek, for our shared appreciation for the simple yet beautiful things in life from indigo to produce, I cherish our culinary adventures and expeditions and I am grateful for all the amazing props you have added to my collection.

Saadia, for your help with our New York shoots and your unwavering support, even in the hardest times, thank you for being an incredible recipe tester and cheerleader.

Cassie Jones, your time and encouragement have been a guiding light for me. A compliment from you is a cherished achievement in the cookbook community, and I'm grateful for the guidance and patience you've shown me.

Sharmeen, despite the whirlwind of your commitments, you found the time to grace our book with a foreword, sharing a reverence for our grandmothers that I deeply cherish. For this, I am eternally grateful.

To our editor, Nicole, for your appreciation and support. I appreciate your understanding and patience.

Finally, to Laura, my compatriot in the wild dance of creation and chaos—our journey has been one of extremes: exhilarating triumphs and harrowing challenges, an odyssey of passion, perseverance, and partnership. That we have emerged, is a testament to our shared vision, a feat I attribute to our unshakeable alliance. For every moment, every trial, every victory, I am profoundly thankful.

—Mumtaz

To Mehreen, for your endless patience, calm presence, sensible and straightforward approach to complicated problems. You kept us moving forward and brought us back to reality when we lost focus. Thank you for being the first person to believe in this project and for being there every step of the food-photography-crazy way.

To Leo, for your charm, your wit, and for carrying on your grandfather's sense of humor.

To Victor, for the endless setups, teardowns, prop organization, living through food photography messes, and for making sure no food went to waste.

To my mother for teaching me through her example that food tastes even better when shared and that fellowship is always the best part of any meal.

To Nicole Frail, our editor, for taking on this monster book with grace and attention-to-detail and for cheering us on all the way.

To the team at Skyhorse Publishing: Abigail Gehring, Chris Schultz, Brian Peterson, and Joseph Sverchek. Thank you for all the behind-the-scenes work.

To my BPG colleagues, Paula, Laura, Emily, Maya, Suzi, and Nate, your creative camraderie makes every design challenge more achievable and more fun.

To Allison, for helping us throw a quinceañera in Central America and for your contributions to the Tropical Table, and of course for the many years of baking shenanigans.

To Renee, for sharing your travel photos, humoring my crazy requests, and for being one of my first baking buddies.

To my co-author and long time friend, Mumtaz: no one can dream up big, culinary artistry like you. Thanks for going on this over-the-top, just-as-we-like-it, up-too-late, delicious journey with me.

—Laura

ABOUT THE AUTHORS

MUMTAZ MUSTAFA is an award-winning graphic designer working in branding, digital marketing, and focusing on book cover design. She is senior art director at HarperCollins Publishers in charge of the lifestyle imprint Harvest Books. A native of Karachi, Pakistan, Mumtaz currently lives and works in New York City.

LAURA KLYNSTRA is senior art director for Revell Books and a freelance graphic designer and photographer. Previously, she worked as art director at Hyperion Books and at HarperCollins Publishers in New York City. She is the co-author and photographer of *Christmas Baking* and lives in Michigan with her family and a menagerie of dogs, cats, chickens, and ducks.

Follow them on instagram @spiceandsugartable.